Swift's
Silver Mines
and Related Appalachian Treasures

Michael S. Steely

D1570659

The Overmountain Press

JOHNSON CITY, TENNESSEE

ISBN 1-57072-036-3

1 2 3 4 5 6 7 8 9 0

Contents

Dedication

This book is dedicated to my wife, Lettie, for putting up with me for almost thirty years and for keeping me on the straight and narrow; to Roy Price, who has always offered support and friendship; and to the late Michael Paul Henson, who truly was the "Dean of Appalachian Treasure Hunters," whether their quest was searching or researching.

Dear reader,

Michael Paul Henson died a few weeks after writing this very special introduction. During the years of researching this book, I often saw or called Michael Paul, and the information herein owes much to him and his endless efforts to preserve Appalachian folklore. It is with great sadness that we mourn his passing.   —M.S.S.

Introduction

Nothing can stir the heart and imagination so much as the lure and fascination of hidden treasure. The lost silver mines of John Swift have caused the pulse to quicken in young and old throughout Appalachia for over two hundred years.

In this area a silent, unseen legion of people are busy exploring, digging, prospecting and searching for the Swift mines. Their trust is in no one, their activities are secret. Their guide may be an old map, a newspaper clipping, a legend, a rumor, sometimes only a whisper.

I have made several trips to the areas where it is believed the lost mines are located, and while I have heard the story of the lost mines numerous times, there is still a thrill in listening to a mountaineer tell his version as his forefathers have been telling it for nine or ten generations.

The country Swift described is still rugged, and in some places almost inaccessible. It has changed little in the last two hundred years. The mountains, like the oceans, are silent, and guard their secrets well.

Perhaps, after all, the story is just a fanciful tale, and somewhere Jonathan Swift, pirate, Indian trader, miner and smuggler, is laughing at the joke he perpetrated on ten generations of "treasure hunters" that have sometimes been called fools, visionaries, and dreamers.

But without dreams man cannot exist, so he seeks the elusive, sometimes the unobtainable.

The story of the lost silver mines of John Swift is such a beautiful legend, and so much a part of Virginia, North Carolina, Kentucky, Tennessee, and West Virginia folklore and history that I almost hope they are never found. They should always be there, just to be looked for.

Michael Paul Henson
Jeffersonville, Indiana
January 6, 1995

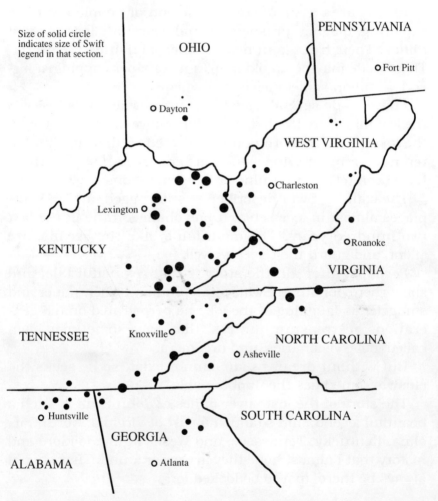

Size of solid circle indicates size of Swift legend in that section.

OHIO

PENNSYLVANIA

O Fort Pitt

O Dayton

WEST VIRGINIA

O Charleston

Lexington O

KENTUCKY

O Roanoke

VIRGINIA

TENNESSEE

Knoxville O

NORTH CAROLINA

O Asheville

O Huntsville

GEORGIA

SOUTH CAROLINA

ALABAMA

O Atlanta

Throughout Central Appalachia are dozens of tales of lost silver mines, including those of Jonathan Swift. These legends stretch from West Virginia to Alabama and go back to the 1600's.

Foreword

As with many Appalachian natives, I first heard of Swift's Lost Silver Mines as a child, in fantastic stories passed down for generations within my family. Like a prince on a white horse who is the dream of starry-eyed young country girls, or the "someday my ship will come in" attitude of many poor families, the mysterious silver mines and the possibility of stumbling across Swift's treasures tugs at the hearts of many people.

Although I have occasionally tramped the mountains and crawled through caves with the Swift legend on my mind, my actual search has been research. My positions with various newspapers in Tennessee, Kentucky, and Virginia and my later travels as a book sales representative in the Southeast have aided my continual quest for "Swift" facts. I have spent many hours in local and regional libraries finding dusty references to the subject, copying unpublished manuscripts, and tracking down as much information as I could find.

My association with the bookstores and treasure writers has brought me most texts published on Swift and other lost silver mine tales. The research and subsequent creation, along with Roy Price and Joanne Watts of Jellico, Tennessee, of the "Swift Silver Mine Lost Treasure Weekend" has introduced me to fellow "Swift" buffs, published treasure authors, researchers, and new friends.

Of all the articles and little books I have read on Swift, I believe this is the most complete and objective that has ever been written. The Swift legend has grown so large over the past 230 years that no book could ever include everything on the subject. I have, however, attempted to include all that I feel is worthwhile, although I must admit some "journals" and several related stories have been summarized and condensed in order to be included.

The interesting thing about the Swift Legend is how it plays in the recorded history of central Appalachia. Although it is nothing more than a footnote in some texts, other works contain several pages about the lost mines. Certainly many of the early settlers and frontier leaders believed in the tale, and spent much of their time looking for lost treasures. More than a few have lost their lives in the pursuit.

Even today, as we approach the twenty-first century, the Swift legend has thousands of devotees, many actively looking for any clue they can find. My hope is that this book will become a useful tool in their efforts, and an aid to fellow researchers.

The debate as to the truth of the lost silver mines continues, and I have found myself on both sides of the issue. I came to the search as a skeptic, and now find that I am what can best be described as a "soft believer." The chance that the mines and hidden treasures exist is more likely than not, for two main reasons: Some of them have been found, and silver coins, bars, and relics have been located.

I know, because I am one of the finders.

Michael Paul Henson, known as the "Dean" of modern Swift silver mine hunters, wrote extensively on the legend, as well as other lost treasure tales, ghost stories, folk humor, and history. Henson was sought out by people from across the nation for clues to various caches and was well respected within the growing community of treasure searchers and researchers. (Photo by Mike Steely)

Silver Arrowhead Points
to Swift's Legendary Mine

For more than two hundred years, white fortune hunters have scoured the Appalachian Mountains, from the Blue Ridge to the Blue Grass, for clues, marks, signs, and hints of the legendary lost silver mines chronicled in Jonathan Swift's journal. I've spent many years crawling through caves, rock shelters, and ancient yellowed pages of manuscripts in search of anything that could point to the lost mines, and was becoming convinced that the entire two-century search was nothing more than a huge historical hoax.

I was preparing a lengthy manuscript to dispute the silver legend, complete with references, cross-references, and the like. That, however, was before a bright winter afternoon on the south side of Pine Mountain near the Kentucky-Tennessee boundary. I was hunting treasure and my metal detector blipped, and suddenly my mind changed. I went from serious skeptic to possible believer in less than a heartbeat.

I have often hunted the Pine Mountain area between Pineville, Kentucky, and Jellico, Tennessee, for relics. The area is alive with tales of Civil War troop movements by Generals Morgan and Kirby Smith, with stories concerning Indian mounds at the gaps of the long mountain at both small towns, and with constant tales of Swift's Silver Mine.

My own attention to the Swift legend began in 1970 when I was actively exploring caves along the Pine Mountain fault while editing the Bell County weekly newspaper. I began as a skeptic, admittedly an interested skeptic because of the footnote the legend made in regional history, until that snowy winter excursion.

Since Pineville, I've tramped up and down the 123-mile

length of the single, pointed mountain. The peak, which averages about 2,500 feet high, runs from the Breaks of the Sandy on the Kentucky-Virginia border to the barrens of Scott County, Tennessee, at the headwaters of the Big South Fork of the Cumberland River.

Of the thirty-six different versions of Jonathan Swift's "journals," maps, and waybills, Pine Mountain is mentioned by name or by description in most. Areas along the historic buffer between the Kentucky-Tennessee wilderness and the colonies that figure importantly in the numerous searches for Swift's mine include the region of the Breaks, the Sandy River headwaters, Pound Gap, Straight Creek and the headwaters of the Red Bird River, Clear Creek, and Furnace Ridge in Bell County, Kentucky, and Primroy Hollow in Campbell County, Tennessee.

But when my detector bleeped, I thought perhaps I had found a piece of coal company script, a shotgun shell casing, or at best, a "V" nickel. When I slid my hunting knife blade into the soft sand of the shadowy rock shelter, I felt an object through the knife handle. I knew it was larger than a nickel, and thought I must have turned up a zip-top can of Vienna sausages.

When I cleared the earth and saw the palm-size arrowhead, I was at first delighted, then confused and puzzled. The earth-colored relic must have been lying in the same spot for hundreds of years, probably dropped by someone spending the night in the shelter of the sandstone bluff, or sitting beneath it to get out of a rainstorm.

I figured that for it to provide a signal, there was some iron ore in the makeup of the arrowhead. At best I thought it might be copper. But with the years of discoloration on it from the surrounding earth, it was impossible to tell anything about it other than it was located with the detector.

That in itself is unusual for arrowheads. Actually, you would have to describe the relic as more of a spearhead because of its size and shape. A Cherokee store operator at the Indian Nation in North Carolina told me the object, which he admired greatly, was probably carried by a chief or a medicine man.

A couple of weeks after discovering the relic, I took the dirt-coated arrowhead and several 1930's coins I found near moonshine still sites on the north face of Pine Mountain to a jeweler in Kentucky and asked him to clean it. He disappeared into the back of his shop and returned with a large smile on his face. Using acid and another solution, he had cleaned away the brown stain, and the dirt color was replaced by a dull gray.

"I thought it was lead," he said, washing the acid off and handing it to me. "But I believe it's silver."

My heart leaped, and my mind raced through the hundreds of hours of research I'd done on the silver mine legends. Just to be on solid ground I asked another jeweler to test it. He used a solution on the relic and confirmed that the silver content was about 85 percent, with the rest made up of impurities, including ash.

The second jeweler also told me something that was even more interesting. He said, after his testing, that the arrowhead was made of one piece of silver, not from melted (or smelted) coins. The work on the piece was apparently done in some ancient time simply by heating a good-size chunk of ore and beating it into shape.

I searched my references for some mention of silver arrowheads, but only came up with a reference to a silver tomahawk legend involving the Shawnee brave Huraken in the Carter Cave, Kentucky, region. Carter Cave State Park Naturalist John Tierney and I spent several hours talking about the local wing of the silver legend and guessing about the silver arrowhead.

Tierney said that the possibility of a silver deposit being near the surface of the earth was likely only in two places in Appalachia, one of them in Bell County, Kentucky. The rock shelter in which I found the unusual precious relic is less than twelve miles from the Bell County line, and only one-half mile from the earth fault that would bring the valuable metal near the surface and make it available for mining.

I went to my cross-references again, and found various mentions of Indians working the silver mines prior to the arrival of Swift and his mining crew in 1760. The legend was passed down through countless generations of settlers from Pennsylvania to Georgia by word of mouth. Roughly, here's the ancient history, prior to the arrival of the "colonials" and the years Swift worked the deposit.

The earliest mention of the silver mine somewhere in Appalachia began among the Shawnee and Cherokee, who apparently worked the ore first for jewelry and then for bullets. The use of lead and silver ore being used by the Indians for ammunition is mentioned by Jenny Wiley, in her recollection of being kidnapped by the Shawnee.

Following early crude mining by these tribes, the Spanish may have arrived, via DeSoto or a wing of his exploration. Cherokee legends tell of Spanish miners and Indians being enslaved to work the ore.

Early English explorers among the North Carolina Cherokee report Spanish mining activities just across the Smoky Mountains in the Cumberlands.

The French followed the Spanish into the wilderness, and are rumored to have allied with the Shawnee and mined the ore for shipment back to France to help in the war against the English. In between the Spanish, French, and later English or colonial operations at the legendary mines, the Indians continued to work them.

With the removal of the Shawnee following wars with the Cherokee in the 1700's, and then the physical removal of the Cherokee Indians by legislation in the 1830's, the location of the silver mines was lost. Over the past hundred years dozens of Indians and those of Indian descent have returned to Kentucky and eastern Tennessee to search for the left-behind treasure.

The legend actually assisted in the settlement of some of the more rugged areas of southeastern Kentucky, with families following rough maps to isolated regions, settling, and spending every spare moment searching for clues. It has led to mysterious deaths of searchers, arrests and trials for violation of private property, and even to snake bites.

Copies of the "journal" have been found behind old chimneys, in trunks, Bibles, even rolled up like precious papers in vaults. Maps are still sold for top dollar, then copied and recopied. Bulldozers and backhoes are rented and used in the continuing search.

Yet after more than four years of research in local, state, regional and private libraries; after more than 400 pages of accumulated legend; after bruising my knees in dozens and dozens of caves and bumping my head on more than a few rock shelters, I did not believe the legend. I did not believe it because every scientist I spoke to told me there was no large amount of silver ore in Appalachia.

That was before I found the arrowhead.

This silver arrowhead was discovered on Pine Mountain near the Kentucky-Tennessee state line.

The Fact and Fiction of
John Swift's Lost Silver Mines

"It is near a peculiar rock. Boys, don't ever quit looking for it. It is the richest thing I ever saw."

These were supposed to be the last words ever uttered by John Swift just before he departed this life. And so Indian trader, hunter, explorer, profiteer, counterfeiter, sea captain, and silver miner Jonathan Swift left this earth, a clue to his now-famous lost silver mines on his lips.

Swift is said to have died about 1800, some thirty-nine years after he claimed to have entered the wild mountains west of the colonies, and after an exhausting dozen years or so in which he attempted, with the help of many new settlers in several states in mid-Appalachia, to relocate the fabled mines. His appearance in Virginia, Tennessee, and Kentucky is noted by early historians as being fact. Whether the man was actually Swift or a pretender, whether the mines and the many cache sites he claimed ever existed, and whether the entire legend is fictional or reality is yet being questioned.

Yet with every legend there is a grain of truth.

Sometime before the colonial settlement of the Appalachian Mountains and the territories to the west of the long chain, Swift and a crew of men claimed to have penetrated the wilderness. There they were said to have located, with the help of regional Indians and even a French friend, several ancient silver mines.

Swift and his crew, by most accounts, mined, smelted, and produced bars, tugs, and coins out of the native silver from 1761 to 1768 or so, finally being driven off by hostile Shawnee and Cherokee Indians.

During trips back and forth from their various homes,

which ranged from Kent Colony and Alexandria, Virginia, to Philadelphia and the Yadkin Valley in North Carolina, the silver miners were forced to abandon part of their year's silver production here and there.

Eventually all work was abandoned, the mines closed and concealed, and according to some legends, a huge amount of silver in coins and bars was hidden in a large cave. Plans were made to return following the Indian Wars, and retrieve the cache. But hardship befell Swift and his crew.

Swift, who is said to have been a successful shipping merchant in Alexandria by most accounts, sailed to England to obtain the financial backing he needed to expand his mines. There he was thrown into prison for his outspoken support for independence for the American Colonies.

When he was released after many years of confinement, Swift found himself aged, ill, and blind. He had prepared a journal of his adventures and returned to the region in an attempt to rediscover his mines and resume operation, or at least recover the cache in the great cave.

Yet the territory around his many mines, following 1770, had changed much. Settlers had flooded in from the colonies, and many of the old paths and landmarks had been altered.

Swift's search at various places in Kentucky, Virginia, West Virginia, and Tennessee failed to relocate the mines. During these hunts, Swift gave or sold various people copies of his now-famous journal. Most accounts have the "original" journal being left with Mrs. Renfro of Bean Station, Tennessee.

At last, frustrated and ill, Swift died with the clue to the location of a silver mine uttered with his last breath.

The visitation of Swift in the newly settled regions of the southeastern United States rekindled rumors within the region that go back to the ancient Indians. The directions, landmarks, carvings, and clues he left behind in the various "journals" and in the traditions and lore told from father to son for more than 200 years has created a huge legend of romantic wilderness adventure, Indian troubles, greed, murder, and unbelievable riches.

Many people, even today, believe that the treasures of John Swift do indeed exist, and are waiting to be found.

The search for silver mines in Appalachia began long before Swift's 1760 adventure began. Ancient Indians mined silver, copper, gold and semiprecious stones and ores from caves and bluffs in the region, and traded with distant tribes for the ores. Excavations of mounds and graves have turned up interesting pieces, including weapons and jewelry fashioned long before Europeans ever entered the mountains.

The Spanish and French explored the region with the purpose of locating the rumored mines, and the Spanish may have had several gold and silver mines in North Carolina, Georgia, Alabama, and Tennessee. Swift's journal, or versions of it, mention French and Spanish miners operating a silver mine near one of his digs.

Although not highlighted in most historical accounts, many of the first colonial explorers, including Gist and Boone, made observations about precious metals they suspected of being in the area. Rumors of Spanish mines circulated in Colonial Virginia and North Carolina as early as 1700. Expeditions were sent into and beyond the Blue Ridge Mountains in search of the illusive mines.

The Cherokee, Creek, and Shawnee have tribal legends of silver mines, and many times have returned to their old homeland to seek out hidden silver caches left there by their ancestors.

Early settlers in West Virginia, Virginia, Tennessee, Kentucky, southern Ohio, western North Carolina, upper South Carolina, northern Georgia and northern Alabama heard the tales of lost mines, and many spent time searching for the treasures. When a mysterious old man appeared in their area prior to 1800, claiming to be John Swift, he was welcomed and assisted wherever he went. Dozens of families with descendants still living in the area claim to have helped Swift in his frustrating search for his lost mines.

Wherever Swift went, he seemed to have had a copy of his famous journal which he shared, or sold, to those he encountered. Apparently none of the "original" versions survived, yet hundreds of people believe they have a copy of the journal Swift wrote. Although each copy follows the main tale, all vary in descriptions of landmarks, names of his mining crew, and directions to the mines.

As noted by the late Scott Partin of Frakes, Kentucky, some of the settlers of central Appalachia originally came to the area to look for the mines. Eventually they returned to their homes in the coastal states and brought their families back into the mountains to settle. The search for the lost mines then fell to their children, and their children's children, etc., each with a copy of their great-grandfather's Swift Silver Mine Journal and Map.

Mix into this tradition (which Ed Henson, Director of Kentucky's Recreational State Parks, calls the state's "oldest folk tale") the official and unofficial interest in the treasures by state and national leaders, and you create a powerful legend. Add into the brew the likes of John Filson, James Harrod, John Sevier, George Washington, Thomas Jefferson and Daniel Boone, and you have an eternal tale of romance, death, injury, mystery, rebellion, Indian attacks, and bloody murder.

Only a handful of those searchers over the years are mentioned in regional histories, but countless people have no doubt tramped the hills from Pittsburgh to Birmingham in search of the mines or the caches reported left by Swift.

Modern searchers looking for the mines or the cache sites use everything from long-distance metal detectors to calling on ancient spirits to assist them. A few searchers are actually "researchers" and comb the pages of books, magazines, and manuscripts in search of clues or new information. Even fewer people can be truly called treasure hunters, following up their research with physical searches of a suspected area.

"I hope it's never found," Michael Paul Henson said in 1994. Henson, the dean of Swift treasure hunters and a noted author and speaker, explained that if a mine or a major cache was found, then the search would be over and the tale concluded.

It is possible, however, that portions of Swift's treasures have been found. There seems to be evidence scattered here and there that recoveries have been made.

Yet the main find, whether it be the huge treasure hidden inside the Great Cave of the Shawnee or one of the Swift mines, has not been reported, and hundreds of people still believe.

Beneth a rock shelter like this one Swift claimed to have camped while mining silver from a nearby bluff. Early settlers in Bell County, Kentucky, found a silver smelter and the skeleton of a European man below the natural "rock house." The above shelter is in the "Doublehead Silver Mine" region. (Photo by Mike Steely)

The Classic Swift Journal

Almost anyone who is interested in the Swift legend is familiar with Michael Paul Henson. Over the years he had offered more information about the tale than anyone, and continued to be the chief contact for those researching the tale.

Henson's *John Swift's Lost Silver Mines*, first published in 1975, continues to be the "bible" of the lore. While he had written, spoken, and researched many other treasure, folk, and ghost tales, his knowledge of the Swift legend is recognized as superior.

Swift and the legend are also included in Henson's *Lost Silver Mines and Buried Treasures of Kentucky* and *Lost, Buried, and Sunken Treasures of the Midwest*. His *America's Lost Treasures* contains hundreds of clues to sites around the United States. Any extended review of the Swift lore would be incomplete without a tip of the hat to Henson, who has personally assisted the author and many others in research.

So it is with Mr. Henson's permission that I am presenting part of the extensive journal he found and published. For a complete version, any interested person should obtain a copy of *John Swift's Lost Silver Mines* from Mrs. Michael Paul (Nancy) Henson, P.O. Box 980, Jeffersonville, Indiana 47131.

"I was born October 3, 1712, in Philadelphia, Pennsylvania, my ancestors first came to America in 1637. I went to sea, when a boy, after several years of sailing I became captain of a ship. I married Desiree Ann Swift, April 21, 1748. When I left the sea in 1752 I settled in Alexandria, Virginia."

Surprisingly, most of the above statement can be traced through official records and found to be true, more or less.

One researcher found a John Swift born October 3, 1727, in Philadelphia, and marrying Desire F. Swift on September 21, 1752, and then leaving that area.

The "Loyal collector of Customs" in Philadelphia in 1750 was one "John Swift."

By other accounts Swift claims birth in Salisbury, England, in 1712 or 1689. Still others have him born in Portsmouth, England. As far back as 1667, one Jonathan Swift was living in Kent Colony, Virginia, and one version of the journal has him from Kent. Another John or Jonathan Swift resided, in 1776, in Northumberland County, Virginia, and had lived there since 1759.

Interestingly, one Jonathan Swift of Alexandria, Virginia, was the holder of two land grants on the Green River in Kentucky in 1795 and 1809. From Deed Book "A" of old Franklin County, Kentucky, comes the following:

"October 18, 1801. Jonathan Swift of Alexandria, Virginia, Merchant, to Wm. Mattock Rogers of Boston, Suffolk County, Massachusetts, all interests in tracts called Springfield on Green River, Hardin County, Kentucky."

Other land grants in Kentucky, including one in 1809, were issued to Jonathan Swift of Alexandria and to Swift's by the name of Thomas, John, Flower, etc. One deed, on file in Frankfort, Kentucky, to John Swift is for land in Christian County.

Henson's copy of the Swift Journal has Swift writing that he became a trader among the Cherokee and in the "Tennessee Country" while many other versions have him as a longhunter or trader among the Shawnee in the Ohio Valley. Other versions have him with no connection with the Appalachians or western territories prior to his service with the colonial forces under George Washington at Fort Duquesne.

Henson's copy reflects the service with the British against the French at Duquesne, having Swift return to Alexandria to resume his Indian trade and to become a silversmith. He has Munday as "George Munday" and coming to Swift as a captive during the Fort Duquesne battle, having served the

French as a "White Indian."

Munday, here, says he was born in 1735 on the Great Lakes and tells of his father and brothers hunting for furs and minerals south of the Ohio River about 1750, being captured by the Indians after discovering and working an old silver mine "somewhere on the headwaters of Big Sandy Creek."

The Indians carried Munday off and forced him to mine silver at various places. Having been befriended by Swift, Munday agreed to guide him into the wilderness and show him the various mines.

Swift sails to Cuba and hires two men, Guise and Jeffries, who were experienced miners. The names appear, in variations as Gist, Guess, Guest; Jeffries or Jeffers is Jefferson, in other versions of the journal.

After returning to Alexandria, Swift acquires the help of several men he had known while serving under George Washington: James Ireland, Abram Flint, Samual Blackburn, Shadrack Jefferson, and Issac Campbell. These associates are also listed in other versions, along with many others, with spelling variations of their names.

Swift and the crew depart Alexandria on June 21, 1760, enter the distant mountains and cross the Big Sandy "near its headwaters," then continue west until they find three different mines.

"We located the other mines by traveling along a great ridge, leading in a southwesterly direction, until we came to a large river, the name of which was unknown to us. Thence north to a large and very rocky creek, thence to the mines."

Most researchers read this, which is similar to several other journal versions, as following Pine Mountain, which begins at the Breaks of the Big Sandy River and ends in Scott County, Tennessee.

Fort Pitt was located at the junction of the Allegheny and Monongahela Rivers. These streams combine to form the Ohio. The fort was situated near the heart of modern Pittsburgh, at the tip of the "Golden Triangle" on Pittsburgh Point. This crossroads community served the emerging nation much the same way as the Panama Canal did later.

The first fort on the site was built in 1754 by colonists from Virginia. They gave it up to the French, who renamed it "Fort Duquesne." In 1758, the English finally drove the French out and built a new fort, naming it "Fort Pitt." Early Fort Pitt workers made tools, wire, and nails, and built boats for pioneer families migrating down the Ohio River.

"Knowledge of Swift's life in the back countries embraced in the head branches of the Ohio prior to Braddock's disastrous expedition is preserved in traditions alone," wrote Lewis Collins. "It is reasonably certain that about the year 1753 he was an Indian trader and it is more than likely that this had been his pursuit for some years previous to that date. It is said he was associated with some Pennsylvania businessmen."

Many accounts have Swift, like other colonial traders and longhunters, joining Colonel George Washington in service to their British homeland against the French during the French and Indian Wars. Swift claims such a service in several versions of his journal, noting that he served with several men who would later become associated with him in the silver mining operations.

The colonial forces with Washington fell beneath the questionable command of English General Edward Braddock, who arrived from England with regiments of regular troops. Before the large force of "redcoats" could reach Fort Duquesne, they were ambushed by the French and Indians and defeated some ten miles from their destination. Braddock and sixty-three of his eighty-nine officers were killed, wounded, or captured.

Washington, in charge of the Virginia militia, fought back in "Indian fashion" against the standing rows of the enemy. Prisoners were taken on both sides, and among the French fighters was one man we know today as "Munday" in the 1758 battle.

By the time Swift and his crew began stopping by Fort Pitt, some 200 families lived there. Just as Indians bothered Swift and his crew, they also pestered Fort Pitt; and in 1763, families living outside the fort took shelter there.

By 1765, Pittsburgh was laid out about 200 yards from the walls of the fort. The Alley copy of the journal notes that Swift and his crew purchased tools at Fort Pitt, and then bought maize from Indians in Ohio on their way to the mines.

Yet some researchers disclaim "Munday" and argue that Swift learned of the mines while trading with the Indians in Ohio and Kentucky prior to the service with the colonial forces.

"While in the great valley of the Ohio bartering trinkets, gaudy cloth, and rum to the Indians for valuable skins, Swift must have obtained his first information of the existence of silver mines in the territory south of the Ohio River, which had been worked in the past," one researcher has written.

"They had been worked, however, by some Frenchmen who lived in what is now Tennessee.

"The mines were in the country claimed by the Cherokee, but which was not then occupied by them. The country had been the home of the Shawnee, and they were familiar with every portion of it."

Another version has Swift taken hostage in North Carolina by Indians and transported into the mountains, there learning of the mines.

"After his escape, Swift made his way through the unbroken forests to the settlements of Virginia," writes Lewis Collins.

Swift, in the Henson version, wrote that the crew built a furnace and burned charcoal west of the headwaters of the Big Sandy "in preparation of our mining."

The following year, in 1761, Swift added men to his crew, including Joshua McClintock, Henry Hewitt, John Watts, Moses Fletcher, Pierre St. Martin, Andrew Renaud, and Seth Montgomery. Montgomery had "worked in the Royal Mint in London" and was knowledgeable about making dies and molds for coining money.

Swift had Montgomery as a partner with him, owning ships together "used in trade on the Spanish Seas." Many researchers read this to mean that Swift actually pirated against the Spanish, hauled the booty into the wilderness, and recoined it into acceptable coins.

Swift permits Munday to use his property in the Yadkin Valley of North Carolina between trips to the mine. By 1761, Swift had also found help from "our friendly Indians," and the large group departed to expand operations at the mines. Several Shawnee, including Chiefs Blue Jacket and Cornstalk, later claimed to have helped Swift at the mines.

The 1761 trip first went to Fort Pitt, where the Frenchmen Renaud and St. Martin joined the crew, along with "several Shawnee."

"We had two workings, the company was divided into two parties, one group went due west (from one of the Forks of the Sandy River, near its headwaters) for a considerable distance. The other went southwest along the great ridge, and each party to work the locations selected the previous year."

On the return Swift and some of the men retraced their trip to the mines back to Alexandria, but were attacked five days into their journey by Indians. Nine days later the Indians attacked again, shooting a hole in their "lading" and causing Swift to lose part of the silver. He buried part of the year's work near a "symbol of a triangle on a large slanted rock, at the mouth of a creek flowing generally north. We did not camp this night until we crossed the Big Kanawha." This passage apparently refers to parts of West Virginia, and much speculation has been made about the cache site.

When Swift and part of his crew, including Montgomery, returned to Alexandria, they found their "shipping" had gone well and they bought five more ships.

In 1762, he departed Alexandria and went by way of Fort Pitt, with a large "pack train" of supplies. When he returned to the mines he found many crew members left there for the winter were ready to go home, although "much work had been done." Here Swift mentions that some of the men "had sailed with me."

After a summer of mining, Swift and some of the men set off for home on September 1, only to be attacked by Indians the following day, not far from one of the mines.

"We left a valuable prize and two horse loads of silver on

the south side of the Big Gap where we marked some trees with our names and curious signs."

Yet Swift then alters his trek home, probably because of being "greatly pestered" by Indians, and exits the mountains to stop at Cassels Woods (Castlewood, Virginia). His path through a "Great Gap" to Castlewood would have taken him through Cumberland Gap, Pound Gap, or the Breaks of the Sandy. On arriving in Alexandria he found his "shipping" was continuing to prosper and he bought three more ships.

Swift wrote that the ships were purchased "from the Scotch Company." Other versions of the journal mention trouble with the "Scottish Company" but do not refer to why or what was transpiring.

In 1763 Swift "doubles" the number of pack animals and then takes a new route into the mines.

"We crossed the New River, thence to the Holston River, thence to a Large Gap in the Mountains," the journal says. Certainly this "large gap" could only have been Cumberland or Big Creek Gap, the only two large passes in the area north of the Holston (which eventually becomes the Tennessee River).

"Here we set our course for the mines near the headwaters of the Big Sandy."

Returning that year, Swift mentions spending three days with "Castleman" at Castle Woods.

In 1764 Swift leaves Alexandria and goes to the New River, crossing at Ingles Ferry and the "large gap," and reaches his "lower mines" some thirty-five days after leaving his home port. The crew, or part of them, leave the mines in November, go by the "Big Gap" and New River, and travel to Munday's place on the Yadkin rather than going on to Alexandria.

The following year they return by (probably) the same route and, realizing a good year of mining, "gathered into a great cave our immense store of precious metal, both the coined and uncoined, and hid them until we would...convey it thence to the trade of the seas." They leave the mine through "a Gap at the headwaters of the Big Sandy Creek."

In 1766, Swift and his men were delayed in their return

to the mines because two crew members, Fletcher and Flint, had a fatal sword fight. Before the duel, the men made wills and "concealed their money in the vicinity of Munday's house on the Upper Yadkin" of North Carolina. Flint was reported to have buried 240,000 English crowns, and Fletcher hid 360,000. Fletcher died six months after the fight and Flint eventually recovered, though missing that year's trip.

Beginning in 1766, Swift refers to his men, or crew, as "the company," indicating that he may have formed some type of legal corporation. He returned to the mines to find that some of the winter workers had abandoned the digs and returned to their homes. He had difficulty in obtaining new men who could be trusted.

In 1767 Swift left North Carolina with the largest pack train thus far and attempted to leave in secret, noting that "several others" had become suspicious of his activities. Here some Swift researchers connect Daniel Boone and other Yadkin Valley longhunters to the Swift legend, contending that Boone and several men tried to follow Swift and find his mines.

Swift apparently spent the year in success, and even stayed the winter, returning from the mines to Alexandria. After two months there he set out again for the mines, staying until October.

On his attempt to return to the colonies, Swift and some of his men were ambushed by Indians "on the Big Sandy," and Campbell was killed. Hazlett and Staley were badly wounded, and shortly after arriving at Munday's home on the Yadkin, Hazlett died. Swift also tells of two horses being stolen during the fight, and of concealing their cargo "at the mouth of a large creek running generally east. We left marks on a beech tree so we could locate it on our return."

In January of 1769, Swift noted that a settlement with the "Scotch Company" was made, although the Scots "took advantage of the nature of our business to extort from us a great sum, not their due." If all he had traded with the Scots was money for ships it is striking that the settlement with them took place on the Yadkin, where Swift claims to have wintered that year.

In 1769, the last year of mining silver in the secrets of Appalachia, Swift and his men left Munday's house in May, going by way of Ingle's Ferry and through the "Big Gap." This was apparently at the head of the Sandy River, as opposed to the "Large Gap" above the Holston River.

Because of increasing Indian troubles, Swift decided to close the operation, settle up with his men, and transport the rest back to the colonies. Yet he found the silver too much to transport, and he and his "company" stored it in "the great cavern of the Shawnee," planning to return for it after the Indian Wars. Here, for the first and only time, Swift mentions that they "had gathered GOLD and silver until we had heaped up great riches." No other place in any other journal mentions gold, although gold is occasionally found with silver, in small amounts.

With the riches gathered in the cave, Swift and his men began to return to their different homes; but finding the loads too great, they stopped here and there to hide the excess.

"We left $22,000 and $30,000 in English crowns on a large creek running near a south course. Close by the creek we marked our names, Swift, Jefferson, and Munday, and other names on a large beech tree with the symbols of a compass, trowel and square."

The "symbols" mentioned here by Swift are believed, by several Swift researchers, to be symbols associated with the Masonic Order. They stretch that connection to come up with an entire "Masonic" twist to the legend, even to a point of involving the "Knights of the Golden Circle" in the theory.

"About twenty or thirty poles from the creek stands a small rock, between the small rock and the creek you will find a small rock of bluish color with three chips made with a gritstone by rubbing it on the rock. By the side of this bluish rock you will find a valuable prize. We left prizes here at three different times. At not great distance from this place we left $15,000 of the same kind of crowns, marking three or four trees with the marks. Nor far from these trees we left a prize near a forked white oak, about three feet underground. We laid two long stones across it, marking several stones close about it with marks of animal tracks and arrows.

"At the Forks of the Sandy, near its headwaters is a small rockhouse on a small branch. We hid a prize underground. It is valued at $6,000. We likewise left $3,000 buried in the rockhouse we camped in, on the right hand side."

The Henson version of the journal has Swift saying that he made three trips to the mines which Swift did not record.

Clues, Marks, and Signs

"The furnace that is built is on the left hand side of a long rocky branch, that heads southwest and flows northeast, in a very remote place in the west," Swift claims in the Henson copy. Like many of his clues in the various journals, this seems a very vague piece of information. Yet some of his clues, marks, and signs are not as vague.

The last part of this version of the journal, which is certainly the longest version yet found, is full of information, including references to "Furnace Creek," remarkable rocks, Buffalo Salt Lick, Half Moon Cliff, an Indian village in a gap populated by "Mecca" Indians, Balanced Rock, etc.

Henson mentions Swift's return to the recently settled region after his release from the English prison and his sad attempt to relocate his mines. He mentions the old blinded man searching, with the help of settlers, in various areas including Twelve Poles Creek, West Virginia.

The noted treasure writer has stated that he believes Swift had at least three mines, scattered from the Sandy River to Bell County, Kentucky, and tells of many findings made in the region, including silver bars, coins, furnaces, carvings, etc.

At random, taking some thirty-six versions of the journal into account, here are some of the "clues" mentioned: Arrows, Rock Arch, Animal Tracks, Balanced Rock, Bear's Den, Bald Mountain, Buffalo Rock, Bullet Holes in Trees, Boxed Canyon, Blue Stone, Caves, Coaling Grounds, Chimney Rocks, Compass and Square, Corn Cob Rock, Curious Marks, Crane, Haystack Knobs, Haystack Rock, Hanging

Rock, High Cliffs, Horseshoe Bend, Horseshoe Carving, Falls of Water, Flag Pond, Hatchet Marks, Indian Stairs, Indian Face Rock, Large Gap, Myrtle Thicket, Names and Initials, Notches in Stone, Pine Knot, Pond with Rock in Middle, Remarkable Rock, Rattlesnake Carving, Flat Rock, Rockhouse, Saddle Gap, Sheepskin Apron, Sky Rock, Lighthouse Rock, Spruce Pine Cove, Stone Monument, Monument Rocks, Saddle Gap, Table Top Rock, Turkey Tracks, Triangle, Tea Kettle Rock, Turkey Carving, Wolf, Zodiac signs, Sinking Creek, Turtle Back Rock, Table Top Rock, Lookout Rock, Face of Man Rock, Half Moon Shelter, Long Shelter, Big Gap, Holly Thicket, Moccasin Gap, Buffalo Head Carving, Indian Reed Creek, Great Cave, and Crows Foot Carving.

Also, from the various journals: Bell carving or Shape, Anchor, Stars, Drying Grounds, Laurel Mountain, Great Ridge, etc.

If the Swift Journals were a hoax or a fraud, whoever wrote them certainly knew the area very well prior to 1800. It may be that, if Swift wrote various versions, his information about the region increased as he spent more and more time there and he included later place names in his text. It is obvious, with the land claim by John Filson, the circulation of journals in Virginia and North Carolina, and early Indian tales, that rumors of lost silver mines existed long before Swift made his "return" to search for his lost mines.

Had no version of the Swift Journals ever been circulated or published, settlers in West Virginia, Kentucky, western Virginia, North Carolina, and east Tennessee would have had suspicions of the existence of silver mines there simply from the silver bars, coins, relics, furnaces, and other clues which have turned up.

Old tools which fell from a bluff in Carter County, Kentucky, were believed to have been used by Swift during the mining and minting of silver. Other objects, like money molds, silver-bearing ashes, and clothing on skeletons found in rock shelters have pointed to Swift's era, if not his mining operation.

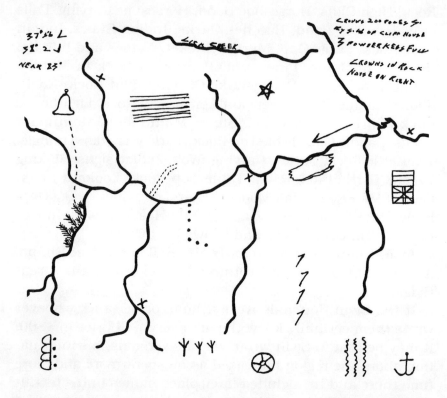

Probably the most prized "Swift map" was first published by Michael Paul Henson in 1975 and is believed by some to have been drawn by Swift about 1769. The map was probably held by noted Swift hunter Robert Alley of Paintsville, Kentucky, and eventually by the late Alva Rice, who passed it to Henson. The original map was much larger, and Henson traced over the thin lines to make them darker.

Versions and Variations

After almost twenty years of research into the legend of Swift's silver mines, I wish I could report that there is one original journal that would offer enough authentic clues to eventually lead someone to find the mine, or mines, or the various caches supposedly hidden from West Virginia to Alabama.

Unfortunately I cannot. For in my search I have found some forty different versions of Swift's journal. Some are very similar and some are totally different. If you add in the "way-bills" and maps floating around central Appalachia, you might have fifty or more different pieces of information, all claiming to be authentic.

Among the different journals are the versions and copies attributed to: Alley, Alley's Uniontown, Granny Anderson, Apperson's, Beasley's, Chief Joseph's, Collins various copies, Cornstalk's, Connelley's, Cole's waybill, Clark's, the Clear Fork copy, and the Cumberland Falls copy.

Also: Dillion's, Dougherty, Caugherty, Deer Skin, Graybeal's, Johnson's, the Kent Colony copy, McMillan's, Lakely's, Forward's, Hopkin's, Haywood's, and the Fugate waybill.

And: Hoskins', McLeMoore's, Monday's, Partin's, Parson's, Pack Train version, Rice's, Rasnick's, Spurlock's, G.W. Swift version, Stringfield's, Timmon's, Terrell's, Reams, Wilson's, Walden's, Young's, Zodiac copy, Shepherd Family's, Simmons, etc., etc., etc.

Even those journals which seem "old" enough to be authentic have had subtle changes by people who have held them, including changes of place names and the insertion of other information they thought might help. Or might mislead.

Often one of these versions is discovered anew, published

in magazines, books, or news stories by people who believe they have found an "original" version. Other people will hide their "journal" in a Bible or with other precious papers, thinking they have the one and only clue to the location of the rich silver mine.

In the journals, Swift himself is called by various names, including "John Smith." His first name is given as John, Johnathan, Jonathan, George, William, George William, Tom, William Matthew, etc. Munday is given as Monday, Munday, Monde, Mundeau, Money, and Mondie.

Journals are also attributed to Monday and Staley, especially in central Kentucky, and the names of those who accompanied Swift as "original mining crew members" vary within many journals. Occasionally the names of noted American families, like Jefferson, appear in the versions.

Swift appears as "An English Gentleman," a Pennsylvania-born merchant in Alexandria, an Ohio Valley trader, a shipping merchant, a pirate preying on Spanish ships, a Kent Colony businessman, and as having never existed at all, being instead a dreamed-up character in a work of fiction by the missing John Filson.

The various versions give Swift's associates as Shawnee, Cherokee, French, Peruvian miners, English businessmen, silversmiths, cutthroats, outlaws, and even Masons.

Over the many years since the appearance of the Swift journals, which we could date at about 1785, copies or versions have found their way into the hands of academics and "experts" who have commented about them. The reviews have been mixed.

Some experts and historians take an objective look at the documents, such as Tennessee's early historian Judge John Haywood and Kentucky Judge Richard Apperson. Others reject the journals outright, and scoff at the idea that silver could ever have been mined in the region. An example is Professor David Dale Owens.

One inquiry into the "originality" of one of the journals was conducted by Francis L. Berkley, curator of manuscripts for the University of Virginia. Unfortunately we do not know which "journal" or version thereof he saw.

Berkley described the journal as "spurious and tommyrot" because the handwritten manuscript was too modern, and the author used the word "smelter," which Berkley said did not come into common use until after the journal was said to have been penned. Berkley even reviewed the paper on which it was written, and said it was "woven" and too modern for 1775, noting that the document had been crumpled time and time again to give it the appearance of being from an ancient time. The ink used, he said, was not durable enough to have lasted the length of time involved.

Swift is said by several legends to have been married in Pennsylvania or in Alexandria, as having romanced Mrs. Renfro of Bean Station, Tennessee, as having a Wyondott or Shawnee wife, and as having married a Melungeon woman.

By the different accounts Swift kills all his fellow miners, and by another Blackburn kills them all, including Swift. In one version, Munday is the financial backer and Swift only a silversmith hired by him.

In one version Swift, Munday, and other original crew members return and reclaim part of the loot hidden in the Great Cave. In another, Munday is killed by Indians when he with others attempts to get the treasure while Swift is in prison in England.

The versions seem to go on and on, in almost endless variations, which is what happens to stories that are passed down by word of mouth. Probably the most accurate are those versions dating closer to Swift's time which were first published after 1800. That is, if the legend itself is true.

A few years ago my friend Roy Price and I would lecture groups about the legend. We spoke around southeastern Kentucky and in Tennessee, each time to a large audience of history or treasure buffs. Roy usually took the "absolutely true" position, and I took the "historically the mines could never have existed" view. This gave us a good balance and the presentations went well, with my being a good skeptic having been a newspaper reporter—until I found a silver arrowhead with my metal detector.

Somehow I could not get my heart into being serious about "never could have existed" from that point on. My skeptical attitude was softened to a point of "possible belief." As I have seen more and more silver relics, including bars, axes, Indian jewelry, and coins, I have softened my position even more.

Today I find myself a believer of sorts in the legend, given all its warts and scars.

Beware the Curse

If you believe in the existence, or possible existence, of lost silver mines in central Appalachia and have plans to search for the mines or the many caches reportedly left here and there by Swift, be forewarned.

When settlers in Kentucky, Tennessee, West Virginia, and western Virginia began following journal directions, waybills or map drawings, they began having very unusual things happen to them. Some would find a mine or treasure sign and make a mental note of its location, returning later only to become totally confused. Others suffered broken limbs, arrest, and even disappeared forever into the pages of history. Some died tragic deaths.

In the Kentucky version of the tale, the Shawnee, who knew of and operated the mines long before Swift, considered the silver and all things associated with it (including their Great Cave) as sacred places. To the south, the Cherokee so feared the Spanish silver miners that they attacked and killed them, lest the tribe be enslaved and forced to mine the ore. Both noble Indian peoples kept their secrets, and little has been passed on to their descendants.

The idea of an Indian curse, or spell, on the silver mines and all things thereof has several noteworthy examples:

Swift himself suffers Indian attacks and wilderness hardships. He is thrown in prison in England, goes blind and becomes ill, and returns to search for the lost mines for years.

Munday and other crew members, if not killed by Indians or each other, are killed while Swift was in prison while trying to recover booty left in the mountains.

John Filson was the first man to mention Swift "in print." He obtained a land grant in 1788, along with Robert Breckenridge, for 1,000 acres in the old "county of Lincoln" to include "a silver mine which was improved about seventeen years ago by a certain man named Swift."

"Wherein Swift reports he had extracted from the ore a considerable quantity of silver, some of which he made into dollars, and left at or near the mine," Filson wrote. Filson set off that same year, apparently to locate the Swift mine, and disappeared. What happened to him is unknown, although some pioneer historians assume he was killed by Indians.

Joe Nickell wrote of Filson in the "Filson Club History Quarterly" and put forth the idea that Filson, who wrote the first *History of Kentucky* and *Adventures of Daniel Boone*, may well have written the original Swift Journal, too. Nickell refers to Filson's known admiration for the English fiction writer "Jonathan Swift," and theorizes that Filson may have been working on his own fiction before his sudden disappearance. The works, which might have been found among his belongings, then circulated throughout the new territories as works of fact.

James Harrod, founder of Harrodsburg, Kentucky, and noted frontiersman, is approached by a man known to us only as Bridges, who tells Colonel Harrod he knows the location of Swift's mine. Although involved in a lawsuit against Bridges, Harrod accompanies the man to near the "Three Forks of the Kentucky River." Harrod is never seen alive again, but Bridges shows up in Lexington, selling some skins and furs and a set of silver sleeve buttons with the initial "H" on them. Years later hunters find a decomposed body in a cave near the Kentucky River, believed to be the remains of Harrod.

Chief Blue Jacket, after contracting with Kentucky investors to lead them to a silver mine, takes them on a long march through the mountains, only to end up in a pow-wow with the Great Spirit and declining to lead them any further.

Lakely, the Cherokee treasure hunter at Bolton Gap east of Pineville, Kentucky, discovers the mysterious carvings he sought and abruptly drops dead.

Returning Shawnee, including descendants of Cornstalk and Blue Jacket, search the mountains of central Kentucky and are reportedly murdered by pioneer settlers.

A Knoxville, Tennessee, couple, in the 1930's, follow an old journal to the Narrows, near Jellico, Tennessee, and find themselves in jail following a gunfight with local police officers.

Roy Price, a much-read Swift researcher, follows a tip from another treasure hunter and crawls into what may be the "Great Shawnee Cave" in Kentucky. An experienced spelunker of several years, Price gets "spooked" and suffers a strange illness for days following the exploration.

James Renfro, a pioneer toll-gate keeper at Cumberland Ford (now Pineville, Kentucky) searched the area of Red Bird, Clear Fork, and Stinking Creek following a copy of the journal. He and his slave are struck by lightning and killed.

Huraken and Manuita, star-crossed Indian lovers, both die tragically.

And there were others, too many to mention, who have been associated with the lost silver mine lore in one way or the other and have experienced much difficulty. As one Swift buff puts it, the closer you get to the treasure, the tougher things become.

Two different Kentucky families, unrelated to each other but with roots reaching back to the first settlement of the territory, became involved in lawsuits against the state over claims to the lost mines.

A modern-day Indian treasure hunter runs into "law trouble" while searching for the lost mine in Tennessee.

The list goes on and on.

Is there a curse? Has a spell by the ancient Indians surrounded the silver mines even before Swift? Does the curse continue even today?

Interesting questions.

While no one is certain as to what happened to John Filson, there is some speculation. Shortly after he disappeared into the Kentucky wilderness, after requesting rights to the region supposed to contain Swift's mine, Swift appeard at Bean Station and began his efforts to relocate his lost mines.

As some have speculated that Filson wrote the Swift journal, or journals, is it also possible that the man who appeared in Bean Station, Tennessee, in southwest Virginia, and at different points in Kentucky, posing as Swift, was actually Filson? My response to that is: Not likely, but interesting. Although we don't know the fate of Filson, or for that matter the definite fate of James Harrod, we do have some clues.

Harold Hackworth was hunting in Madison County, Kentucky, in 1969 and chased a raccoon into a crack in a bluff. When he cleared away the bushes he found a cave, on the Kentucky River near Boonesboro. When he moved a rock blocking the cave, he discovered a large chamber containing several items, among them an old 62 calibre British flintlock pistol, a flintlock rifle, a bullet mold with eight bullets, a coin with the date 1870, and a hunting knife with a tomahawk with the initials "JF" cut into the head. He also discovered a copy of the *Pennsylvania Gazette* dated September 14, 1769.

The initials could have belonged to anyone, but a Courier Journal newspaper article speculated that it might be Filson or John Finley.

Willis Everman, in a 1969 newspaper article, recalled the Hackworth find and speculated that Filson learned of the Swift Silver mines from Boone, who Everman believed searched for the mines.

The likelihood is that the truth of it will never be known.

Before Swift Came the Spanish

Just how far did early Spanish treasure hunters and soldiers of fortune penetrate the Appalachian Mountains? Did the seekers of precious ore only trek to northern Georgia, as some historians believe? Or did the Latins actually explore further inland into the upper reaches of Tennessee, North Carolina, and even West Virginia?

There is much evidence that, in fact, the Spanish and their miners and soldiers extended far beyond their formerly recognized contact with resident Indians, and may have left relics and landmarks as clues to their unrecognized exploits. Scattered here and there—in regional legends, Indian lore, obscure history and manuscripts, and carvings on boulders—is enough to interest any treasure history buff. Even today, clues to the reach of the early Spanish treasure hunters continues to come to light.

"Long before the end of the 16th Century...the existence of mines of gold and other metals in Cherokee country was a matter of common knowledge among the Spanish at St. Augustine and Santa Elena, and more than one expedition has been fitted out to explore the interior," wrote James Mooney in *Myths of the Cherokee and Sacred Formulas*.

"Numerous traces of ancient mining operations, with remains of old shafts and fortifications evidently of European origin, show that discoveries were followed up, although the policies of the Spanish concealed that fact from the outside world," Mooney noted.

Early Spanish mining is also mentioned by William Jones in *Antiquities of the Southern Indians*. He describes underground activities discovered in 1834 on Dukes Creek, in White County, Georgia, including structures uncovered that had notched and shaped logs. Similar hewn logs "bound with iron" bands were found along the Valley River in North Carolina. In the 1800's, several mine shafts believed to be of Spanish origin were discovered in Georgia and western North Carolina.

The remains of an old white settlement were found near Lincolnton, North Carolina, and believed to be Spanish. Found was a fire pit and timbers of "Subterranean cabins" on Dukes Creek. Evidence of ancient mining was also found by the first English settlers near Kings Mountain, North Carolina, about 1750. Within twenty miles of the noted Revolutionary War battlefield park, the mines were believed to be Spanish, and may have been described in 1670 by John Ledere and later, in 1690, by James Moore.

Ora Blackmun's *Western North Carolina* also mentions rumors of early Spanish mining.

"Gold, silver, and copper the Indians mined and used as ornaments. The gold-greedy soldiers of DeSoto prospected for the same metals. For more than a century their sporadic mining attempts probably turned up small amounts of gold and silver, for both appear in many places," Blackmun wrote.

Blackmun also mentions gold in the Blue Ridge Mountains, copper deposits in Ashe, Jackson, Haywood, and Swain Counties, and an interesting section about old feldspar diggings at the "Hoot Owl Hollow Mine."

Virginia Colonial Governor William Berkley authorized an early expedition in 1640 into the state's western region not only to find the long-sought "short passage to India" but to locate silver he learned the Spanish had mined. In 1649 the Virginia colonial government offered land grants and mining rights to persons discovering new territory and minerals in the uncharted regions west. Governor Berkley was told of ore mines "within five days' journey to the west and by the south, there is a great high mountain and at the foot thereof, great rivers that run into a great sea." We know today the mountains were the Blue Ridge and Smoky, and the Rivers were the Tennessee, Ohio, and Kentucky, which become the Mississippi and empty into the Gulf of Mexico.

"And that there are men that come hither in ships. They

wear apparel and have reed caps on their heads and ride beastes like our horses, but have much longer ears," he learned.

Jackson County, Kentucky, far above where many historians credit the Spanish with exploring, was the site in 1872 of the discovery of a four-ounce lump of silver. Nearby was a rock carved in Spanish, with the date "June 3, 1632."

"How much permanent impression the early Spanish intercourse made on the Cherokee is impossible to estimate, but must have been considerable," Mooney wrote.

Legends in North Carolina tell of DeSoto's interest in mining along the Valley River. Don Tristan De Luna led a separate group of 300 Spanish soldiers into the region in 1560, and spent the summer searching for ore. Juan Pardo's expedition, including a 1567 march from Fort Santa Elena, South Carolina, took him at first four days into the interior to the village of Chisca. The Spanish then continued another twenty days to a principal town of the Indians known as Kusa. Along the way the soldiers stayed with different tribes and, at Kusa, they built a small fort. They also visited "Canosi" or "Cofetacque," described as some "fifty leagues from Santa Elena."

Eventually Pardo visited several Indian towns and viewed the "mines of crystal" before marching to "Xuala" in the foothills of the Blue Ridge. The Brooks manuscripts on file with the Bureau of American Ethnology indicate that the gold and other metals mined by the various Spanish explorations were transported to Florida and South Carolina by the end of the 1500's.

While seeking mines and exploiting tribes in Appalachia, the Spanish eventually gained an evil reputation among Native Americans, and many conflicts erupted. The Cherokee feared them and knew that if caught by the white men, they would be enslaved and forced to work in the mines. Near Soco Gap near Cherokee, North Carolina, is a spot called "Skwan-digugunyi" meaning "Where the Spaniard is in the water." It apparently indicates the site of a battle where the dead enemy soldiers were thrown into the river.

Survivors among the Spanish soldiers, including many

Portuguese men, were captured and held. According to Cherokee legend, the men eventually coupled with tribal women and were isolated from the rest of the nation. Chief Attakullakulla told the story:

"As a result of a great battle with the Spanish, six soldiers were spared. Over a period of time they achieved a degree of freedom, took Cherokee wives, and adapted their lifestyles as best they could. When the Cherokee began alliances with other European visitors, including the French and English, the descendants of the Latin soldiers were banished into 'the upper reaches of the Pellissippi' to an area known today as the Clinch Mountains, along the Tennessee, Kentucky, and Virginia borders."

The Melungeons of that region have long claimed to be of Portuguese descent, and gene tests in recent years have proven the link.

The Cherokee referred to the people as "Melungos" and there were other isolated descendants of the Spanish soldiers scattered here and there in Appalachia, including the "Ramps" of Central Kentucky and the "Pedros" of West Virginia.

Near Indian Camp Run, in West Virginia, is a tradition of a lost mine with fabulous buried riches. The origin predates the American Revolution, according to writer Lucullus Virgil McWhorter. In *The Border Settlers of Northwest Virginia, 1768 to 1795*, he wrote that the mine had been worked by Spanish and English adventurers alike, both of whom were nearly exterminated by their Indian allies. Descendants of the survivors, who go by the name of Petro or Pedro, were known on the upper Monongahela as early as 1777, and descendants lived in Randolph County. In 1883, in a cave not far from Indian Camp Cave, some very old tools were found that were made of metal and were "very rusty."

Early longhunter and pioneer tales link the Melungeons with counterfeiting and silversmithing. One legend has the Melungeons mining and smelting silver along the waters of Straight Creek between Pineville and Harlan, Kentucky. The money they supposedly minted were copies of Spanish coins and, according to Colonel W.A. Henderson of Tennessee, the money contained more ore than that minted by the government.

"At one time in my recollection these coins passed current, without question," he wrote.

"Somewhere in the hills they discovered gold and silver," wrote James Ashwell in *Lost Tribes of Tennessee's Mountains*. Possibly the descendants of the Latin soldiers simply mined the same ore their forefathers had discovered.

Further proof that the Spanish went far beyond their historically credited trek includes the discovery of a small copper cross near the mouth of Paint Creek, Kentucky. Plowed up by a local farmer in 1840, the cross was found to have the inscription "Santa Maria" engraved on it.

A silver mine in the Nantahala Gorge in western North Carolina was operated by early Spaniards. After the English began settling the region, three Spanish men were found to have worked a mine near Silver Creek. The settlers were visited by a young man of "Spanish Blood" who had a map of early mining there. He spoke of the site and mentioned "three bushels of money" but apparently failed to locate the cache, disappearing without notice.

Cliff Winkle, a Nantahala Gorge man, reported that he accidentally chanced upon an old Spanish silver mine while looking for a lost cow, but could never relocate it.

Near Chattanooga, Tennessee, close to the path now officially designated as DeSoto's Route, the skeleton of a Spanish soldier was unearthed just inside the mouth of Raccoon Mountain Cave, now a noted tourist attraction. Similar finds have been made further north, including a Spanish helmet found in a north Tennessee rock shelter, and European buttons found with a skeleton beneath a bluff in Bell County, Kentucky.

J.W.M. Breazeale, in *Life As It Is*, wrote that a fort was discovered one mile above the junction of the Pigeon River and the French Broad River, atop the crest of a high bluff. The 8.5 acre site sported a level parade ground, a passage to the river, and posts at one of the gateways. Other unexplained forts, which may have been built by the Spanish for their own protection, have been found, including Fort Mountain in northern Georgia, Old Stone Fort in south central Tennessee, Indian Fort near Berea, Kentucky, and Fort Ancient in southern Ohio.

A large limestone cavern near the Kentucky line in Campbell County, Tennessee, has several unique Indian carvings in the ceiling, including one of a rifle and another of a crossbow. Both weapons were used and introduced (along with the horse) by the Spanish visitors.

Early English explorers along the "Wilderness Road" from Virginia into Kentucky, noted strange carvings on trees and bluffs at Cumberland Gap, including many "crosses." Crosses of Spanish design have also been found here and there throughout mid-Appalachia.

As more and more treasure hunters take to the mountains and fields, further links involving early Spanish silver and gold seekers will certainly be found. There is a lot of unwritten history yet to be uncovered, and possibly a treasure or two.

One recent unofficial find along the Tennessee and Kentucky line on an ancient trail involves fifteen silver bars, each weighing seven ounces, found beneath a flat rock. Another rock is nearby, in the hewn shape of a battle axe, and the remains of Spanish soldiers are rumored to be beneath the stone.

Fort Harrod State Park, Kentucky.

The Cherokee Will Return

There is an ancient tradition among the Cherokee people of silver and gold mines within their vast nation prior to the arrival of the English, the colonial traders, and the longhunters. The tales may actually precede the invasion of their lands by the Spanish in 1540.

Modern archeologist are dumbfounded by the uncovering of copper and silver artifacts from burial mounds in the Tennessee and Ohio Valleys. The scientists, despite growing evidence otherwise, contend that the Cherokee and other eastern Native Americans had no knowledge of mining or smelting ores until the Europeans showed them how to do so.

Yet copper and silver bracelets, ear spools, tools and ceremonial axes and arrowheads found in burial sites several thousand years old prove beyond debate that, like the white man, eastern tribes recognized the value of worked ores, and knew of techniques to produce beautiful and worthwhile products for use and trade.

The origin of silver and the white man's desire for it is reflected in a legend transcribed by James Mooney in *Myths of the Cherokee*, first published in 1891 from field studies beginning in 1887:

"At the creation the Ulunsuti [a holy transparent stone of crystal] was given to the white man and a piece of silver to the Indian. But the white man despised the stone and threw it away, while the Indian did the same with the silver. In going about, the white man afterward found the silver piece and put it into his pocket, and has prized it ever since.

"The Indian, in a like manner, found the Ulunsuti where the white man had thrown it. He picked it up and has had it since as his talisman, as money is the talismanic power tax of the white. This story is general and is probably older than others of its class."

Mooney and others, researching the encounter between the first whites and the Cherokee, indicate that the silver mines existed before the Spanish arrived.

"As the existence of the precious metals in the southern Alleghenys was known to the Spanish from a very early period, it is probable that more thorough exploration of that region will bring to light many evidences of their mining operations. In his *Antiquities of the Southern Indians*, Jones describes a sort of subterranean village discovered in 1834 on Dukes Creek in White County, Georgia, consisting of a row of small log cabins extending along the creek, but embedded several feet below the surface of the ground, upon which large trees were growing, the inference being that the houses had been thus covered by successive freshets. The logs had been notched and shaped apparently with metallic tools."

Mooney also wrote that shafts have been found in Valley River, North Carolina, at the bottom of which hewn oak timbers, banded with iron, were found. Stone fortifications and corrals were discovered at Fort Mountain and Silver Creek, Georgia.

"Ancient mining indications were also reported from Kings Mountain, about twenty miles distant," he noted.

When the Spanish entered the old Cherokee holdings, from Florida with DeSoto and from Charleston, South Carolina, with Juan Pardo, they came in search of valuable ore which they believed was located near a village called "Coca or Xuala" some "twenty days inland."

Mooney and others have guessed at the location of Xuala, he supposing it to be within the territory of the neighboring Creek Nation, but no one has ever located the site. Others suppose the Indian town was in western North Carolina and still others, especially early settlers of western Virginia, believed the village was there. Certainly the Spanish penetrated the nation of the Cherokee much further than the limited expedition claimed by modern historical writers.

DeSoto and his men were credited by Mooney with crossing the Blue Ridge Mountains and descending the Smoky Mountains to the French Broad River in east Tennessee.

All the while, when assisting or resisting the Spanish, the Cherokee kept secret their various mines of precious metals. Possibly they had workings in the Copperhill and Ducktown copper fields, in the gold fields of northern Georgia and southwestern North Carolina, and along Coker Creek in east Tennessee.

Pardo's expedition and plans to set up trading routes and settlements in the region came after DeSoto's ill-fated exploits. While his efforts may indeed lead to the existence of the Melungeons, Pedros and others who still have descendants in Appalachia, some believe the Spanish certainly were resisted, forced back to the coast, or killed by the Cherokee.

The mistrust of the Spanish among the Cherokee is evident in old legends of the battles, which resulted from fear that if captured or conquered, the Indians would be forced into slavery and made to mine the rich ores.

Remains of an old white settlement near Lincolnton, North Carolina, are believed to be Spanish. Cabins built or buried beneath the earth were also found there.

"Gold, silver and copper the Indians mined and used as ornaments. The gold-greedy soldiers of DeSoto prospected for the same metals. For more than a century their sporadic mining efforts probably returned small amounts of gold and silver, for both appear in many places," wrote Ora Blackman in *Western North Carolina.*

James Ledeer and James Moore noted ancient mines being found by early settlers near Kings Mountain, both men making their observations in 1670 and 1690. Moore, who was secretary of the Virginia colony, made an exploration in 1690 and reached a point "within twenty miles of where the Spanish were engaged in mining and smelting with bellows and furnaces, and adding that the Indians had killed the Spanish miners."

Evidence of earlier Cherokee mines was given by Mooney,

who wrote, "from the appearance of ancient soapstone vessels...found in the region...the Indians knew something of smelting."

J.W.M. Breazeale, in *Life As It Is* wrote that fortifications located one mile above the junction of the Pigeon River and the French Broad, in Tennessee, may have been Spanish. In 1780 the site consisted of an eight and one-half acre "parade ground," and posts of one of the "gateways" to the fort.

On a hill on "the old Indian trail" on the west side of the Little Tennessee River, above and opposite Morgantown, Tennessee, in old Loudon County, there were once four trees marked in an odd manner. The common Cherokee tale was that the carvings were made "by Indians to indicate the position of a hidden mine."

After the Cherokee had driven the Spanish off, or isolated their descendants in distant mountains (such as Newman's Ridge) there was a brief return to traditional life. Then the French came.

While never as numerous among the tribe as the Spanish, the French from Canada and Louisiana did establish a growing trading network. While the "Old Indian Fields" near Winchester, Kentucky, and "French Lick" near Nashville might be best-known among Appalachian Indians (and even current historians), there were several other outposts with evidence that the French were living and prospering not only among the Shawnee, but among the Cherokee and Creek as well.

Old maps by the French (and later English) explorers indicate an old French fort or store between the waters of the Clinch and Powell Rivers. Several versions of the Swift journal refer to a French fort or French castle near Swift's route to the mine.

Other versions of Swift's journal indicate that some or all of his "Indian guides" were Cherokee. Certainly some of the later people encountered during his fruitless search to locate the lost mines were Cherokee. Charles Hicks, the noted Cherokee physician in North Carolina, was sought out by Swift in an attempt to cure his blindness.

By the time the English and colonists were establishing Fort Loudoun near present day Vonore, Tennessee, they were hearing stories of silver mines "within twenty miles" of their new fort. Cherokee Indians they came in contact with spoke of the abundance of silver in their nation. Many wore decorative silver ear and nose jewelry and silver arm bands, and even sported rifles and axes with delicate silver workings.

The Swift journals speak of both Spanish and French silver mines within the old Cherokee holdings, one near one of the Swift works. James Dougherty's *The Legend of Swift's Silver Mine* notes that the mines were located "in the country claimed by the Cherokee but which were not occupied by them," apparently referring to northeast Tennessee or Kentucky. The area, he wrote, had been the home of the Shawnee. Dougherty also noted that the mines, or some of them, worked by Swift had been previously worked by the French and Indians, and the French "lived in what is now Tennessee."

Despite attempts to remain peaceful and hold back the tide of colonial settlement, the Cherokee, prodded by the French, eventually waged many bloody campaigns against the settlers. During the wars there are instances where the Cherokee continued to mine silver, including the lingering story of Chief Doublehead's mine on the big South Fork River, somewhere near the current state line between Tennessee and Kentucky.

Although gold mines among the Cherokee, especially those in northern Georgia, are more commonly known, and led directly to the removal of the noble tribe, other silver mines existed and produced silver even during hostilities.

Bob Benge, as noted elsewhere, was apparently the chief of a village located where Rising Fawn, Georgia, is today. Somewhere in the cliffs of Lookout Mountain or other nearby mountains, Benge and his Cherokee, French, and English mixed-blood villagers mined and smelted silver.

It is obvious that he knew the ore and the value of it by his conversations with white captives. It is also apparent that he knew of several sites throughout the old Cherokee claim, including the Breaks of the Sandy River, where silver could be found.

By the time the English arrived in 1756 and began construction of Fort Loudoun on the Tennessee River, the Cherokee had managed to expand their territorial holdings to include all of east Tennessee, much of Central and eastern Kentucky, much of extreme western Virginia and North Carolina, a portion of upper South Carolina, and a sizable part of northern Alabama and Georgia.

The traditional "Swift" region of northeast Tennessee and eastern Kentucky had been wrestled from temporary settlement and claim by the Shawnee through a war of many years which forced the Shawnee into southern and central Ohio. While both nations had outpost villages here and there in the mountains of the Cumberlands and the Blue Grass region, most of these were seasonal, and by the time longhunters and explorers arrived from the colonies, most of the villages were abandoned.

Given the abuse begun by the Spanish and continued by the French, English, colonials, and Americans, the Cherokee took their knowledge of gold and silver to their graves with them, except for accidental discoveries by new white settlers.

Many of the ancient gold and silver mines in Georgia and Alabama are yet unknown to whites. The silver mines of Tennessee, Kentucky, Virginia, North Carolina, and even West Virginia remain a closely held secret even today, except for some occasional Cherokee returning to recover treasure left long ago in the mines, in buried pits, or in sacred caves.

As noted elsewhere, there were and continue to be treks by the likes of Lakely and others of Cherokee descent into the old "Swift" sites. There are other instances which are noteworthy:

In 1871, two Cherokee appeared at the Crabtree farm near Irvine, Kentucky, and spoke to Jacob Crabtree. One was a "young chieftain who was a polite man" and spoke with an Oxford accent, according to Kentucky historian Clark.

The Cherokees explored around Little Sinking Creek to the

Big Sinking, leaving their horses and walking to the site of an ancient mine. They reappeared at Crabtree with two "Buckskins" filled with a "heavy substance," watching over their find with loaded guns. Because of the incident, the community around Irvine, Kentucky, bubbled with rumors of old silver mines.

Maps and journals used by treasure hunters in western Virginia were reportedly obtained from "an old Indian" in Oklahoma.

An old Cherokee mine is supposedly located along Mine Fork of Paint Creek in Johnson County, Kentucky.

The Cherokee and Spanish were said to have a silver mine and silver cave somewhere down in the Nantahala Gorge in North Carolina, as well as mines on Wesser Creek and Silver Mine Creek in western North Carolina.

A Spanish miner might be depicted in this rock carving in the old Cherokee territory. It appears to show a soldier holding something and wearing a pack on his back; and W, X, and Y can be seen along with what appears to be the date "1558." (Photo and drawing by Mike Steely)

Cherokee Chief Doublehead's Silver Mine

In the years preceding statehood for Kentucky and Tennessee, the Cherokee (who had claimed the region for hundreds of years and by 1740 had pushed the Shawnee across the Ohio River) were determined to turn back white settlements.

Several uncontrolled raiding parties ravaged isolated cabins and stations in both territories, killed lone travelers, and kept fear in the hearts of any outsiders. Chief John Watts, a half-breed like his notorious nephew Bob Benge, the red-headed captain of a warring party, waged war with surprise attacks, brutality, and outrages. Watts' principal war chief was an odd full-blooded Cherokee known as Doublehead.

Chief Doublehead was well-named, for when drinking whiskey the fellow lost control of any faculty he had. On one occasion, Doublehead and Benge captured, skinned and ate the flesh of a longhunter they suspected of spying on them.

Doublehead's life was ended not by a white bullet, but by the hands of his own people as punishment for illegally selling Cherokee lands for personal profit. Yet in those years prior to war, Doublehead is said to have had a secret source of income, a very fruitful silver mine which he and his daughter operated somewhere along the waters of the Big South Fork River, near the present Tennessee-Kentucky state line.

Early white traders among the Cherokee had heard tales of silver mines in the nation, and many historians made notes of the tales, one describing the mines as being "within twenty miles of Fort Loudoun" near the Tennessee-North Carolina border.

Silver bars had reportedly been found in a cave near Pilot Mountain in Wayne County, Kentucky, within the Big South Fork region, on the "west side" of said river. Furnaces with traces of silver ore in the ashes were found along the banks of the river, as well as on the Clear Fork River in nearby Tennessee. Treasure hunters have searched on Laurel Creek near Stearns, Kentucky, and around "Father of Rocks" near Jamestown.

The best account of Doublehead's Mines comes from the late Tom Troxell of Scott County, Tennessee, who wrote extensively on the tale. Troxell, a direct descendant of an early white settler and Chief Doublehead's daughter Cornblossom, told a tale of greed and mystery. The story was passed down from the Indian grandmother to generations of Troxells, many of whom continue to live in the area.

Chief Doublehead and his clan held all of the land from the Cumberland Mountain above the Tennessee Valley to the Cumberland River near present-day Burnsides, Kentucky. When seasonally visiting the area, Doublehead and his party stayed in a "large open-front cave or rock shelter" near Monticello, Kentucky. Today the site is known as Hines Cave, in the area of Doublehead Gap and Doublehead Spring.

Chief Doublehead's grave is supposed to be located near Dry Valley, close to the junction of the South Fork with the Cumberland River, south of Burnsides and north of Yarmacraw, Kentucky.

Prior to Doublehead, it is said that the French worked the mine, and some speculation has the Spanish working it late in the 1600's. The Cherokee have legends of the Latin soldiers, and appear to have feared that they would be captured and forced to work as slaves in the mines.

Troxell's tale involves the Princess Cornblossom and her brother, Tuchahoe. The story was first told by Cornblossom to her white husband, "Big Jake" Troxell. Cornblossom said that her brother had gone off to lead a group of white men to the silver mine at about the time of the close of the American Revolution. Tuchahoe traded with them, using a "passel of silver" to obtain a rifle, powder horn, and a fringed shot pouch. One of the men talked the brave into showing him the mine and Troxell recounts the name of the white man as

"Hans Blackburn."

Ironically, one Hans Blackburn is listed as one of the crew members of John Swift's silver mining crew, which mined in the region some ten years earlier. Several of the crew returned to the area following Swift's English imprisonment, and possibly the two Blackburns are, indeed, one and the same. Swift mentions a French mine near one of his southern ore sites.

Cornblossom told Jake Troxell that the mine was marked with "a buffalo head carved on a tree, a rattlesnake carved on a rock, and an inland pond with a rock and tree in the center." In this tale, Blackburn was accompanied by his "hired man" whose name was Monday, another Swift crew member.

Cornblossom said she became suspicious of the men and went to the mine to check on her brother. When she arrived she found that they had murdered Tuchahoe. While the white men were busy "loosening the bars of silver," Cornblossom crept into the mine, grabbed a rifle, and ran off into the darkness.

The Cherokee princess knew that Blackburn would be returning to his "workshop near Fonde" (Kentucky), and ran to Turtleneck Ford along the trail, where she hid in ambush. She got the aid of two braves and the three went to the ford, today called "Cracker's Neck," some three miles west of Stearns, Kentucky, on Ponco Creek.

The Cherokees found Blackburn camped in a rock house, today called Camp Dusty. Cornblossom took aim and shot Blackburn through the heart with the same rifle her brother had purchased from him. The two braves gutted the thief, filling his belly with rocks, and tossing the body into the creek.

Tuckahoe's Path, leading the white men to the mine, begins at Little Indian Rock House on Laurel Creek, two miles east of Stearns, at a "point used by silver mine hunters to this day to reckon their course," wrote Troxell.

Cornblossom said that Tuckahoe was struck on the back of the head with a pickaxe by Blackburn. He and Monday, whom she called "simple-minded," threw her brother's body into a crevice between two rocks, covering it with leaves, brush, and rocks.

About 1890, several Indians traveled to Stearns in search of the mine. A smelter and mine shaft is reportedly known in the area of the Little South Fork by members of the Dobbs family.

An old map gives directions to the Doublehead mine, beginning in McCreary County, Kentucky, and says to "travel for one day from the Little Indian Shelter near Stearns." One day's time, in Indian walking time, is about twenty miles. The mine is said to be found between Father of Rocks, a "mound atop a mound," and Ridge Cliff.

Another old map from the hands of Tom Troxell himself, and given to me by Michael Paul Henson, does not locate the silver mine but lists all of the landmarks, the Silver Mine Trail, and Turtle Neck (Cracker Neck) Ford.

From his *Legion of the Lost Mine*, Thomas H. Troxell identifies Chief Doublehead as Chief Chuqualataque, and writes that the whites nicknamed him "Doublehead." The powerful chief was reportedly born near Somerset, Kentucky, about 1750 and lived for a while at Doublehead's Cave, now called Hines Cave, on the Little South Fork of the Cumberland, near Monticello.

At the cave, warring Cherokees often met to plan their campaigns. Other notables met with Doublehead there. Doublehead married a half-French maiden by whom he fathered Princess Cornblossom and Tuckahoe.

Big Jake (or Jacob) Troxell was born in Philadelphia in 1757, and had served under General Washington in the Revolutionary War. His military service was to come in handy as he assisted his new Indian relatives defend their homeland.

Father of Rocks, said to be the location of another ancient silver mine, is today called "Pilot Mountain," and stands along the highway between Monticello and Jamestown. There, in 1780, a small group of white intruders was headquartered, illegally hunting and prospecting the Doublehead territory.

Troxell, Tuckahoe, and other braves surprised the white men there, and all of the enemy were killed. Among them was a Watauga region settler from eastern Tennessee known as Bill Dyke. When Troxell recognized Dyke's clothing as being part of a British uniform, he decided to give him a proper burial, near the rock shelter campsite where he was attacked. Tom Troxell identifies the site as lying along King's Creek on the west side of the river. Found among the belongings of the dead men was evidence that they had in fact been robbing Doublehead's region: furs, skins, and several silver bars.

Following the funeral, Jake Troxell and the Indians built a large barge, and floated down the Cumberland to the French trading post in Nashville, where they traded the goods.

The Search for Shawnee Silver Mines

Did the Shawnee have silver mines somewhere in the vicinity of the Ohio River? Why is it that the tribe is associated with so many silver legends in the Midwest and Southeast? Is there anything to stories linking Chiefs Blue Jacket and Cornstalk to the mining and smelting of this precious ore?

Anyone seriously reading the early histories of Kentucky, West Virginia, or Ohio cannot help but bump up against the mighty Shawnee in two instances, wars and treasures. Folklore among the whites and Indians tells of the Shawnee showing French traders a silver mine somewhere in Kentucky. The tribe had worked it prior to the French, and possibly before the Spanish.

As white settlers began moving into the Ohio River Valley, they heard many tales of the mines. Even those who discounted such treasure tales began to reconsider when descendants of the original Americans showed up in their new communities to look for hidden wealth left behind by the removed Indians. Throughout the "old west," from Cumberland Gap to Chicago, Indians have returned occasionally to their forefather's lands, guided by maps and ancient directions, to recover booty.

Some early pioneers believed so strongly in the old tales that they went "straight to the horse's mouth" for answers, bringing in the very Indians said to have taken part in the mining. James Galloway, a veteran of campaigns against the Shawnee, relocated his family from Lexington, Kentucky, to Xenia, Ohio. In prior years he had ridden with fellow Kentuckians to attack this area, and had fought against the tribe here when it was headed by the noted white Shawnee Chief Blue Jacket.

In the spring of 1800, Galloway, aided by funds from old Kentucky friends, brought to his home his former enemy and another chief. Blue Jacket had been hired to "show them a great silver mine" somewhere along the Red River, one of the headwaters of the great Kentucky, according to Galloway's son. An agent of the venture, Jonathan Flack, went with the Shawnee for several months in an attempt to relocate the mine. In the rugged country of eastern Kentucky, Blue Jacket sought permission of the great spirits to reveal the location, but permission was denied. He halted the venture because of poor health and eyesight, and promised to send his son to complete the search. The great chief died in 1810 at age 56, of cholera. His son did not return to search for the treasure, but there is some evidence that his grandson did.

Blue Jacket was formerly known as Marmaduke Van Swearingen. He had been captured as a teenager near his home in West Virginia. Being an Indian buff, he quickly adapted to the lifestyle and rose quickly to a place of importance. He became a leader in a nation of leaders that included Chief Cornstalk, Black Snake, Pucksinwah, and Chiksika.

Unbeknownst to Galloway and Blue Jacket until after the war years, both were actually related through marriage of the white families. This no doubt helped Galloway secure Blue Jacket's service. Both Blue Jacket and Cornstalk are mentioned in frontier legends as having assisted French, and later English, outlaws in locating and mining silver.

Seventy years after Blue Jacket abandoned his attempt to relocate the mine, another Shawnee appeared in Little Mud Lick Creek, Kentucky, carrying a number of "rude maps" which he believed would lead him to casks of silver coins hidden by his forefathers. This lone Indian was later identified as Peter Cornstalk, a descendant of both Blue Jacket and Cornstalk. The maps he carried, according to Chief Charles Blue Jacket, had belonged to Blue Jacket.

Young Cornstalk stayed at the mouth of Little Mud Lick for four or five weeks, and was seen along the high bluffs of the big bend of Paint Creek. One day after the Indian passed a large crowd of settlers at the mill with the saddle bags of his horses jingling with what sounded like coins, the brave's horse was found wandering, unattended along the creek, absent of both Indian and saddle bags. A year later, a skeleton found in a bluff of Big Paint Creek was identified as that of the brave by the buckskin it wore and presence of colored beads. Years later, Chief Blue Jacket told Kentucky historian Lewis Collins that the mine was found in a Great Shawnee Cave, which also served as a storehouse for the coins. The Indian cavern was supposed to extend from one side of a mountain to the other.

"They very carefully covered the entrances to the caverns when they departed the country," Collins wrote. The historian placed the cave much further to the east, near Pound, Virginia. "There is a secret society among the Shawnee which preserves many of the old traditions, and this Great Cave has some significance in the ritual of the order," he wrote.

Two years after Peter Cornstalk's disappearance in 1872, a local man, Noah Branham, found a bar of silver near Rule's Mill. He sold it to Enoch Fairchild, a gunsmith, for two dollars, and Fairchild used it for years to make gun sights. Branham said he found the silver while digging a roadway around a hill, beneath tall bluffs.

Mud Lick Creek is located in Johnson County, Kentucky, and has been searched for silver for hundreds of years. Certainly the descriptions given of the area where Peter Cornstalk had been searching could easily be located by modern treasure hunters equipped with much more adequate equipment than anything available to the pioneer families.

Throughout the annals of Kentucky history the occasional piece of silver unexpectedly pops up. A bank in Granson reportedly has a bag of counterfeit coins made from silver mined on Tygarts Creek in the early 1800's. A bar of silver was found at the head of Smokey Creek in Carter County in 1890 on the land of Dennis Burchett, and silver bars were found near the Lewis Cabin in the same county. Historian William Connelley reported that cinders found by early settlers were used to extract silver and make spoons and other silverware.

Yet legends of Indian silver mines are not limited to Kentucky or Ohio. The Cherokee have their own version of the tales, and many of their stories also center on Kentucky. Long-time enemies, the Shawnee and Cherokee are said to have fought over both the silver and the Kentucky territory, long before the settlers arrived.

Stories of silver mines in the Blue Ridge and Appalachian mountains involve western Virginia, West Virginia, northern Georgia, North and South Carolina, and even northern Alabama.

Jenny Wiley, kidnapped by the Shawnee a hundred years later, was taken to a camp near the mouth of Mud Lick. She later told of being forced to smelt lead for their bullets. The warriors left her in camp and returned to her in less than thirty minutes, with raw lead. It is debated whether this camp was on Mud Lick Creek or Oil Springs in eastern Kentucky.

Kentucky historian Thomas D. Clark wrote fairly extensively of early silver mining and referred to "The Blue Jackets" as being involved with the operation.

While most of the stories of Shawnee silver revolve around Kentucky, there is a growing body of information that the Indians also had a much closer source of the ore. The principal town of the Shawnee was called Chillicothe, and while a present city in Ohio has that name, it is far from being the original village. Old Chillicothe is, in fact, located between Xenia and Yellow Springs. Today simply called "Old Town," Highway 68 splits what was once a half-mile long Shawnee community.

Is it possible that James Galloway brought Blue Jacket from the western reservation and was steered to Kentucky by the chief because the mines were, in reality, almost in Galloway's back yard?

Captives of the Shawnee were taken from Old Town, blindfolded, to Massie Creek, where they were met by warriors with heavy sacks of lead or silver ore. The white slaves were forced to carry the bags back to the village.

Professor Roy S. King of the University of Arizona wrote about the mines and a map pointing to two locations in Green County, Ohio. Following removal from Ohio, Shawnee parties returned often to the area, camping in a glen near Yellow Springs, and hunting treasure in the area of several pre-settlement excavations.

William Albert Galloway, in his *Old Chillicothe*, tells of ancient excavations on Caesar's Creek, southeast of Xenia, where timbers were found in two vertical shafts by pioneer families.

At Glen Helen, near Yellow Springs, a local college student blasted a cliff face and found a small vein of silver near the falls of the east fork of Yellow Springs. Two round, stone-filled holes are located near the foot of "Devil's Backbone," a high ridge of Massie's Creek.

Except that Old Town is an ideal setting for an Indian settlement, today's passing automobile drivers have little reason to recognize the little community for the historic site it is. Not only was Old Chillicothe a principal Shawnee village, it was also there that Simon Kenton ran the gauntlet, Daniel Boone was held captive and adopted into the tribe, and forces under George Rogers Clark swept down and burnt the place to the ground. Nearby, the great Chief Tecumseh was born, and there, off and on, resided Blue Jacket and Cornstalk.

The village extended along the eastern ridge. It included a council house and several log cabins, and had a population at its zenith of about 2,000 warriors. Through the site, as Highway 68 does now, ran a great trace that led from the Great Lakes to the Cumberland Gap and on to Florida.

There is much evidence that the Shawnee and earlier Indians worked silver long before the arrival of the French or English. In 1819, a Marietta, Ohio, street building brought forth a silver belt buckle and a silver ornament atop a sword scabbard. The mounds at Circleville produced a small elk horn sword with silver insets. Thirty or more silver and copper ear ornaments were recovered from another mound in the Little Miami Valley.

So, if there is no truth to the legends of Shawnee or other eastern Indian silver mines, as the experts tell us, where did the ore come from?

Is it possible that somewhere in the hills of Kentucky or the knolls of Ohio, hidden silver mines exist even today, awaiting some accidental discovery during coal mining or highway construction? Will some subcontractor building a subdivision unearth a cache or break into the mouth of the Great Shawnee Cave?

Or will some weekend treasure hunter stumble across a dusty diary or an old text in a small rural library, and simply walk to the site based upon long-forgotten information?

The Silver Cache of the Great Shawnee Cave

For more than 200 years people have been searching throughout Appalachia for John Swift's Lost Silver Mines. A few wiser souls have searched for silver coins and bars hidden or dropped by Swift or his crew. After some ten years of searching through tons of manuscripts, old maps, newspaper clippings, and old waybills, I believe we have all overlooked something fairly obvious.

There is certainly much to debate involving the various legends of the lost silver mines, and each state or region seems to have its own version of the tale, a story that Kentucky's Director of Recreational Parks, Ed Henson, says is his state's oldest folk tale. Yet folk tales are rarely recorded by historians, and certainly Swift and his silver claims were so noted.

Kentucky's noted historian, William Rouse Jillson, wrote several notes on the legend, including the following: "If this interpretation is correct, it may well be that inside the mythical 'Great Shawnee Cave' near the Breaks of the Big Sandy Valley lies a treasure-house of silver and gold coins awaiting the coming of some unknown Alladin."

Jillson's predecessor, John Filson, also believed the silver tales, and even put in a claim for one of Swift's mines some "forty miles north of Martin's Station [Rose Hill, Virginia]." Unfortunately, Filson never followed up his claim, disappearing in the wilds of the territory while searching for the treasure.

Some modern Swift buffs believe the great cave is located near a striking formation known as "The Towers" at the Breaks State Park, above the waters of Russell Fork.

There is some evidence that the Shawnee used the cave long before Swift and his crew stored their ore there. Legend has the tribe, which claimed the region until about 1730 but lost it to their historic enemy the Cherokee, using the cavern to hide their women and children from the enemy. The Indian legend has the cave extending from one side of the mountain to the other.

About twenty years ago a "great cave" was discovered near Whitesburg, Kentucky, and was sported in newspapers as being the legendary treasure trove. It proved not to be, nor was it very extensive.

Pound Gap, Virginia, on the Kentucky border, was long thought to be the site of the treasure cave. Early longhunters called the pass "Pound" because of the sound their horses hooves made when crossing, as if the gap was hollow beneath.

The Kentucky River country was also thought to be the home of the great Shawnee caverns. Several Kentucky capitalists, along with Xenia, Ohio, pioneer Major Gallaway, hired Shawnee Chief Blue Jacket to return from his western reservation and show them the cave. Blue Jacket, a white captive gone Indian, led the men into the area of the Kentucky River but then, after praying to the tribe's ancestors, declined to show them the cave.

Blue Jacket spoke to Kentucky historian Lewis Collins about the great cave, telling him that Swift's principal mines were located nearby, and confirming that Swift and his miners "made it a storehouse for all their surplus production of silver."

Collins wrote that Blue Jacket and Chief Cornstalk went into the cave on more than one occasion and worked the mines with Swift.

One of the Swift journals recalls the storage in a great cave of "our great immense store" of precious metals "both coined and uncoined and hid therein until we could in the providence of God convey it thence to the trade of the seas."

Several tales have Swift sneaking into the cave at night and murdering each of his crew members, one by one, only to discover that he alone could not remove the treasure. So the survivor seals the mouth, hoping to relocate it someday and recover the wealth.

Swingle's Cave above Olive Hill, Kentucky, is better known today as "Counterfeiters Cave." Rangers of Carter Caves State Park take visitors on a brief walking tour each day, repeating old Indian legends there about a brave, a squaw, and a silver tomahawk. They also repeat local legends about the cavern, pre-revolutionary silver mines in the area, and the place being used to mint coins.

Looking for the Great Shawnee Cave, or venturing into any cave, can be dangerous and exhausting. The knowledgeable spelunker goes well-prepared for anything that might happen. Here, Roy Price and Jimmy Arnold take a "breather" after a couple hours of exploration. (Photo by Mike Steely)

The area of the famous Lost Silver Mines of Appalachia, rumors of which circulated in the American colonies long before Jonathan Swift claimed to have mined ore at various sites in the 1760's.

Silver Mines of Melungeons

Probably the most unique legend of the Cumberland Mountains is the persistent rumor of secret silver mines operated by a mysterious race of people known today as the Melungeons. Until very recently it was anyone's guess as to the origin of these dark-skinned, black-haired, blue-eyed people.

Now, after more than two hundred years of unfair persecution and wild speculation, it has been shown that the folks living in the isolation of the mountains between Kentucky, Tennessee, and Virginia are who they claimed to be all along. They, in fact, are descendants of the Portuguese.

Since early Scotch-Irish longhunters first encountered these "original" settlers, already living in cabins in the midst of Cherokee and Shawnee-claimed territory, two romantic questions have persisted. One, who they are, is now settled. The other, where they found, smelted, and minted silver, remains unanswered.

Until DNA testing of modern-day Melungeons verified the Portuguese and Mediterranean stock (along with some American Indian, African, European, etc.), speculation had spanned groups from The Lost Tribe of Israel to The Lost Colony of Roanoke Island. Until this century, the dark population was classified as People of Color, Mulatto, etc., and denied not only voting rights, but in some cases property and even wedding permits to "white" neighbors.

Oddly enough, had anyone bothered to ask or listen, the Melungeons have always claimed to be Portuguese. Yet many had forgotten how they came to be in the Appalachian Mountains, and the elders occasionally explained that they were the children of shipwrecked sailors.

Encountering the Melungeons was not limited to the Cumberlands. Here and there throughout the inland eastern United States similar peoples were encountered by explorers and settlers. In the Dungannan area of Virginia they were called "Ramps" and were said to be talented in counterfeiting.

In West Virginia they were called "Pedro's" and thought to be the descendants of early Spanish silver miners or soldiers. In South Carolina they were called "Brass Ankles" and elsewhere were known as "Redbones," "Turks," "Lungeons," etc. Many Indian nations, including the Cherokee, Catawba, Powhatan, Lumbee, and Pamunkeys have members who share similar characteristics with Melungeons.

N. Brent Kennedy's *The Melungeons, the Resurrection of a Proud People*, deals squarely with the issue, and puts forth a reasonable answer to the question of origin.

Kennedy, a descendant of the Melungeons, writes that Spanish explorer and adventurer Juan Pardo made several trips into the region from a home base at Santa Elena, near modern-day Beaufort, South Carolina. Much of the expedition's efforts were treasure hunting, looking for gold, silver, and other precious ore and gems along the Indians of the Blue Ridge, Smoky, and Cumberland Mountains.

Pardo, who Kennedy says spelled his first name "Juao," may have been Portuguese himself, serving the Spanish as so many of his fellow countrymen did at that time. Early in his efforts he placed groups of miners and soldiers at specific "forts" along the route. On one voyage to Spain he returned with women and children for some of the men.

Many of the soldiers in the Spanish ranks, especially among the lower ranks, were men from North Africa, and Moors from Spain, Portugal, etc. The implanted population of dark-skinned Europeans and North Africans treated the local Indians better than DeSoto had in previous years and, for the most part, lived in peace and pursued their goal of locating gold and silver.

When the Spanish lost their North American claims these "implants" had been living in the mountains among the Indians for generations. Many had been forgotten, and others felt no reason to return to Spain. Others may have been killed by local tribes or disappeared into Indian bloodlines.

Cherokee Chief Attakullakulla told his tribe's version of the origin of the Melungeons. It started with a great battle with the Spanish, probably at Soco Gap near modern-day Cherokee, North Carolina, and ended with six soldiers being spared. Over a period of captivity, which happened in the 16th Century, the men gained a measure of freedom, married Cherokee women, and adapted themselves somewhat to village life.

While some may have lived in villages, others probably moved off and began their own settlements. When the Cherokee were forced into alliances first with the French and then the English, the descendants of the Latin soldiers were banished to "the upper reaches of the Pellissippi." This is exactly where early colonial longhunters and explorers discovered the Melungeons living, and pinpoints what we know today as Melungeon settlements on the headwaters of the Clinch River.

Jean Patterson Bible's *Melungeons, Yesterday and Today* also wonders about their origin, and includes legends of stranded sailors from the Middle East before the time of Christ. John Sevier, himself of French blood and noted as one of Tennessee's founding fathers, quizzed about the Melungeons and wrote of them as "Welch Indians." He also noted, in 1810, that "they have yet some small scraps of old books remaining among them, but in such tattered and destructive order nothing intelligible remained."

"They call themselves Portuguese, which they pronounce 'Porter Ghee,' and were found in the regions mentioned by the first pioneers of civilization here. As a body they were as concrete as the Jews, and their descendants are still to be found," wrote Samuel C. Williams in *Early Travels in Tennessee Country*.

In *Tribes That Slumber*, about the Indian tribes of Tennessee, the Melungeons are claimed to be "Yuchis or the lower tribe, the Tomahattans." With the "Yuchis" DeSoto is said to have searched for gold and silver in the Appalachians, much further south than the current Melungeon domain.

Mrs. John Trotwood, late historian and former head of the Tennessee State Library, believed as Kennedy does, that the Melungeons were of Spanish and Portuguese descent who settled in the region prior to the American Revolution.

Although the people of Melungeon descent are still to be found in the mid-Appalachians of Kentucky, Virginia, and Tennessee, the years and social injustice and even twentieth century "freedom" have scattered them throughout the nation. Many have little idea of their origin and have, out of necessity, claimed to be French, Black Dutch, Black Irish, Indian, etc.

By the time the isolated Melungeons had encountered colonial visitors in their midst, they were already speaking broken English which they apparently picked up from their Indian friends. Much of their former language, or languages, had disappeared, and they even began to adapt English versions of their historic Latin names.

From the time of first contact with white hunters and long into settlement, right up to current times, the Melungeons have been linked to treasure in the region, especially lost silver mines. Early settlers believed the darker people possessed treasure maps, and were surprised that many had coined silver. Given that the Melungeons were, in fact, descendants of Pardo's soldiers and miners, the idea that they had found and mined silver within their mountains was understandable.

Some of the speculation was echoed, or resounded, in Haywood's *History of Tennessee*, in which this early Tennessee judge notes that the Melungeons had secret silver mines along the waters of Straight Creek, which runs along the north base of Pine Mountain between Harlan and Pineville, Kentucky, only a few miles north of the historic "Newman's Ridge" in Hancock County, Tennessee, the best known "home" of the Melungeons.

A family named "Mullins" was supposed to be makers of silver money in the area of the creek. This name is common among the Melungeons and, in the 1870's, one Jackson Mullins is recorded as having been convicted in Abingdon,

Virginia, of counterfeiting.

An ancient "stone fort" was said to have been found on the waters of Straight Creek, reflecting the idea of the "forts" established by Pardo's party. The forts were said to be either on "Laurel Branch or at the junction of Stoney Fork and Straight Creek," according to a Bell County, Kentucky, manuscript.

Kennedy wrote that Jack Mullins, known as "Brandy Jack" was convicted of counterfeiting and served eight years in the Wise County, Virginia, jail. His uncle, Sol Mullins, was known as "Counterfeit'n Sol" and ran out "Spanish milled dollars" in the late 1800's. Sol is said to have mined his ore somewhere in or near the Breaks of the Sandy River.

The Melungeon researcher puts forth the idea that Swift's assistants, or some of them, were Melungeons, and that Swift himself "was evidently married to a Melungeon woman." Some legends point to Swift in union with a Wyandott woman while in Ohio or Kentucky, but Kennedy claims a Melungeon liaison as well.

Remarkably, in the list of Melungeon family names of Portuguese adapted to English, there appears some of the last names of Swift associates, such as Martin, Stanley (Staley), Campbell, Watts, and in early census records not published by Kennedy, there appears "Swift."

Also, within the list of Melungeon-related names is "Swindall." The same name (or Swindell) appears in Carter County, Kentucky, legends of silver and counterfeiting. Gibson, Fletcher, Munday, and Anderson were also popular names in the community.

Some Swift buffs claim that the Melungeons were really descendants of Swift's own mining crew, as opposed to making up the crew. Possibly it was both.

"Uncle Lewis" Hopkins of Newman Ridge is said to have a map to silver mines which mentions Moccasin Gap. He is said to have obtained it from a Captain Jarvis, a Mexican War veteran from Sneedville, Tennessee.

Swift's mention of meeting "Mecca Indians" somewhere west of the Blue Ridge Mountains, who lived in a mountain gap, and in some versions of the journal near Moccasin Gap (Kingsport, Tennessee), could have been a reference to the Middle Eastern appearance of the Melungeons. Kennedy writes that Swift probably had some Melungeons among his crew, and brings forward an odd claim, that Swift married a Melungeon woman.

How did the Indians, French, Spanish, or Melungeons separate the silver from the raw ore?

J.W.M. Breaseale, in *Life As It Is*, wrote: "They dug the ore from the earth and placed it in a large pile of timbers, commonly called log heaps, which, being set on fire, melted the lead (or silver) out of the ore, and ran it down together in large masses."

Later miners, like Swift, built rock furnaces or smelters, for the "melting," and the ore was caught in a basin carved in the rock below the smelter, running off into a trough and then dipped out. Then the molten ore was poured into forms in clay, sand, or rock and allowed to cool.

There is some evidence that early Indians simply fired the ore and let the silver cool down in small clumps, working the clumps into shapes by hand to produce animals, tools, or ornamental arrowheads.

Silver finds exhibited at Tennessee's annual "Swift Silver Mine Lost Treasure Weekend" include "fingers" of ore apparently molded in sand, small square bars, and wedge-shaped "axe" bars.

The most obvious result of smelting is, as expected, the immediate production of coins. The Spanish Milled Dollar, or Piece of Eight, was the most acceptable coin during Swift's lifetime, yet the various legends have Swift and his crew also producing French and English coins. By one example of a find along the Nolichucky River in Tennessee, there is reason to believe that German coins of this period were also minted by secret silver miners.

While the records have not been published or produced, there are old tales in Virginia and North Carolina that Swift was arrested for counterfeiting but acquitted when his coins were found to contain more silver than those produced by the official government mints.

Other tales relate the same information about the coins produced by the Melungeons of the region and, in some cases, by other silver miners of lesser notoriety. If a counterfeited coin contains more pure silver than one produced by an official mint, there is a question as to whether the counterfeiter understands how such money is valued.

MELUNGEONS

SILVER MINE LORE

The Heart of the Lore, Red River Gorge

Modern-day visitors to Campton, Kentucky, might be puzzled by a historic marker there which gives a brief summary of the local version of the Swift's Lost Silver Mine legend. The metal sign is only a hint of the years and years of search in the state's beautiful and rugged Red River Gorge.

Aside from the fact that many of the landmarks, carvings, and signs Swift lists in his various journals are identical to those found in and near the gorge, it is presumed that Swift himself was there in his elderly, blinded years and called on local settlers to help him relocate his famous, or infamous, lost mines.

Because of that fruitless search, or because of rumors that Swift actually operated mines there from 1760 until 1769, many places and landmarks now refer to him or his descriptions: Lighthouse Rock, Half-Moon Rock, Rock Bridge, Haystack Rock, Buffalo Rock, and the most telling of all, Swift Camp Creek.

One researcher actually places Swift's camp not only in the town of Campton, but at the site of the "most pretentious hotel in the place." From the time of settlement until the modern-day search by people like the Shepherd family and others, the Red River Gorge has been haunted by Swift.

The Red River Gorge Legend
Aunt Becky Timmons and the Search for Swift's Mine

Thomas Clark, author of *History of Kentucky*, has written: "When Cud Hanks was in his grave, old Mrs. Anderson, whose husband had been intimate with Swift, took up the search. She had records and maps and went looking for the 'remarkable rock'."

Hanks, of Campton, is said to have tramped the woods

round the Kentucky town constantly looking for the lost silver mine. The old man claimed to have known Swift personally and had "firsthand information" about the mine's location.

Clark says that much of the legend involved the Red River area, and the people living there recall it involved places like Campton, Swift's Creek, Upper and Lower Devil's Creek, Trace Fork, Tight Hollow, and Pine Ridge. Within the area of what is today called the Red River Gorge are many rock formations, gullies, and other landmarks very similar to those in most versions of Swift's journal. Many people in Kentucky point to Carter County, Bell County, or elsewhere as the possible location, but central Kentucky old-timers immediately think, and talk, of the Gorge area.

In his later fruitless search for the mine, one account has Swift associating with the new settlers of the territory, including men named Townsend, Tye, Anderson, Spurlock, and others. Some of these men were said to have been given (or to have bought) copies of his journal.

Townsend is said to have met Swift while the elderly fellow was exploring "down in the gorge," and to have aided Swift and his latter-day crew by feeding them and escorting them to Lexington, where in his final days Swift gave Townsend his journal.

A portion of one Swift Journal, offered by Mrs. Roy Cecil, editor of the *Wolf County News*, seems to give local landmarks, as follows:

"...about twenty or thirty poles from this creek (running in a south course) stands a sharp rock. Between it and the creek you will find a small rock of bluish color, with three chop marks with a grit stone, by rubbing the rock. By the side of the rock you will find the prize we left three different times.

"...not far from here we left another prize in a hole and laid rocks and twigs across it. It has plate value of $5,000 in crowns buried in the rockhouse up in the crack of the rock.

"...go between them (a hanging rock and one that has fallen) and you are near the spot, you will find three ledges, first, second, and third. Between the second and third ledges you will find the opening of the mine beneath a red sand rock on the top of the cliff.

"...we walled up the entrance with masonry form and stuck a rock in the opening the size of a salt barrel.

"...up the side of the cliff (across the creek) you will find a hole that resembles a door. We call it the 'Door Supposed.' You can stand on the rock there and point to the mines."

One local family claimed several years ago to have located Swift's mine on property they owned. They offered to sell it to the Kentucky Department of Parks.

When a representative of the state arrived he was taken blindfolded to the area of Timmon's Arch in the Red River Gorge. He was shown a pit and chunks of something like mica. Recognizing the mine as being on federal land, he reported it as such. A few years later the state developed a slide show about the legend, and when the family chanced to see it, they filed suit against the state.

Swift's companion Anderson, who may have been John or Joseph, is said to have linked up with the old silver miner in southwest Virginia, and accompanied him into Kentucky on the search, eventually ending up in the Gorge. In the same company, or in a separate search with Swift, was Colonel Tye, said by some legends to be Swift's "right hand man." Clark wrote:

"Blind John, once more in Kentucky, was unable to go into the woods by himself, so he went exploring on the arm of his constant companion, Anderson. It was pitiful to see the old man hobble over the rocky ground, up the cliffs, and across the mountain streams, searching frantically for the site of his former mining adventure. For fourteen years he searched for the Kentucky El Dorado, but never with success. In 1800 the old man died, broken in body and spirit."

One John Anderson, of Anderson's Blockhouse at the head of Carter's Valley near the Tennessee and Virginia state line, is said to have operated the first and only mint in the

Old Southwest Territory at nearby Eaton's Station, near present-day Kingsport, Tennessee.

Anderson built the blockhouse (a fortified station) in 1777, and it sheltered travelers on their way from Virginia to Kentucky. The station stood "in a narrow valley in present Scott County, Virginia, two miles east of the ford over the North Fork of the Holston River." His land grant was issued in 1774 in old Fincastle County, for 98 and 64 acres "on both sides of Clinch River."

Old lady Anderson, also known as "Granny Anderson," claimed to have cooked for Swift when she was a little girl. She died at age 95 in Wolf County. The county seat of Wolfe, Campton, is said to have been named such because Swift's party camped there (camp town).

Colonel Tye, probably John Tye, was with a party of men searching for the mine in Whitley County "before settlement," when the group was attacked near Pine Mountain between present-day Williamsburg and Pineville. Tye's son was killed, and an old man in the party was wounded. The account appears in Whitley County history and also in Tennessee history, since incidents near the then-unmarked state line were recorded in both states. The Tennessee accounts give Tye's companions as John Burlinson, Sherrad and Thomas Mays, and John Tye, Jr. Swift is not named, but the incident occurred on January 5, 1795, during the years of the last search.

Colonel Tye reportedly obtained a copy of the journal directly from John Swift. The same copy is rumored to have been "left with friends" in Uniontown, Pennsylvania, before Swift sailed for England, was imprisoned, and later returned to locate his mines.

Michael Paul Henson wrote that Swift returned to Pennsylvania and picked up his journal. Tye here returns with Swift to Kentucky and may have been with Swift at Bean Station, Tennessee, when he resumed his search. The Indian attack against Tye's party took place very close to Henry Bolton gap, in the Frakes area, a region that has for centuries been involved in the search.

Another silver mine buff of the Gorge area was "Long George" Spencer of Glen Cairn. This noted fiddle player owned a store when the railroad was built up the river valley, and divided his time between reading the Bible, running his store, fiddling, and prospecting.

Most of Spencer's search was for the "remarkable rock" with a turkey track print carved into it. He claimed to have seen the grave of Swift's "partner" J.C. Blackburn, and that the marker had a date of 1825. Eventually Spencer came to believe that God wanted no one to find the silver mine. He said that many times, while he was searching for the treasure, odd things would happen to him.

By far the most effort, time, and money spent on locating the silver mines in the Red River Gorge area can be credited to Aunt Becky Timmons. By some accounts she had been close friends with Granny Anderson (believed by some to be Swift's daughter), and had in her possession journals Swift had left with Colonel Tye, and then with a Colonel Torwood. She came into the possession of the journal about 1863.

It should be noted that the "Tye Copy" of the journal was similar to, if not an exact copy, of the journal carried by William Spurlock, which passed to Robert Alley, then to William Connelly, then to Lewis Collins, etc.

Mrs. Timmons, wrote Clark, was believed to be a mystic and was directed in her search by a series of taps on the table. She searched for the "Turtleback Rock" where three white oak trees drew from the same stump.

Another account has Rebecca Timmons coming to the Gorge in 1863 and buying most of the land there. She hired local men to dig here and there. Emerald Lykins described the lady as having her men all over the country, digging holes and blasting rocks, switching men from job to job.

An old newspaper article republished in the *Kentucky Explorer* described the lady as "Rebecca Pocahontas Timmons" and gave her maiden name as "McIntyre." By some accounts one of Swift's early mining crew was one Joshua McClintock or McIntyre. She reportedly was born in 1828 in Mason County, Kentucky, and moved to the gorge with her second husband. Nearby Campton, at that time, was known as Swiftsville!

Mrs. Timmons' search, or at least the initial phase, was assisted by "a group of Louisville men" in a syndicate. The Timmonses bought a farm near where they believed to be the location of the long-lost mine.

One of the Timmonses' business partners was a William Forward, or Forwood, who is also known to be a partner of Robert Alley. In fact Forward is said to have gotten a copy of the journal from someone in Uniontown in 1840, according to the Draper Papers. Forward is also linked, in Johnson County, Kentucky, to Alley and the search for lost mines in that area.

Some researchers believe that Forward got his journal copy directly from the hands of "Swift's son" who agreed to share any find. One story claims that Forward came first to the Red River Gorge, and five years later brought in the Timmons family.

Forward left them there and returned to Louisville to attend his business. In a few years the Timmons small fortune ran low and they opened a sawmill to help finance the search. When Forward died, his son came to the Gorge occasionally to oversee the treasure search. When he died of drowning in Florida, his son Samuel came to the area and continued to contribute money toward the location of the treasure.

For thirty years the Timmons couple searched in vain. After her husband died, Aunt Becky Timmons continued, however, growing old in her effort. She eventually took a New York partner and a "practical miner" from the west known as S.A. Hazelton.

The fruitless effort continued until Mrs. Timmons could look no more. Before her death she is said to have built a small one-room hut on the second ledge of "Half Moon Cliff," and to have lived there alone.

When she was found dead, nothing of value was left except a large envelope addressed to a physician in St. Louis. A local farmer dropped the package in the mail, not knowing that it contained the precious copy of Swift's Journal.

Hazelton is said to have continued the search in the Gorge area for fifteen years following Mrs. Timmons' death. She died in 1902, and is buried atop a hill near her old homestead. Timmons Arch, deep in the gorge near where she believed the mine to be, is named for her and her husband's search, which not only passed to Hazelton, but to Nannie McQuinn, Mrs. Williams, and the "Smith Brothers."

Forward's search was led by local mountaineer Jackson Tutt, who excavated near a then-schoolhouse site in the "Calaboose" area. He said they found metal some two hundred yards southwest of the school site, and dug up a red sandstone rock from fifteen feet below the surface. The rock has three hatchet marks in it.

He also said that Mrs. Timmons got small amounts of silver from the Buffalo Rock and that he, Tutt, had found a vessel a mile from the "lighthouse," used for melting ore. Tutt also said that he found the bones of two men in the Half Moon Rockhouse on Sun's Branch, one-half mile from the lighthouse.

Square McQuinn, a native of the Calaboose area, was hired as a scout, and located many landmarks for Mrs. Timmons that Tutt couldn't find. He found the "Monument Rocks," the "Indian Stairsteps," and from atop the stairsteps, pointed out the Half Moon Shelter across the valley.

The Half Moon Shelter was blasted, but the debris filled the hole. Three other shafts were blasted and excavated, each forty-three feet deep, in attempts to reach the mine believed to be behind the shelter.

So ends the saga of Aunt Becky Timmons.

The overwhelming attraction of so many treasure hunters to the Gorge area of Red River was that many, if not most, of the landmarks that appear in their copy of the Swift Journal can also be found in and near the Gorge. Also, some of the rock and tree carvings mentioned in the journal were found by early settlers, including Swift's name carved in a rock, turkey tracks, an Indian stairway carved in a bluff, and

"S.J.M." found carved at Devil's creek. The initials supposedly stand for Swift, Jefferson, and Munday.

"Close by the creek we marked our names, Swift, Jefferson, and Munday, and other names on a large beech tree with the symbols of a compass, trowell and square," part of the journal reads.

Problems in finding the mine, or mines, in the Gorge have been attributed to the condition in which Swift and his crew left the diggings. Swift claims to have walled up the opening and then to have put twigs and earth across the entrance so that it appears as any other part of the landscape.

Most searchers in the area also believed that there was more than one mine there, possibly two, as part of a three mine workings Swift had in the mountains. In fact, current searches span from Carter Caves above Olive Hill and Paint Creek near Paintsville to Pound Gap and Pine Mountain between Pineville and Jellico, Tennessee.

One clue to the location of one mine in the area of Swift Camp Creek comes from the Draper Papers, a collection of manuscripts of Central Appalachia during the period of Swift.

"Seven miles above the mouth is a natural rock bridge, and on the northeast side of the creek a short distance is a branch. Follow the branch to its head, then climb the ridge leading to the highest part on your right.

"Go along the ridge to a point that is higher than the others where a large rock seems to have fallen from above. Go in between them, this is where we obtained the ore."

Rock Bridge, which spans Swift Camp Creek, is said to have had, at one time, a map or curious carvings on it, but the signs have since been defaced.

During Swift's "latter day" visit to the Red River Gorge with Colonel John Tye, the men were said to be looking for "a creek with three forks, with the remarkable rock at the mouth of them. The rock had "turkey tracks" carved in it pointing backwards to one of the mines," according to a magazine article written by Harry M. Caudill.

An excellent hiking guide to the Red River Gorge has been written by Robert H. Ruchhoft, a professor of history at University College, Cincinnati. The guide gives a brief history of silver mine legends there, but the author discounts the tale.

"Swift's descriptions of visible land marks do match several well-known geographic features in the Gorge area," he wrote. Although Ruchhoft gives five sound reasons as to why the gorge cannot be the location of a silver mine, he also mentions several sites there which are identical to those mentioned in the old journals, including the Rock Bridge, Haystack Rock, Half Moon Shelter, and Sky Bridge.

He also notes that many ancient Indian campsites beneath the rock bluffs may have been destroyed by people searching for silver, as well as destruction of "honey holes" by searchers who thought they were forms or dies for silver ore.

Other landmarks in the Gorge area named for the legend, aside from Timmons Arch, include Silver Mine Arch, Turtle Back Rock, Indian Stairway, Needles Eye, and Indian Head Rock. Other rock formations in Tennessee and Virginia also have similar titles and appearance, although few are collected in such a small area as Red River Gorge.

Whether the connection with Swift came from the actual location of one of his mines there or his unsuccessful search there prior to 1800 (or both) is not known. Certainly a continual treasure hunt for mines and silver caches began around the beginning of that century and lasted, in the Gorge, until the place came under state control. Today a hike through the Red River Gorge is an exciting visual and physical experience, even for those visitors who have never heard of the lost silver mine legends, or couldn't care less. A walk there by historians and Swift buffs is a bit more interesting, and there is often a tendency to get off the paths and poke into a hidden cave or turn over a few rocks.

Despite the warnings and the common knowledge that the area has been searched and searched again, Swift buffs are not easily discouraged.

Silver and Clues Found in Gorge

A rock jutting out over Swift Camp Creek was found that had a five-inch outside circle and three-inch inside circle carved into it. An arrow was carved through the center of both circles and many believe the clue points to a silver mine.

Jim Rose found a large stone in 1937 near Campton that was proven to be 85% gold, 15 % silver. The find touched off a rush to prospect the region, and rumors of the old lost silver mines of John Swift took on new meaning.

In 1964, Indians visited Lower Devil's Creek searching for a carving like "101," where they said they could dig up the skull of an ancient Indian princess. Locals believed they were actually looking for lost silver mines.

In Joe Nickell's 1980 article in *The Filson Club History Quarterly*, he takes a broad look at the Swift legend from a couple of unusual angles, including the position that Filson may have penned the original "journal," and that there may be several secret "Masonic" clues within the text. Nickell also takes note of some interesting public records:

"April, 1791. Levi Cleveland withdraws his entry of 200 acres made on January 5, 1791, on Warrant No. 15132. Eli Cleveland and John Morton enters 1483 acres of land on two Treasury Warrants No. 15232 and 12128 on a branch of Red River to include an Old Camp in the Center where there is some troughs at said Camp on the branch side. The said Camp is a place difficult to access Supposed to be Swift's Old Camp and others including a mine said to be occupied formerly by said Swift and others."

The Filson entry reads as follows, 1788:

"Robert Breckenridge and John Filson as Tenants in Common Enters 1000 acres of land upon the balance of a Treasury Warrant No. 10,117 about sixty or seventy miles North Eastwardly from Martins Cabbins in Powells Valley to Include a silver mine which was Improved about 17 years ago by a Certain man named Swift at said mine, wherein the said Swift Reports he has extracted from the ore a Considerable quality of Silver some of which he made into Dollars and left at or near the mine, together with the apparatus for making

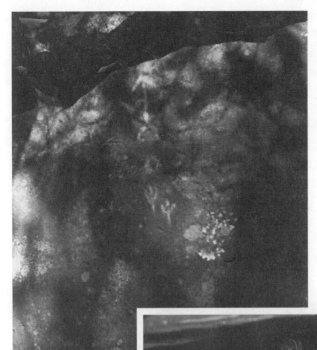

Turkey tracks cut in rocks are often sought by lost silver mine hunters because several legends have the signs leading to buried silver treasure. These signs, along with two "triangles" were found recently on Pine Mountain.

The author turns soil below treasure symbols in a low rock shelter. Mike Steely usually researches treasure legends in libraries or archives, but occasionally he gets into the Central Appalachian Mountains for some "on hands" adventures. (Photo by Roy Price) the same, the land to be in a square and the lines to run at the Cardinal Points of the Compass including the mine in the Centre as near as may be."

While Nickell says that no mention of Swift is given before that date, he fails to mention the numerous tales of silver mines among the Cherokee, Shawnee, Spanish and French within the area. He also fails to note that, during the time of the Filson land claim, Swift had not reappeared in the region, most legends having him in an English prison during the roamings and writings of Filson.

In fact, some "journals" and other traditions have Swift returning to the region to reclaim his lost mines as late as 1789, although knowledge of his mines must have spread throughout the region through his crew members or their families.

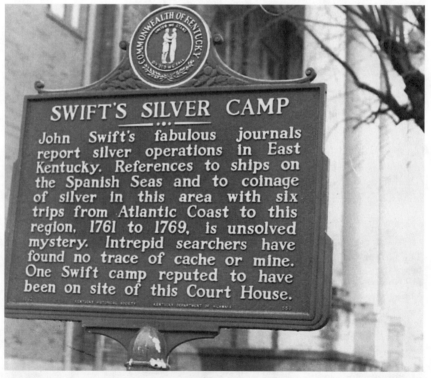

SWIFT'S SILVER CAMP

John Swift's fabulous journals report silver operations in East Kentucky. References to ships on the Spanish Seas and to coinage of silver in this area with six trips from Atlantic Coast to this region, 1761 to 1769, is unsolved mystery. Intrepid searchers have found no trace of cache or mine. One Swift camp reputed to have been on site of this Court House.

This historical marker sits on the courthouse lawn in Campton, Kentucky, retelling the region's oldest folk story. Red River Gorge, nearby, has been searched for Swift's treasures since the 1770's. (Photo by Mike Steely)

Spurlock, Alley, and the Cornstalks

Within the various legends of lost silver mines in Appalachia there are undertones of the fabulous ore being linked to the American Indians who originally lived and hunted in the region. Even Swift himself mentions his companion, George Munday, being captured by Shawnee and forced to labor in one of the mines. In fact, several of the Swift journals mention Indians as being part of his mining crew.

Tales of silver mines in the Southeast actually go back long before Swift's nine-year adventure began in 1760. While most researchers point to Spanish exploits of the area in the 1600's, and the Latin search for gold and silver primarily among the Cherokee, some historians point to the recovery of copper and silver artifacts from Indian burials that long precede European visits to America. Certainly there is a continual legend among the Shawnee and Cherokee about hidden silver mines, and much interplay between the tribes and those early and later treasure hunters seeking the location of old digs, the hidden coins and ore, and sharing tales about the legend.

It is possible that members of both tribes may have returned to the region following their removal in the 1830's and, by using information passed down within their tribes but never shared with whites, recovered some of the wealth left behind by Swift, his crew, and the forefathers of their nation.

I've written about Chief Blue Jacket and his trip to Kentucky as the guide for a rather extensive search for the mines in association with Colonel James Gallaway of Ohio and several pioneer capitalists. In the end the old chief begged off, telling his bosses that the Great Spirit would not allow him to take them to the mine. The noted chief, who was in fact a colonial white teen captured by Shawnee and adapting their lifestyle, promised that he would send his son back to help in their search. The son apparently never assisted the search, but his grandson may well have returned to Kentucky and located part of the hoard.

A similar event occurred in 1871 near Irvine, Kentucky, when two Cherokee braves and a squaw visited Jacob Crabtree. The small party spent much time on the Little and Big Sinking Creek and departed the area with two buckskin sacks "heavily laden."

Blue Jacket's descendant came to Mud Lick Creek in Johnson County, Kentucky, about the same time. A large Shawnee village reportedly occupied the junction of Big and Little Mud Lick Creeks until about 1774, and may have been the site where Virginia captive Jenny Wiley made her escape. The white woman wrote that the Shawnee obtained lead and silver from a mine somewhere near one of their campsites, and says that she was forced to help smelter the ore.

Whether the return of Indians to central Appalachia periodically is linked to Swift's Silver Mine or the recovery of tribal "banks" left behind long ago before the removal is not known. Some surely returned simply to view old sites, find abandoned graves, or simply out of curiosity.

The search by Blue Jacket's descendant was described by noted Kentucky historian Lewis Collins, who wrote that the Shawnee "carried with him a number of rude maps by the aid of which he said he had come to that particular locality and he said that by their help he expected to discover some casts of coined silver concealed by some Shawnee, among them his ancestors, while in the service of John Swift more than a hundred years before." The Shawnee was known as "Cornstalk," and was later identified by Charles Blue Jacket as the grandson of Peter Cornstalk. The maps he carried were said to belong to the "original" Chief Blue Jacket.

In Johnson County, Cornstalk remained more than a month in 1870 near the mouth of the Little Mud Lick Creek, and was seen along the high cliffs at a big bend of the Paint Creek, downriver from Rule's Mill. When he visited the mill, several local people noticed he had "buckskin bags" which were filled with something and slung over his horse's back. The Indian was walking and driving the horse before him as he passed, and it was known that several local men much prized the horse. Collins wrote that the crowd around Rule's Mill that day had been drinking and had taunted and teased the Indian. When one troublemaker approached Cornstalk and shook the buckskin bags, the others swore they heard the jingle of silver coins.

The next morning the horse was found wandering along the creek bank without bridle, saddle, or buckskin bags. The Indian was not seen again.

Several years later, among the cliffs of Big Paint Creek above Rule's Mill, along with buckskin moccasins worked with colored beads, the remains of a man were found. Rumors around Johnson County were that one or more of the drunken troublemakers had murdered Cornstalk and had taken his property, including the mysterious bags.

Two years after the disappearance of Cornstalk, a local man, Noah Branham, reported finding a silver bar at the mill site. Branham sold the bar to Enoch Fairchild, a local gunsmith and violin maker, and told him he had located it while digging and widening the roadway around the hill. Fairchild used the ore for beads in the sights of rifles he made and repaired.

About 1840 more of the silver turned up when Presley Larkin, known as "Daddy" Larkin, found a number of bars near where "the road crossed the stream known as Big Paint Creek." The bars were said to be found near a rock bottom where the stream is shallow and known as Flat Rock, near Deep Hole. The silver was sold to Henry Dickson, a silversmith, who made several ornamental pins and broaches.

"Mrs. Susan Joynes Connelly, one of the pioneers of Eastern Kentucky, wore one of those broaches for half a century. It was unquestionably pure silver," Collins wrote.

Much of the interest along the Big Sandy River came as a result of the activities of Robert Alley, who moved to Johnson County about 1859 and remained there until his death in 1890, all the years searching for the lost silver mine. The east Tennessee native had earlier sought the treasure in the Cumberland Gap area and other portions along the Tennessee, Kentucky, and Virginia state lines.

Alley chanced upon an odd fellow known as William Spurlock (or Turlington). Some accounts have a "Spurlock" as being a member of Swift's mining crew, others give the name as an associate of the late Swift in his efforts to find the lost mines.

Alley believed that Spurlock had the original copy of Swift's journal. The copy, worn and beaten with age and use, was barely readable. Spurlock is said to have kept the journal neatly between two thin cedar boards, wrapped in sheets of blotter paper, to protect it from the elements.

Spurlock always seemed to have money and, in fact, had loaned Alley money and was visiting to collect when Alley talked him out of a portion of the journal. Spurlock told Alley he had received the journal from his grandfather. The "Alley Journal" eventually found its way into the hands of Judge Richard Apperson, of Mt. Sterling, who once held the original land patent to the Big Sandy Region. The journal then passed to William Connelly, who wrote about the tale, the searchers, etc.

The journal details Swift's visit and names "Sandy Creek" and "Forks of the Sandy" and many other unnamed landmarks that are in or near Johnson County. Spurlock has been described as an "erratic character" who roamed Tennessee and Kentucky in search of the lost mines, and may have actually recovered some of the silver. Robert Alley reported that Spurlock "always carried large saddlebags containing money."

Thomas Clark, the noted Kentucky historian, wrote that scenes of Swift's activities were along the Paint River and "hence, old silver legends have become so widespread that even at this late date (1937) the Paint River localities are occasionally excited over reputed finds of the Swift cache."

The Alley copy of the journal mentions places along the Big Sandy during the entire eight or nine years of activity by

Swift. Among those mentioned are the Forks of the Sandy, the "Big Gap" which some read as Pound or Breaks, others as Cumberland Gap, Cassel Woods (across the Cumberland Mountain in Virginia), the Great Kanawha, the Guyandotte (West Virginia along with Wheeling Creek) and once "went out through a gap at the headwaters of the Big Sandy Creek."

The journal also refers to the "Great Cavern of the Shawnee" where Swift and the crew stored huge amounts of silver ore and coins. Speculation as to this cave being located near Pound Gap has existed since the first longhunters entered the region. The name "Pound" comes from the gap once called "Pounding Gap" because horsemen reported hearing their hoof pings echo (or pound) as if the mountain were hollow.

Dr. Lige Rasnick, in researching the legend on the Sandy, noted that the "grandfathers of Morgan Lipps, Core Holbrook, Eli Hill and old man Castle" accompanied the ailing Swift on his later search for the mines, and were with him at Nancy Gap, in Sandy Ridge, when he broke down and cried because of his unsuccessful search. Later searchers of the area included Hick Baker, Elijah Rasnick, Noah K. Counts, Kelly and John Erwin, Dr. Rasnick himself, and others. Many were apparently led by a map said to belong to James Simmons of Johnson City, Tennessee. The map, rumored to be made of deerskin by Swift, was bought from an Oklahoma Indian and purports to say that the mines "were on the fourth ridge from the Blue Ridge," which they believed to be Sandy Ridge.

In 1921, rumors spread throughout southwest Virginia that the mine had been found on Jenny's Creek, two miles from Paintsville, Kentucky. Another account, in 1926, pointed to Johnson County as the place where some old silver coins were found.

Jillson noted that a cave of considerable size is located due south of Blue Head Knob of Pine Mountain, as is another known as "Lost Cave," and writes that both were believed to be sites of Swift mining activities. Pound Gap is said to be in "reverence and sacred remembrance by the Shawnee." Chief Blue Jacket reportedly claimed the great cave as near Pound and had several mouths. He told Kentucky historian Collins that some of "the principal mines worked by Swift" were in the area of the great cave.

"Cornstalk and Blue Jacket's father went into the cave on more than one occasion, and had worked the mines with Swift," Collins wrote.

The Paint Creek name for the stream near Paintsville comes from the surprising marks early white settlers found on trees, tree roots, and rocks along the creek. Earlier Indians had decorated the place with various unusual carvings and paintings. There were drawings of birds, buffalo, deer, and other animals, as well as unknown symbols. Most of the art work has since faded or been defaced. Paintsville, as an early settlement, was said to be surrounded by Indian mounds and graves.

The area around the town is dotted with rock shelters, one said to be the captive site of Jenny Wiley. Nearby is the former site of Harmon's Station, the frontier outpost to which she fled after breaking loose from her Shawnee captives.

In her account of Wiley's ordeal, *The Captive*, Caroline Gordon retells the story through the pioneer woman's words. She describes the mine and how its ore had to be smelted, and the rock shelter.

"It was the biggest rock house ever I saw, running all along one side of the cliff. The old chief took a way up the side of the cliffs, the rest of us followed....

"We walked along a narrow ledge and come to the rock-house."

The rock house (or rock shelter) was said to be in a hidden valley near many ancient rock drawings, some "as big as a man." Above the shelter was a large elm tree with a huge rattlesnake painted on it. Later historians identified the spot as being along aptly named "Jenny Creek" in Johnson County.

In fact, some claim that several landmarks in the area are named for Swift: John's Creek, for the man himself, and Tug Fork, for the small "tugs" of silver he smelted out. Other stories have both waters named for other historic visitors and events.

In *The Big Sandy Valley*, Kentucky historian and surveyor William Rouse Jillson wrote the following:

"There is a tradition commonly found throughout the Big Sandy Valley and elsewhere in eastern Kentucky...that an English gentleman of education and means by the name of John Swift, came into this portion of Kentucky annually from 1760 to 1769 at the head of a composite company of Englishmen, Frenchmen, and Shawnee Indians for the purpose of operating certain silver mines."

In several versions of the Swift journal, including the one obtained from Robert Alley, which the east Tennessee native reportedly obtained from William Spurlock, who got it from Mrs. Bean in Bean Station, Swift mentions many trips back and forth on the Big Sandy.

"Reports of the existence of Swift's silver mines have been accredited to Johnson, Floyd, and Pike County," Jillson noted.

The journal carried and prized by William Spurlock and then by Robert Alley is probably the most complete, and is claimed by many to be the closest to the original Swift manuscript, if not actually the original. This journal has had an interesting history.

If legend is correct, the journal was presented by John Swift to Mrs. Renfro at Bean Station, Tennessee, sometime before 1800, while he was attempting to relocate his silver mines. His initial search to rediscover the old mines began there, at the Clinch Mountain foothills, and then stretched for an unsuccessful twelve years or more into Bell and Whitley Counties in Kentucky, up to Wise County, Virginia, across the Breaks of the Sandy to Pike County, Kentucky, down the river to Maysville, Kentucky (then Limestone), and down to the Red River Gorge area. While most tales have him leaving his journal with the Bean Station widow, still others have him giving copies to people who helped him along his way and assisted him in his search.

The journal may have passed from Mrs. Renfro to James

Renfro, of Cumberland Ford (Pineville, Kentucky) who relocated there from Tennessee. After his accidental death while searching for the mine, his widow came into ownership of the journal. How it passed from her to Spurlock isn't known, but Spurlock was known to have searched the area of Cumberland Gap, just south of Pineville, before moving his search to Kentucky. Robert Alley, later a Johnson County, Kentucky, school teacher, was also known to have searched for the lost mines in the Cumberland Gap area prior to relocating to Kentucky.

It should be noted that Alley reported being able to copy a large portion of the journal, but not all of it. It is likely that the copy of the journal which came into the hands of Tennessee judge and historian Haywood was probably a duplicate of the Spurlock/Alley journal.

What follows is a partial copy of the Spurlock/Alley version of Swift's Journal, judged by many to be one of the best and most complete. Material about the year of 1760 was not available as of this printing. The journal is very similar to the one published by Michael Paul Henson in *John Swift's Lost Silver Mines*, but much of the language and events differ.

The following apparently comes to us by way of Judge Apperson:

Started on the 25th of June, 1761, from Alexandria, Virginia, and came to Leesburg; thence to Winchester; thence to Little's; thence to Pittsburgh; thence to the headwaters of Wheeling; thence to the Little Kanawha; thence to the Big Kanawha; thence to the Guyandotte; thence to Great Sandy Creek; and from thence to the Great Ridge bearing in a southwesterly direction; and from thence to a large river the name of which was unknown to us; and from thence to a large and very rocky creek; and from thence to the mines, where we remained from the 18th of July to the 26th of October, 1761, when we left them and returned over the same way we had taken to come out. And on the 28th of October our scouts discovered six savages; by altering our course we avoided them. On the 30th we were pursued by savages, but we escaped from them. We saw no more of the savages until the 9th of November, when they fired on us and shot a hole in our lading which soon enlarged and spilled the silver. We fired in return and they must have fled for we saw no more of them; we did not camp this night until after we had crossed the Kanawha. We arrived at the settlements without further conflict, December 2nd, 1761.

April 15th, 1762. We this day started back to the mines. We arrived there on the 10th day of May without accident except the spilled rum.

August 1st, 1762. We this day left the mines to return home. We came to a sudden halt and camped a short time on the 2nd of August when we were alarmed by savages. We escaped from them and camped on our creek. We were greatly pestered but came through safe; we left a valuable prize on the south of the big Gap where we marked some trees with our names and curious marks. From this place we went to Cassell's Woods, and from that place we went to Virginia, where we remained until the next spring, 1763.

We then started on the 1st day of May, 1763, and came to New River; and from thence to Holston; and from thence to the Cumberland Valley.

Here we set our course and went to the place where our mines are situated, arriving there the 2nd of June, 1763.

We remained here until the 1st of September, when we set out for home. We went through Cassel's Woods, and stopped with Cassellman for five days. From Cassellman's we went to the settlements, and arrived home October 12th, 1763.

We started from home on the 1st of October, 1767, and got to the mines on the 4th of November, 1767. We stayed until the 1st of April, 1768, when we set out for home. We went by the way of Sandy Creek, meeting with nothing material on the way to the settlements.

We left Alexandria on the 4th of June, same year, 1768, and arrived safely at the mines on the 1st of July. We remained here until the 26th of October, 1768. Arrived at home on the 24th of December. Our horses stolen by the Indians was a great loss to us as we were compelled to conceal and leave their lading at the mouth of a large creek running due east.

We left our homes in North Carolina on the 16th day of May, 1769, and started for the mines. We went by the way of the door in the Cumberland Mountains and arrived at the mines safe and sound 24th of June, 1769.

We stayed at the mines until 19th October, 1769. On that day we started home, and went by the way of Sandy Creek. At the Forks of Sandy we lost two of our horses, stolen by savages, and here we concealed their lading, a great loss to us, but we escaped with our lives, and got safe home 1st December, 1769.

I was at the place again, and came by the place where we left the two-horse loads, and the valuable prize, and found all things as we left them in 1762 and 1763. [1768]

On the 1st September, 1769, we left between $22,000.00 and $30,00.00 in crowns on a large creek running near a south course. Close by the creek we marked our names, Swift, Jefferson, and Munday, and other names on a large beech tree with compasses, square and trowel. About twenty or thirty poles from the creek stands a small rock, and between it and the creek you will find a small rock of a bluish color with three chops made with a grit-stone by rubbing it on the rock. By the side of this rock you will find the prize. We left prizes here at three different times. At no great distance from the place we left $15,000.00 of the same kind, marking three or four trees with marks. Not far from these trees, we left a prize near a forked white oak, and about three feet underground, and laid two long stones across it, marking several stones close about it.

At the Forks of Sandy, close by the fork, is a small rockhouse which has a spring in one end of it, and between it and a small branch we hid a prize under the ground. It was valued at $6,000.00. We likewise left $3,000.00 buried in the rocks of the rockhouse.

Directions to the Mines

The furnace that I built is on the left-hand side of a very rocky creek at a remote place in the West. To find the best ore, climb up the cliff at the left-hand side of the furnace and go a due south direction until you strike a small branch nearby. Go to the head of the branch without crossing, and you there see my name on three beech trees. From these trees go due east to the top of a low ridge. Pass a small knob on top of the ridge to the right-hand when you will see a big rock which has fallen from a high ledge. Behind this fallen rock we got our best ore. This vein runs northeast and southwest, lying and being in latitude 37 degrees and 56 minutes N. And ore is also found in latitude 38 degrees and 2 minutes N. By astronomical observations and calculations you will find the location of both these veins of silver ore to be on the 83rd meridian of longitude or very close to it.

Description of the Country

The creek heads southwest and runs northeast. It abounds with laurel. It is so cliffy and rocky that it is nearly impossible to get horses to the furnace. So extremely rough is the way that we rarely took our horses nearer than six or seven miles of the place.

There is a thicket of holly a quarter of a mile below the furnace and a small lick a mile above. There is a large buffalo lick two miles from the small lick on another creek that we called Lick Creek. The creek forks about three miles below the furnace and the left-hand fork is the furnace creek. Below the forks the creek is a small stream of water running generally in a north-easterly direction.

Between the forks and holly thicket you will find my name on a beech tree, cut in the year 1767, and about one mile below, you will find Munday, Jefferson and Swift's names in the year 1762, 1765 and 1767.

Between the small lick and the furnace is a remarkable rock; it hangs out quite over the creek, and the water runs under it.

The mountains and hills are covered with laurel and water courses so much that a man can not get along without much difficulty where paths are not cut. Most of the mountains and hills have but little timber and are poor and barren. North of the furnace about three miles is a larger hill seven or eight miles long upon which there is good timber of different kinds, but south of it there is little timber worth notice.

Furnace Creek forks about three miles above the lick, and in the forks upon the foot of the hill you will find three white oaks growing from one stump. On each of them is cut a small notch with a tomahawk. We sometimes went to a salt spring up the right-hand fork, and came this way back which was the cause for our marking the trees.

From the door in the Cumberland Mountains, on the top at the north, you will run north, forty degrees west, we supposed forty-one miles, and if on the right course you will find trees marked with curious marks all the way. In the course we crossed many creeks and one river.

The first company in search of these mines was composed of Staley, Ireland, McClintock, Blackburn and Swift.

We concealed much silver in bars and crowns in the Indian cave. Set your compass on the west side of the furnace under the rockhouse, and go due west fifty poles, when you will find a tree in this form _____. Set your compass at the second turn and go south twenty poles and you will find a large tree and a limb growing out of the south side near the ground; under this limb we buried four ten-gallon kegs full of crowns.

Set your compass on the south side of the furnace and steer south two hundred poles and you will find a tree that grows in this form_____. Set your compass at the second turn and go south twenty poles. Under the large limb of a big tree which leans down the creek you will ind ore. You cannot miss finding the furnace if you find the _____.
Here the old journal ends.

Colonel William McMillan, of Clark County, Kentucky, had a copy of Swift's journal sometime after 1788, and formed a company to search for the mines. The company consisted of eleven other men.

Colonel McMillan's version of the journal included clues involving phases of the moon and signs of the Zodiac.

In Laurel County, according to Lewis Clark in *History of Kentucky*, a quantity of iron was discovered along with some "appearance of lead" and the find renewed interest in the old legend.

"Swift's old mine is supposed to be in this county," Clark wrote.

Turkey Tracks, carved in a rock and pointing backwards toward one of Swift's mines, were one clue to finding the treasure in the Red River Gorge area. These carvings were photographed by Doug Belcher on Lower Devil's Creek near the noted Kentucky gorge.

Daniel Boone's Silver Mine

Mention Kentucky, the Wilderness Road, or Cumberland Gap and many people immediately associate them with Daniel Boone. It seems that Boone was everywhere in east Tennessee, Kentucky, and even West Virginia. And everywhere he went he carved his name and "kilt a bar," or so it is claimed.

Actually not only was Boone not the first colonial explorer in the region, he himself had a guide. John Finley, who had been an Indian captive and longhunter, and piloted Boone and others along the Great Warrior Path which Boone later "blazed" to become the Wilderness Road. Finley had been preceded by Dr. Thomas Walker as early as 1750, who named many of the landmarks, including the Cumberland Mountains, Cumberland River, etc.

Numerous other explorers, adventurers, longhunters, land speculators, and traders explored the region prior to Boone. One of these may have been John Swift, who some believe first entered Kentucky as an Ohio Valley trader among the Indians in Ohio and Kentucky.

Some versions of the journal and related legend have Swift associated with Pennsylvania businessmen and Colonel John Tye in Uniontown. Daniel Boone's father, Squire Boone, Sr., moved his family from Pennsylvania to Yadkin Valley of North Carolina about 1752. Many Swift associates, by some versions even Munday, lived in the Yadkin.

Daniel, as a young man, carried furs and supplies to Salisbury, another town associated in the Swift legend. Then, in 1755, both Boone and Swift served under Washington with the British in the campaign against Fort Duquesne.

In 1760, while Swift claimed to be starting up his mining deep in the Appalachian Mountains, Boone was serving

North Carolina in the militia against the Cherokee. By 1767, with Swift well into whatever activity he actually did in the isolation of the wilderness, Boone had joined with his brother, Squire, and others for an extended hunt in the same region of the rumored silver mines.

Swift, in one version, tells of Yadkin Valley neighbors becoming overly interested in his activities and complained about Boone, and others, attempting to follow his party across the mountains to the mines.

Several men who knew Boone in the later days of Kentucky's settlement also knew of Swift or his mines, and these included John Filson, Robert Breckenridge, Eli Cleveland, John Morton, James Callaway, and James Harrod.

Filson, known now as Kentucky's first historian, wrote a book on Boone, made a land claim for the area including Swift's mine, and walked off into the wilderness to disappear forever.

Harrod, founder of Harrodsburg and noted Kentucky patriot, followed a man named Bridges to the "three forks of the Kentucky River" in search of Swift's mines, and was never seen again.

A 1769 hunt by Boone in the region included his brother-in-law, John Stuart. The Stuarts (or Stewards) settled near Flat Lick, north of Cumberland Ford (Pineville), and were visited there by Swift in his search to relocate his mines.

Stretching a supposed Boone/Swift connection even further, Boone was hired by Judge Richard Henderson to make the 1769 expedition. Henderson's eventual "treaty" with the Cherokee for land in Powell Valley and Cumberland Mountain along the Tennessee and Kentucky line was found to be illegal, and settlers there were removed. Henderson traveled into the region in 1775 with Boone and others. In 1812 William Henderson, apparently a relative of Richard, and Shelton Partin joined a party of hunters which ventured into the Cumberlands. Scott Partin, a descendant of both, wrote in a *Cincinnati Inquirer* article in 1916 that "Aside from hunting and farming, they settled in South America (the Frakes, Kentucky, area) for the purpose of finding Swift's Silver

Mine." He noted that the men had a copy of the Swift journal upon their arrival in the area of North Carolina.

During Daniel Boone's many years of hunting, trading, and exploring the region, he was captured by Indians and forced to lead them to other longhunter camps, where the unwelcome whites were banished back across the mountains, or even adopted by Shawnee Chief Black Fish. One is said to have disappeared for a year or so into the wilds of Kentucky, and never accounted for his lost time there.

In a newspaper article in 1967, Jim Jayde explored the connection between the two men, and seems to point to a secret Boone silver mine on the South Fork of the Kentucky River in the general area where James Harrod was searching. Jayde notes that the location fits the description given by Filson in his land grant application of "40 miles north of Martin's Station."

He also quotes Swift as saying, "Take me to the three forks of a large stream to which I shall direct you. When I stand at the three forks I will be able to point out the direction so clearly that you will be able to find the mine and the buried treasure."

He noted that Boone and Swift "must have crossed paths many times."

Jayde recalls Swift's unsuccessful search to relocate his lost mines, and Swift's death in Lexington, Kentucky. He has Boone and others searching for the lost mine prior to Swift's return from the English prison.

The best connection Jayde gives for a connection between the two men is from old Clay County records. He says that an old silver mine was found near the Clay County line on the South Fork. The name "D.Boone" was discovered carved into a large rock near the mouth of the mine, and cinders found there revealed gold and silver.

The mine, Jayde wrote, was on "the land of Able Bishop" and his heirs, and within the "40 mile" claim of Filson, near a high knob, opposite the mouth of Sexton Creek. A small creek which drains into the South Fork is called "Meadow Creek." Jayde refers to an 1819 deed which includes Meadow

Creek, formerly owned by Jesse Boone and Daniel Boone, Jr., and being deeded to William Strong as 1000 acres.

Another "Meadow Creek" is located a few miles to the south, on Bullskin Creek of the Big South Fork, or Red Bird River.

"With a reasonable amount of research, the above-described Boone tract of land should be easily located. It is believed that the land is situated close to the mouth of Sexton Creek, and if so it would include the old mine shown on the map," Jayde wrote.

Currently the site may fall just inside Owsley County. Jayde noted than an 1883 report in Frankfort indicates that gold and silver ore were found in Owsley County on Buick Creek. He also wrote of rich lead ore being found in 1866 in Owsley and Wolfe Counties.

Daniel Boone, shown in this early 1800's portrait, may have had a silver mine in Kentucky. Although nothing is mentioned in his life of the secret mine, a deed may tell another story.

Northeast Kentucky Legends

Most tourists' only real contact with the legend of lost silver mines comes during a visit to Carter Caves, between Morehead, Kentucky, and Huntington, West Virginia, near Olive Hill, Kentucky. There, aside from viewing the bluffs, staying in the state lodge, or hiking the hills, they can tour the caves. One cavern, today known as Saltpeter Cave, was once known as "Counterfeiter's Cave" and is linked historically with the legend of lost silver mines.

John Tierney, state ranger and naturalist, is a knowledgeable Swift researcher and often tells the story. Tour guides stop at a little pit inside the cave and tell visitors about the old Indian legend of romance and silver.

The area of Carter and surrounding counties is littered with old tales of silver mines, buried silver treasures, and Indian lore. From Morehead to Olive Springs, from the Red River Gorge to the mouth of the Big Sandy River, the search continues and occasionally someone will claim to have found the mine or another piece of the puzzle.

The legends there began with an old Indian legend.

An Indian brave called Huraken fell in love with an Indian princess from another tribe. The lovely young woman, Maniuta, was forbidden to see Huraken, so the brave searched the countryside for a gift for her father, hoping he could buy her hand.

The brave Huraken was gone so long in his search that Manuita feared he would never return and threw herself off a bluff to her death.

Meanwhile, Huraken's long search ended at a silver mine he discovered. From the deep part of the cave, later known as

Swindle's Cave (Counterfeiter's Cave) he dug silver, smelted it down, and made a beautiful tomahawk of it. He beat the metal out on an anvil, and made a peace pipe as its handle. When he returned with his gift he learned of Manuita's death.

Huraken secretly carried off his lover's body and dug her grave inside the cavern. Manuita's father and his warriors caught Huraken and tied him up in the woods to be eaten by wild animals, but rain loosened the straps, and he wandered through the forest mourning her death.

Eventually he returned to her village, requesting that they allow him to go to the cave before killing him. The warriors escorted him to the cave, where he entered, never to be seen again. Huraken's silver tomahawk lay undiscovered for years until a local settler named Ben Henderson found it.

When the cave was opened in the 1780's, early white explorers found the open grave of Princess Manuita. Numerous Indian relics were found, and according to another story, the mummified remains of the princess. Henderson reportedly found the tomahawk, made of one piece of silver, under a cliff in Smokey Valley. A silver bar was found on Smokey Creek in 1890 by Dennis Burchett.

Sometime after 1788, Colonel William McMillan of Carter County formed a company to search for Swift's mine. The company consisted of himself and eleven other men. He had a copy of the "original" journal, which directed searchers to look during certain phases of the moon and signs of the zodiac.

Ranger Tierney has said that the "Princess grave" may have been dug by over-enthusiastic tour guides of earlier times. He also said that early names have been found in the caves, including that of Simon Kenton.

Sometime prior to 1840, possibly many years prior, a man named Swigle, or Swindell, counterfeited coins at Carter Caves; hence the name "Counterfeiter's Cave." Local legend says he was helped by Jonathan Waite and Billy Johnson. They mined their ore along Kinniconick Creek and smelted it down at the old "Boone Furnace." Even Daniel Boone was believed to have been involved with silver mines. The Commercial Bank of Grayson is said to have a bag of counterfeit coins made of native silver from Tygert's Creek in the early 1800's.

A Lewis County legend has French silver miners on Kinniconick (Kinny) Creek, and identifies one of them as "Deburttes." He supposedly told a story of being in the area about 1775, and being forced off the works by attacking Indians. The only survivor of the French party was a certain McCormick. With McCormick, the Indians opened a silver mine on Kinny or Quick Run Creek, the best ore being found on Laurel Fork. Later silver miners in the area of Lewis County included Jonathan Waite of Adams County, Ohio; Joshia Sprinkle, George Wright, Andrew Beaty and others, including a man known simply as "Shepard."

An old prospector along Kinny and Triplett Creeks looked for the mine there, and found the remains of a silver smelter. Triplett, Kinniconick and Tygart Creek all head up into the hills between Lewis and Carter County.

J.W.M. Breazeale, in his *Life As It Is* published in 1842, tells of the early explorers and longhunters who first entered Kentucky, and makes the following statement:

"When these hunters made their excursions in 1761 into the country we have been describing, there were no white inhabitants west of the Blue Ridge, except a few men who were working at the lead mines."

The writer identifies the mines as operated by a man named "Swigle," and placed them in Jefferson County, Tennessee, six miles east of Mossy Creek, in a large cavern. Possibly Swingle moved north to Kentucky, and worked the Carter County mines. Kentucky historian Lewis Collins wrote that Colonel G. Terrell furnished him a copy of a Swift journal belonging to Wood C. Dollins, of Mount Sterling, Kentucky.

The Lewis family, pioneers of Carter County, found silver-bearing cinders near their cabin. A silver spoon with the date 1774 was found near Grayson, possibly made from a silver bar. Two Shawnee visiting Carter County in 1850 searched around McGlure and Cedar Run for several weeks, and told a white man they stayed with the Indian legend of Carter Caves. A cave near Tygart's Creek is located near an ancient Indian flint quarry.

Cedar Run Creek played heavily in another local silver mine legend involving a French silver miner named Howard LeKain. Swift's journals, or most of them, mention that a nearby silver mine was operated by the French while Swift and his crew labored "at the upper mine."

LeKain reportedly discovered silver, with a little gold, between Carter City and Wesleyville, Kentucky. The legends are similar, with LeKain mining silver, building a smelter, using local Indian helpers, coining Spanish milled dollars, and hiding the treasure in a cave.

"The cave descended straight down six or eight feet, levelled off, then went down another ten feet," Michael Paul Henson wrote. LeKain capped off the mouth with a flat rock. Inside he carved the date 1774, and outside he carved a snake on a large rock, its head pointing to the hiding place. All of his coins were dated 1711.

Later in his life, after escaping from Indians, he took his Indian wife and settled in Louisiana, writing directions to his treasure on "waybills" and directing searchers to Cedar Cliffs and Ring Rock Springs, which were across from the cave.

In 1890, LeKain's grandson, Robert Tinder, returned to Carter County to look for the treasure cave. His directions, or waybill, were left with the family of Charles Stamper, but were destroyed by fire in 1905.

Stamper, of Olive Hill, is said to have located a silver mine in 1910. He had to end his mining because of a mineral rights dispute. Silver ore was found on the Stamper farm while a well was being dug, some forty feet below the surface.

William Everman was a Carter County surveyor who followed the LeKain legend and, in a tale to Estelle S. Rials of the Ashland, Kentucky, *Daily Independent*, said the ore came from a vein near Carter City. The cave was located in 1964 in Wolfe County, Kentucky, it was reported, by the Mountaineer Mining and Exploration Company of Clarksburg, West Virginia. Ralph W. Griffin announced the finding of the suspected "Silver Mine" one mile south of Pine Ridge, within a mile of the Mountain Parkway on the John Adams Farm.

The company members went some thirty feet inside the opening and were stopped by a four-foot thick stone. Griffin said the find ended six years of searching, and the company planned to return to drill and dynamite the blockage.

Another concern, Swift Mines, Inc., was also searching Wolfe County that same year, but closed down its operations because "dirt access roads in Kentucky made it impossible to continue the search." Their search was along Chimney Top Creek.

Treasure signs have reportedly been found near Pine Ridge in Wolfe County. Ralph Griffith believed the signs pointed to the site of Swift's mine. The skull of "an Indian Princess" was sought by three Indian visitors to Wolfe County as late as 1964. They explored along Lower Devil's Creek looking for the mark "101" carved in a rock or tree. The Indians communicated with Charlie Booth of Campton.

The *History of Kentucky* tells of "ancient tools and instruments" that fell from the cliffs of Carter County, and which were examined by well-respected men who believed them to have been used in smelting and coining silver.

"A bar of pure silver was found many years ago near a small mill in Carter County. It was thought to have been smelted from ore obtained from the silver mines said to exist in that county.

"One of the first settlers of the county found near his cabin a quantity of cinder of such unusual color and weight to induce him to have it tested by an expert," wrote William Connelley in *History of Kentucky*.

"This was done and the result was a considerable amount of pure silver which…was converted into spoons. These spoons are in the possession of the family," the historian wrote.

Between Louisa, Kentucky, and Morehead, on Devil's Fork

in Elliott County, is a bluff known as "Silver Mine Cliff." In 1889 John Boykin prospected the area and found silver in a "gray granite-like stone very hard to mine." Boykin was directed to the area by an old Indian who claimed the mines there had been worked by the French and his ancestors.

The man found silver and brought it as ore samples to Morehead, where an assay indicated the silver's worth at only about $80 per ton. He nevertheless mined the silver in his crude way for years, and then moved out west for better diggings.

In a manuscript penned in the 1770's, the renowned Chief Joseph told of four silver mines in Elliott County on Caney Creek of the Little South fork. The mines are marked by a carving of a crane on a cliff near the mouth of the creek, reportedly near Newfoundland.

It should be noted that most modern "Swift Buffs" point to the northeast Kentucky legends as being part of Swift's "upper mines."

Ouasiota Pass, near Station Camp Creek in Jackson and Estill Counties, was a natural gateway for early travelers. In *Indian Trails of the Southeast* by William Edward Myer, he mentions traces of ancient Indian settlements there.

"A vein of so-called 'silver ore' is said to have been found in the region, but it was probably galena, the vein of which contains very small traces of silver. Many such veins were worked to a slight extent by the fires, but they soon found that the value of the ores which they contained were very much less than the cost of extraction."

Myers said the ancient Indians used the lead ore to mix a silver-white powder for body decorations, and possibly for bullets.

In the *History of Clay County*, Mr. and Mrs. Kelly Morgan wrote of Swift's Silver Mines that "scenes of these activities were along the Red Bird River."

William Huff, a companion of Theo Robinson, explored for the lost mines in the area of Quicksand Creek, near the Floyd and Knott County line. In 1926 some silver coins were found in Johnson County.

Hobert Fannin reported, in 1982, finding "spider webs" of silver woven in limestone on Devil's Fork and Laurel Creek near the Elliott-Rowen County line. He also pointed to Caney Creek, in Elliott County, and a silver vein there. Fannin took a lease on property in Greenup County, where he found silver that weighed 2.86 ounces per ton.

John Tillman was said to have counterfeited coins from a secret mine, thought to be one of Swift's, on Laurel Fork in Morgan County before and during the Civil War.

North central and eastern Kentucky was held by the French prior to the colonial settlement there, and the most noted outpost was at Old Indian Fields, near Winchester. Longhunter John Finley, who led Daniel Boone and others into Kentucky, was held captive there in the 1750's. Old stories have the French and Indians in the area killing several white hunters and miners near the village site, and finding much money on the bodies. The coins were hidden or buried nearby, and several old coins were found some 200 years later.

Early French leader Chartier headquartered at Old Indian Fields as early as 1745, and a store or trading post also operated there. Colonial traders camping along Lulbegrud Creek, named by Kentucky explorer and historian John Filson, were attacked and robbed of about 1600 pounds of goods.

Filson, who some modern historians believe actually penned the Swift journal as a work of fiction, camped along Lulbegrud Creek with Daniel Boone and others, naming the stream from the book *Gulliver's Travels* by the English writer Jonathan Swift.

The state's first historian and biographer of Daniel Boone was the first to file a land claim for an area "70 miles" north of Martin's Station (in extreme western Virginia) containing a mine worked by one John Swift. Filson fell to the notorious Swift Silver Mine curse, venturing off into the wilderness and never being seen again.

Finley escaped from the Old Fields ("Eskippakithiki" in Indian) in 1753, returning to North Carolina's Yadkin Valley, home of Daniel Boone and several of Swift's mining crew members.

Two Cherokee Indians came to Irvine, Kentucky, in 1871, and stayed at the farm of Jacob Crabtree. The leader was described as polite, and spoke with an English accent. They searched for a lost silver mine on the Big and Little Sinking Creeks, returning to Crabtree's with a buckskin sack filled with something very heavy. Many yet believe they found the treasure or a cache left behind by their forefathers. Their search heated up local talk of the old silver mine.

About the same time a prospector found some twenty-seven pots, each about eighteen inches in diameter, at Ashley and Bone Cave on Lower Devil's Creek. Lower and Upper Devil Creeks are headed some six miles from Campton (see page 77).

The Ashland, Kentucky, newspaper, in 1983, published a sizable account of several northeast Kentucky men who took a reporter to what they believed to be one of Swift's mines. The treasure hunters included Jeff Hughes and son Rick of Ashland, John Byrd of Carter City, and Haskell Wright and Buck Click of Greenup.

While the location of their mine was not published, they reportedly found it and removed a stone from its mouth. They shoveled the dirt out and went inside the formerly sealed shaft, located at the base of a bluff. Twenty feet from the mouth they found the mine sealed again with a crumbling reddish material they believed to be the "same silicate used in their furnaces."

About forty yards from the mouth of the mine, or cave, they found another shaft, this one running horizontally and reaching back about 125 feet. A three-inch hole was seen there in the limestone. Outside was a trench leading away from the cliff's base, apparently used for horses and sleds coming from the mine.

Three miles from the mine shafts, the men located another mine, near a rock shelter. Assays of rocks from the area indicated that a small amount of silver was present. The "dateline" on the story was Morehead, Kentucky.

Also discovered, beneath moss and debris, were several initials carved in the rock believed to belong to Swift's crew, including "J.S." and, nearby, the word "Mine." The "J.S." carving had the date 1767. The Kentucky men also found a piece of silver with a metal detector, believed to have been "sliced from an overflow of a mold," according to a local jeweler.

To keep the site of the find secret, the men took the reporters, including G. Sam Platt, senior editor of the *Daily Independent*, to the site blindfolded.

Archibald Dickinson is said to have discovered a lead, zinc, and borate vein somewhere on Drennon's Lick in Henry County. In 1780 he also found lead and silver ore there.

William Rouse Jillson in *Collected Writings* wrote: "I have heard of black lead mines upon the _____ waters of Kentucky, but I have not been able to procure any certain information respecting them. Imlay's (map) reference was undoubtedly to the lead, zinc, and borate vein at Drennon's Lick."

Drennons was considered a regular hunting ground of Indians. Later the lick became a popular "medical spring" prior to 1850.

Dickinson swapped his findings at the lick to Colonel Robert Johnson and some other men for 900 acres of land. Silver was supposed to be found in 1872 on the Judith L. Marshall farm near the Kentucky River in Henry County.

Drennon's Lick is located on Kentucky Route 83 near Gratz. In July of 1773, Jacob Drennon and Matthew Braken, directed by an old Delaware Indian, reached the spot. George Rogers Clark had a deed for 400 acres there in 1779. Six miles from Drennon's is an old abandoned lead mine.

Mary Verhoeff, a Filson Club member, devoted much space in her *The Kentucky Mountains, Transportation and Commerce, 1750-1911* to the silver mine legend and wrote that "considerable time and money has been spent in search of silver ore...yet no indication of any deposit of silver ore worth exploration has ever been discovered in Appalachia...though it is beyond dispute that occasional silver-bearing ore has been found in exceedingly small quantities.

"The legend of Swift and his concealed silver mines and treasure...may be left to those who wish to believe it. Legends concerning the silver mines antedate the Revolutionary War and are still current in the Kentucky mountains," she said.

Laurel County, according to Maude Ward Lafferty, was the scene of searches for Swift's mine, along with adjoining counties. In her *Lore of Kentucky*, she retells the Swift legend and the Bean Station romance with Mrs. Renfro, and lists Swift's associates as James Ireland, Samuel Blackburn, Harman Slately (Staley), and Joshua McClintock.

Lafferty also writes that Swift and his men may never have had a mine, and came to Kentucky with silver obtained through pirate adventures, there in secret to "mine" coins.

Theo Robinson was a noted character who searched the area of Quicksand Creek, in Knott County, near the Floyd County line. Another Quicksand Creek resident, William Huff, is also said to have searched the area for treasure.

A Carter County man, Charlie Stamper of Olive Hill, is said to have mined silver in 1910 for some Ohio men. Because of a dispute over mineral rights, the mining was stopped, according to Henson. On the Stamper farm, silver was reportedly found while digging a well, some forty feet below the surface.

About 1750 Howard LeKain, whom some believe was half French and half Indian, left the old Louisiana territory and ventured into the Ohio Valley, lured there by rumors of silver mines. Other French fortune hunters had already traveled to the area, and reports were very favorable.

LeKain became friendly with Indians in the area and married a maiden, then was adopted into the tribe. Following information from the tribe, he prospected what is now northeast Kentucky and found a vein of silver in the hills of present-day Carter County. He also found a deposit of gold nearby, and for several years worked the ore, making bars and minting rough coins.

When the English and Americans began coming into the region, LeKain decided to abandon his mines and take as much as he could back to Louisiana. But over the years he had mined and smelted more than he could carry. Looking for a hiding place, he decided on a cave with a small mouth along the waters of Tygart Creek. From the cave he could look out and see Cedar Cliffs.

LeKain got help from his Indian friends, and hid a large amount of his works under a pile of rocks deep inside the cave. He left the area remembering certain landmarks, including Cedar Cliffs, Tygart Creek, and Ring Rock Spring. To ensure that he could relocate the cave, he carved a snake on a nearby rock, and then sealed the cave's entrance with a boulder.

LeKain and his wife made it safely to Louisiana, and there raised a family. He died when his daughter was four years old. She grew up and married a man named Tinder. Years later the silver miner's daughter had a son, Robert Tinder, who was later to find a map drawn by his grandfather among the family belongings.

About 1819 a new settler stumbled into the cave and found a carving that read "LeKain, 1774" but was not aware of the silver and gold, and did not find the cache. As odd as it seems, the settler moved to Kansas and encountered Robert Tinder, telling him the story of finding the cave and the carvings.

Tinder eventually traveled to Carter County and, with the aid of the old map and the Stamper family, found the cave. Yet when he and his helpers tried to clear away the rocks and dirt, the cave fell in, covering the floor where his grandfather had hidden the silver and gold. Twice he attempted to recover the treasure, once by drilling a shaft into the chamber, but his efforts failed. Robert Tinder is said to have died in 1903, and was buried near Tygart Creek.

Among the similarities in most versions of Swift's Mine are the stories involving counterfeiting. Whether Swift obtained the ore from his mine or transported it into the wilderness to mint in secret, certainly the idea of a hidden silver mine would cover any suspicion that the silver was stolen. So many different coins were in use within the Colonies in the years following the American Revolution that it would have been simple to pass fake coins, especially if the metal was pure.

According to *A Guide Book to United States Coins*, 27th edition, by R.S. Yeoman, the most popular and accepted coin of the time was the Spanish Milled Dollar. It was valued at "eight reales," and often called the "pillar dollar" or "Piece of Eight."

These coins were minted in Mexico City, Bolivia, Chili, Colombia, Guatemala, and Peru. In 1974 the value of a piece of eight of common date and mint mark was $25 to $35, if in fine condition. The manufacture date for the coin was 1732 to 1772, making it the ideal coin to counterfeit for use in the new continent. The Spanish coins were "the principal coins in the American Colonies, and the forerunners of our own silver dollar and its fractional divisions."

Every few years someone will claim to have found one of the lost silver mines. Newspaper articles like the following appear, and when the claim is discovered to be a hoax or a mistake, nothing is printed about it. Examples, from a 1914 article:

"The mystery surrounding the location of the famous Swift's Silver Mine...it is believed, at last, has been solved by a recent find on a farm near Beattyville, Lee County, Kentucky.

"...together with relics of John Swift...which go to prove Swift's mine may have been at this particular spot.... The evidence is arousing much interest among people in this section, as well as of mining experts at the state university.

"The property in Lee County is owned by Miss Lula Derickson, of Lexington, and her brother, John H. Herickson, of Jackson."

These unusual carvings, found in Elliott County by Jerry Dunn, may point to several silver mines in the area. What appear to be dates actually are not, and dozens of other unusual symbols are carved in the bluff top. (Photo by Jerry Dunn)

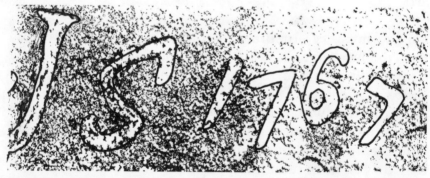

The initials of John Swift and a date (JS 1767) found by Jeff Hughes, Haskell Wright, and others which led to the finding of a very old mine shaft and other "Swift" indicators somewhere in northeastern Kentucky. The initials and date were outlined by the author.

That's the Breaks, Sandy

The beautiful, wild Breaks of the Sandy is a striking water gap between Kentucky and Virginia above the Big Sandy Valley. Russell Fork flows through on its way to join the Big Sandy River. In this deep rugged gorge, with rapids of five miles in length, are abrupt bluffs that stand a thousand feet high above the stream. On the Virginia side is a remarkable rock known as "The Towers," which rises 1600 feet above the base of the gorge.

Shawnee legends tell of a great cave and Swift's silver mines being there and at Pound Gap. Both noted landmarks are in the northeast end of the very long and ancient Pine Mountain.

By some versions of the journal, especially that of William Spurlock and Robert Alley, Swift built a furnace and burned charcoal within the Breaks, from there going southwest along the base of the mountain to the lower, or southern, mine.

Many versions of the journal have Swift and his mining crew traveling from Alexandria, Virginia, to Fort Pitt, down through West Virginia to the Forks of the Sandy River, and then on to different mines. Several times Swift is said to have departed the mines by way of the Breaks, going through the mountains to camp at Castle Woods in Virginia.

Jillson wrote that, although he simply thought Swift and his men were counterfeiters who brought pirated silver into the mountains to be recoined, this activity may have occurred near the Breaks.

"If this interpretation is correct, it may well be that the mythical 'Great Shawnee Cave' near the 'Breaks' in the Sandy Valley is a treasure-house of silver and gold coins awaiting the coming of some unknown Aladdin."

He also noted that local folklore link a cavern known as

Bluestone Cave with the "great cave" lore, which was believed to stretch from one side of the Breaks to the other.

"Thence to one of the forks of the Great Sandy Creek," one journal reads. "Near its headwaters. We had two workings...the other went southwest along the great ridge."

Carol Crowe Carraco's *The Big Sandy* tells of rumors of silver mines "of the English trader Jonathan Swift" and of land surveys by a young George Washington. She retells the story of Swift building furnaces at "the Breaks of the Sandy," and has him as a "pirate, preying on Spanish silver ships." She seems to agree with Jillson that the silver was carried into the mountains instead of being found there.

Talk of silver mines flourished in 1921, when an old mine was reportedly located on the land owned by C.C. Mead, on Jenny's Creek about four miles from Paintsville.

In 1926, several silver coins and pottery were found in the hills of Johnson County.

"At the forks of Sandy we lost two of our horses, stolen by the savages, and here we concealed their lading, a great loss for us."

And:

"At the forks of the Sandy, close to the fork, is a small rock house which has a spring in one end of it, and between it and a small branch we hid a prize under the ground. It was valued at $6,000. We likewise left $3,000 buried in the rocks of the rock house."

So goes but two entries in versions of Swift's journals. On several occasions, the miners either entered or left Kentucky by way of the Big South Fork and the region, especially the Breaks of the Sandy gorge, which play an important part in the lore of the lost mines.

According to the Spurlock version of the journal, Swift and his crew built furnaces and burned a charcoal pit somewhere in the beautiful and rugged gorge. From there the crew went to the southwest along the mountain (Pine Mountain) to where they found "other mines." Most journals refer to these as the "lower mines."

Swift's crew, when arriving on the north side of what is now the Kentucky/Virginia state park, cast lots to see which crew members would work which mines. Jillson places Swift on the Sandy River "toward the headwaters" of Paint Creek, near present-day Paintsville, Kentucky.

Two streams in the tributary network forming the Big Sandy River are said to have been named for Swift: John's Creek, after John Swift's travels there, and Tug Fork, supposedly named for the "tugs" of silver the Swift crew made to carry back to their base in the colonies.

William C. Kozee, in *Pioneer Families of Eastern and Southeastern Kentucky*, noted Swift's Big Sandy travels and places him at the present-day Louisa, where the party divided up to work the upper and lower mines.

Most journals list Swift's first venture (in 1760) to locate the mines as being through Fort Pitt and down to the Forks of the Sandy, with one group continuing up the West, or Louisa fork.

Paint Creek, near modern Paintsville, got its name from the surprising Indian art work found there by early settlers. Colorful drawings of birds and animals, including a buffalo, were found on the bluffs, along with unusual writing and signs. Most of the old art work has since faded.

On Paint Creek is a rock house, or shelter, with "a circular opening out" into it to allow entrance. Nearby the settlers build Harmon's Station, where white captive Jenny Wiley returned after her capture by Shawnee. Wiley, in papers recounting the captivity, tells of being forced to work while the Indians went off from the shelter to mine lead.

The Breaks of the Sandy park is striking, the only water gap in the mountain except for Pineville and Jellico. Russell Fork flows through the gorge on its way to becoming the Sandy River. The deep gorge, with its many rapids in its five-mile length, has 1,000 foot cliffs on either side. The most "remarkable rock" is on the Virginia side of the park, and is called "The Towers." It rises 1,600 feet above the stream. Shawnee legends about a great cave and Swift revolve around the Breaks and nearby Pound Gap. Stores of silver, minted into coins and in bars, are said to rest in the Great Shawnee Cave even today.

Jillson's *Big Sandy Valley* gives the following:

"Salt was made from several salt springs in the region, especially on the waters of Tug Creek, Middle Creek, and Beaver Creek. At the Middle Creek springs, which Daniel Boone visited in 1767 and 1768, works were well-developed by 1795, and after 1800 supported a considerable local industry. There was a tradition through the land about the existence of silver and lead mines toward the headwaters of Paint Creek as early as 1759. These mines had been visited by John Swift as early as that year. This was confirmed by Jenny Wiley and other returning captives; the mines were known to have been used by the Indians from early times for the manufacture of lead bullets.

"Over a century has passed (now two centuries) and the exact location of these far-famed mines is still unknown and shrouded in mystery."

A young George Washington was involved in surveying land in the western frontiers of Virginia. Jillson said that he probably made the first land survey west of the Big Sandy Valley. He places the future first president in the region between 1767 and 1770, at the same time as Swift. Oddly enough, one of Washington's biggest supporters following the American Revolution was one John Swift of Alexandria, Virginia.

Swift became a founder of the "Washington Society."

Five years after George Washington visited Kentucky, Thomas Jefferson hired two men to go into the Big Sandy Valley and survey a tract of land that would be "along the coordinates that John Swift gives." This land, according to one historian, was plotted in what is now Wayne County, West Virginia.

Judge Richard Apperson, of Mt. Sterling, Kentucky, is listed by Jillson as holder of "the original patent to the big Sandy tract" granted in 1792. Apperson, as already noted, also held another valuable possession, a journal he believed to be Swift's original writings.

A map, said to be that of Alley and Spurlock's, belonged to Alva Rice of Oil Springs, Kentucky, who got it from a relative who said it came directly from Alley. Whether this is the same as the one in the hands of Apperson is not known, but Rice saved it for future treasure hunters and historians by presenting it to noted author Michael Paul Henson.

The map has been reproduced often and appears in Henson's *John Swift's Lost Silver Mines* as well as Ralph Volker's *Mysteries of the Mountains.*

It may be the same map as that which fell into the hands of William Forward of Louisville, Kentucky, who is said to have obtained his copy from someone in Uniontown, Pennsylvania, about 1840.

Henson says the map is almost an exact enlargement of Licking River near West Liberty, Kentucky, and "very close to the 30 degree 56 minute and 83 degree longitude" given in a Swift journal.

The "Draper Papers" indicate that the map and journal were taken to Uniontown by Colonel John Tye, or left with him by Swift. Another version has Swift traveling to Uniontown and picking up his journals and maps after being freed from the English prison; he is supposed to have taken them into the mountains to assist in his effort to find the lost mines.

In 1921 rumors spread through the area that one of the lost silver mines had been found on Jenny's Creek, two miles from Paintsville. In 1926 rumors again carried word that a find of silver coins had been made in Johnson County.

When Theo Robinson died in 1927, the death of the well-known "silver mine hunter" kicked off more tales of Swift and his activities. Robinson was known to search around Quicksand Creek in Knott County. Other quicksand searchers were Long George Spencer and William Huff.

In his *Jenny Wiley County*, C. Mitchell Hall wrote that the tradition still abounds as late as 1972. Hall described Swift as "an English gentleman of education and means" and has him "trained at the Tower of London." He retells the building of furnaces and burning of charcoal in the forest along the Big Sandy.

The Big Sandy region drew some interest from Thomas Jefferson, five years after George Washington reportedly visited the area to survey. Jefferson hired two men to go into the Big Sandy Valley and survey land "along the coordinates that John Swift gives." According to one researcher, this land was plotted in what is now Wayne County, West Virginia.

In one "Big Sandy" version, Swift reports that "at the forks of the Sandy, close by the fork, is a small rock and it has a spring at one end of it. Close to the spot we marked our names. Between it and a small branch we hid a prize under the ground and it is valued at $6,000."

"At several points in eastern Kentucky," historian Jillson wrote, "purported remains of old furnaces have been found."

"The Towers," a wind- and rain-cut natural monument at the Breaks of the Sandy, on the Kentucky-Virginia border, is supposed to be another site where Jonathan Swift hid a cache of silver. Local legend points to the late 1730's as the time frame, some thirty years or so before most other stories of Swift's silver mines.

This view of The Towers was snapped from the Breaks Interstate Park. Southwest Virginia tales have Swift, in another account, leaving the state through the Breaks area, traveling down Russell Fork and the Sandy River to the Ohio, and then on to Limestone, Kentucky (now known as Maysville). (Photo by Mike Steely)

Southeastern Kentucky Legends

"According to legend there is a hidden treasure buried way up in the hills of Stinking Creek in Bell County. Only the Indians know where it may be, and some have met with disaster trying to find it," wrote K.S. Sol Warren in *The History of Knox County, Kentucky.*

Stinking Creek is located in Bell and Knox Counties, and flows into the Cumberland River through Flat Lick below Barboursville. Just across the mountains to the north is the Red Bird area, also playing a role in the old Swift tale. Located just off the old Wilderness Road (now Highway 25E) north of Pineville, the headwaters of Stinking Creek once were the route of the Great Warrior's Trace, which linked the Gulf of Mexico with the Great Lakes, an ancient version of a modern Interstate highway.

One of the first searchers of Stinking Creek and Red Bird, following Swift's fruitless attempt to relocate his lost mines there, was James Renfro.

Renfro came to Pineville, then Cumberland Ford, about 1800, the same year many accounts give as Swift's death. There he operated a public tavern, and kept the ferry (or ford) tollgate for Isaac Shelby. Shelby had built the place, and the holdings included a large livestock corral for passing travelers' horses and livestock.

Renfro, it is said, soon became wealthy and his business and success was reported in the *Knoxville Gazette* on November 19, 1822. The old tavern was torn down during the Civil War by Union forces, and the wood was used for military buildings, probably at Cumberland Gap.

The original toll at the ford was established by Colonel Joseph Crockett, father of David Crockett. Renfro and other local men often pleaded with the state of Kentucky to allot more money to keep up the road.

When Renfro wasn't running his businesses, he spent much time looking for Swift's lost mines. His search was apparently not limited to the headwaters of Stinking Creek, for he also held land grants to the High Cliff area of Pine Mountain near Jellico, long rumored to be another site of the lost mines.

Renfro is said to have a copy of Swift's journal and probably was related to the "Mrs. Renfro" of Bean Station, Tennessee, to whom Swift left the "original" journal. Some researchers believe he was, in fact, her son, having originally moved to Kentucky from old Claiborne County, Tennessee. If he received the journal from her or was, as some believe, Swift's love child by her, we will probably never know. The fact that he was an adult when he relocated to Pineville adds only poor speculation to the latter.

Renfro and a young black slave were searching the Stinking Creek area on July 29, 1835, when both were struck by lightning and killed. His wife then became the "Widow Renfro," of course, and there Pineville lays additional claim to the legend. Add to the local lore the claim that in its early days Pineville was settled by a man named Bean and you get another boast: the little town was "Bean Station."

Local historian F.F. Fuson wrote that Renfro actually came to operate the ferry about 1821. He died without a will, and the property passed from him and his wife, Dorcas, to his son, James Jr., in 1832. The young Renfro also died without a will, and the property came into the hands of James T. and Josephus Renfro, his sons, and then went to J.J. Gibson in 1860. Fuson wrote that he personally knew the Widow Renfro in 1886 and that she was a "very old lady."

One James Renfro had been a member of the first court of Claiborne County, Tennessee, in 1801, and was on the Donelson voyage from Long Island, Tennessee, to the Nashville area.

Near Flat Lick lived the Stewart family, descendants of James Steward, a survivor of the Cherokee massacre at Fort

Loudoun, Tennessee. Steward descendants still live in the area, and it is said that Swift visited the family while on his final search. James was an avid believer in the lost mines and may have died while looking for the treasure.

Pineville and Bell County may continue to expand its claim to the legend, apparently involving Swift's "lower mines," by pointing to Melungeon silver mines and smelters along Straight Creek, which runs along the north base of Pine Mountain from near the old ford, and heads in Harlan County.

Various limestone caves and rock shelters in the region have been searched for the treasure, including Rocky Face south of Pineville, Furnace Ridge on the Clear Creek west of Pineville, and Henry Bolton Gap just beyond Frakes.

Cannon Creek, between Pineville and Middlesboro, drew a man named Bob Beasley. He arrived there and hired a lot of local men to dig a deep hole in the bluff called Rocky Face (or Rock Face), near Ferndale, according to John A. Robbins.

"I've heard that Beasley had an old, old map he thought located the silver mine said to have been operated somewhere in the Cumberland Mountains many, many years ago by an old man named Swift," Robbins' statement read.

"Beasley drilled and drilled...all summer, and at last, he got so secret he wouldn't even let his work hands see what came out of the hole. Finally, when he went to leave, he filled the hole up. The place has been called Beasley's Hole ever since," the statement concludes.

Prior to 1921, a group of unidentified investors blasted away the side of a large bluff in their search for the silver. Fuson's *History of Bell County* locates the bluff between Pineville and Harlan on a large cliff across from the Cumberland River. In a *Pineville Sun-Courier* story, William Ayers said the men "for some time conducted their explorations and excavations on the Cumberland River, but without success as far as could be learned." The site, on the south side of the river, is in an area locally known as "Seven Sisters."

West of Pineville, along the north face of Pine Mountain and one-quarter way up the mountain, is a large pit believed to have been dug by some ancient people. It was found by the first white settlers and is ninety feet deep, now filled almost completely with dirt and rock. Local old-timers say the hole was dug in search of silver and gold.

Swift's journal, or some versions thereof, mention that Swift and his crew often ventured into the mountains by way of Moccasin Gap. Most researchers place this pass above Kingsport, Tennessee, yet a Moccasin Gap is also located above Straight Creek's Kittle Island Branch near the beginning of Camp Creek.

Some versions of the journal also have Swift entering Kentucky on various trips to the mines by way of Cumberland Gap and along the old warrior trail, crossing at Cumberland River (now Pineville). The topography of Bell County, especially on Pine Mountain at the water gap called "The Cumberland Narrows" fits well into Swift's descriptions of the landmarks.

Even such descriptions as "Indian Stairway" can be found within Pine Mountain State Park atop the mountain overlooking the County Seat.

The late Scott Partin, benefactor of Frakes, Kentucky, east of Pineville, is surely the "grandfather" of the Swift legend in southeastern Kentucky. Partin wrote much on the subject, including publishing in a local newspaper two different versions of the journal.

Partin's search went back to his grandfathers, who originally came to the area to search for the silver mines and passed down their information to him. As a result, he knew Pine Mountain intimately.

"Uncle Scott's" version is much different than those journals circulated in central Kentucky, beginning with the surname of Swift, his birthdate, various locals and landmarks, etc. Nevertheless, the Partin version follows the same basic story. It is said that this version contains the exact words followed by his forefathers in their continual search for the silver mines. Each generation of Hendersons and Partins continued the search, including Scott. Members of the family also assisted other searchers, including a North Carolina Indian known as Lakely.

Lakely came to the area in the 1930's, armed with a cryptic yellow pad, and hired several local men to help him locate certain carvings on an isolated bluff. After some time, Lakely was taken atop a cliff at Henry Bolton Gap, on the current Bell-Whitley County line between Clairfield, Tennessee, and Poplar Creek, Kentucky. The bluff line is immediately beside the paved road near the high saddle gap, and a few of the old "treasure" marks can still be seen today, including the main symbol, a box or circle with a triangle cap and two bent arrows coming out the bottom.

Until recent years there were several letters or symbols carved just above the main symbol, which were: HEP-ODLINDTOMI. By 1881 the letters had been so faded by vandals and weather that only TOMI was visible.

Where Lakely got his information is not known, but one Swift legend says that he abandoned his search to relocate his mines because of illness and blindness. He traveled to North Carolina to see Charles Hicks, a noted Cherokee medicine man and physician, hoping for a cure. Whether Lakely was searching for caches left behind by Indians or for part of Swift's treasure isn't clear, but most believed he was in search of one of the buried loads of silver Swift left behind after being attacked by Indians on his return from the mines.

Various copies of the journal claim such:

"We left a valuable prize and two horse loads of silver on the south side of the Big Gap where we marked some trees with our names and curious marks," one version says.

Another version has a cache being buried near the top of a "saddle gap" following an Indian attack, with certain carvings left in the rocks, including a saddle, or an actual saddle of a dead horse of one mining crew member being hung from a tree near the gap.

Lakely carried with him a large yellow pad that contained pages of odd writings. When taken to the site of the marks, he became excited and told the men that the marks meant he was very near the treasure. Then, it is said, Lakely died suddenly and was buried in a local cemetery. The belongings, including the mysterious yellow note pad, were turned over to the Bell County Sheriff. Pages of the cryptic writings have been published by various people, and people even now follow the secret text in their search.

While the Henderson-Partin search involved all of Pine Mountain between Pineville, Kentucky, and Jellico, Tennessee, most of the venture took place around Furnace Ridge near Chenoa. There the settlers found several clues they believed linked the area to Swift, including a rock shelter with a smelter in it. On the other end of the rock house they uncovered the skeleton of a European man, identified by the buttons on his clothing. Scott Partin also wrote that his forefathers found, near Furnace Ridge, carvings left by Swift and his crew.

But Partin's ancestors must have been surprised to encounter "Merry Cartwright" still living there and claiming to have been brought to the area by Swift to cook for his party.

"I have in my possession William Swift's descriptive maps about the mine and how he came to find it." Partin, born in 1867, also claimed to have unearthed a "tool about six inches long, made sharp on one end and round on the other, with a ring around the end; various types of crucibles such as used for melting metals; and some human jawbones with teeth" from the cliffs near Chenoa.

Judge John Haywood, the noted Tennessee historian, wrote, "On Clear Creek are two old furnaces, about halfway between the head and the mouth of the creek, first discovered by hunters in the time of the first settlement of this country. These furnaces exhibited very ancient appearances; about them coals and cinders, very unlike iron cinders, as they have no marks of the rust which iron cinders are said uniformly to have in a few years. There are also a number of like furnaces on the South Fork, bearing similar marks, and seemingly of very ancient date."

Other early histories tell of furnaces (or smelters) being also discovered on the Clear Fork, which also heads just west of Henry Bolton Gap, a few miles from the head of the Clear Creek. Clear Creek drains Pine Mountain's southern side from Frakes, including the Log Mountains between Frakes and Middlesboro, and empties into Cumberland River just south of Cumberland Ford, now called Pineville.

Near Chenoa, three cast iron kettles were found in a small cave, or rock shelter, on "The Fox Farm," with traces of silver found in the remains of ashes near old furnaces. During construction of the now-abandoned railroad that served Frakes from Pineville, railroad workers reportedly dug up another large iron pot where the old bed crosses Furnace Ridge Creek.

The "furnace" was, according to a 1790 survey by Hugh Ross, "near the edge of said creek" and "near an old Indian grave."

Swift apparently visited the site in 1791 in his search to relocate his mines, along with several other men.

William Ayers wrote, in the *Pineville Sun* in 1925, that Swift or some other "lucky explorer" operated a furnace for the production of silver. "There is a mountain known as Fork Ridge, running northeast between Big Clear Creek and Little Clear Creek, at the foot of which is a spacious cavern of the kind locally called a rockhouse. This spur has been known for many years as "Furnace Ridge" and was so-called because of the tradition...."

At times the search for Swift's mine in the area became fever-pitched. It was interrupted by the Civil war, and Partin wrote: "In the date 1860 to 1870, there was a man who came to this country and stayed with my Grandfather Henderson and he was a counterfeiter. He had a silver mine in Pine Mountain, where he got his silver ore and my grandfather had a blacksmith shop that he used to run the metal out."

Partin wrote that when the man, identified as "Willoughby," left the area, he left his money molds with Henderson.

"I have seen them many times. My grandfather kept them

hidden, and would never allow them to be used again," Partin wrote.

Beneath a small rock shelter in Henry Bolton Gap, the author inspects a spot indicated by his metal detector.

The "keystone" to the Lakely Treasure is pointed out by Roy Price, a longtime Swift researcher.

Kentucky Silver Cache
Found Near Old Treasure Signs

That Sunday began with some work on the manuscript to a new book when the telephone rang. On the other end was a well-known treasure hunter and fellow writer who informed me that a major find had been made not twenty miles from my home. More notably, it had been found not fifty yards from some old treasure carvings that hundreds of people, including myself, had viewed and detected around.

The caller told me the finder had called him and announced that he had recovered some fifteen silver bars from the site, and had been guided there by another clue familiar to me and dozens of other people: an old yellowed pad filled with cryptic writing.

A few weeks later, during an annual September meeting of treasure hunters, the lucky finder attended and privately showed me photographs of the find and the anchor-shaped rock that covered the bars, a rock I must have stepped over often when taking others to see the old carvings.

A local fellow I've known for years told me that he was shown one of the bars, which the finder accidentally dropped onto the road pavement, and it "chimed like a bell."

Where was the find? Where was if found? Who found it?

I'll tell you everything but who, because I don't have permission to reveal his identity. He says he's not finished with the site, that there are more caches there, including a large one that I won't publish here.

Let's call the finder Larry.

In 1932 a stranger named Lakely came to Bell County, Kentucky, and sought out local help in locating some odd carvings. The man was apparently part Indian and told the people around the Frakes area that the signs would lead him to the location of treasure hidden there by the Cherokee before their removal to Oklahoma. He was so serious in his search that he rented a cabin and hired members of the Partin family to help in his search.

The Partin family, along with their kinfolk the Hendersons, had a long history of treasure hunting and had originally settled the area to look for Swift's Lost Silver Mines. A descendant, Uncle Scott Partin, wrote many newspaper stories about the legend and his family's effort, including some information about silver finds, counterfeiting, and other searchers.

One day Lakely was sent word that some carvings had been found and went to the site, about two miles west of Frakes, in an unusual saddle of Pine Mountain known as Henry Bolton Gap. For years people had searched around a small natural arch there called the "Needle's Eye," which also contained several carvings, including turkey tracks and a large overhang that looks like a huge turtle.

Lakely went to the spot with the Partins and was shown the carvings, which can be seen today atop a small bluff overlooking the gap road on the border of Bell and Whitley County, Kentucky. Some have since speculated that the carvings were done by a county line survey crew, or an early state line survey party. The Tennessee line is only about three miles to the south, but was disputed between North Carolina and Virginia from before the time either were states, and up until the 1830's.

The carvings, which were much more complete and visible when Lakely saw them, read HEPOLIONDTCMI...HF, along with two nearby deeply carved circles, a triangle with a line through it, an arrow, and a circle with a triangle cap and two bent legs at the bottom with arrows.

When Lakely saw the carvings, it is said he announced that he now knew exactly where the caches were buried, and that all of them would be rich. Then he dropped dead.

When his body was being prepared for burial, the Sheriff of Bell County was given the cryptic notebook, which is said to have contained a map. Sheriff George Gibson kept the map for years, and eventually the Partin family obtained it.

Treasure hunter Michael Paul Henson published a story on the carvings, and indicated that silver-bearing cinders were recovered a few miles away in 1972 at an old smelter site near Chenoa, sparking interest in the old carvings again.

Larry, or finder, did a brilliant thing. He obtained a copy of the old map and cryptic writing, reasoned that if Lakely were Cherokee or part Cherokee, that someone in Cherokee, North Carolina, might be able to read the mysterious writings. He went to the Indian community, found someone to look at it, and they read it like you or I would read a book. The code was broken.

Within Lakely's manuscript were directions to several cache sites near the gap. Larry simply took the directions with him, went to the treasure signs, and followed the now-readable map.

He was led to a large flat rock carved like a ship's anchor, with the top notched as if a rope went around it. Above the anchor was a triangle in the rock, with a dot in the middle. Below the triangle he dug twenty inches and uncovered fifteen silver bars, each about seven ounces, and all of them wedge (or axe) shaped. One of the silver wedges had a stamp in it which appeared to be that of a Spanish king, the size of a piece of eight.

Early one morning in the snowless December of 1994, I called my fellow researcher and treasure buff, Roy Price, and we drove up to the gap. We parked below the bluff and walked up to the carvings. From there we went across the knoll and looked at some other vague marks that were discovered the previous year by Choctaw treasure hunter Tommy Veal. Then we went around another knoll and rested beneath a low rock shelter, talking about the Lakely legend.

On our way back toward the carvings, we decided to see if we could find where "Larry" recovered his silver bars, and chanced to drop down to a low bluff not fifty yards from the carvings and easily seen from the signs. There, on the upper end, was a pit some three feet deep, freshly dug, put there by someone who was very serious about digging.

We came away with renewed interest in the treasure sites at the gap, realizing that the little-known pass had been used for thousands of years, wondering how many yet unfound caches remained.

Silver bars, in the shape of axes or wedges, are lined up atop the dirt which had covered them. The old Lakely map apparently led to the discovery of the bars, one of which had the imprint of a Spanish king, somewhere in the wilds of Pine Mountain between Jellico, Tennessee, and Pineville, Kentucky.

Uncle Scott's Version

In 1812, a party of longhunters, surveyors, adventurers, and land speculators was organized in the colonies to explore what was then the wilderness of Tennessee and Kentucky. Among the men to sign on were William Henderson and Shelton Partin. The group followed in the footsteps of Richard Henderson's party in 1775, which included Daniel Boone.

The 1812 group traveled through Cumberland Gap and visited pioneer settler Richard Davis, on Davis Creek near present-day Middlesboro, Kentucky. They then followed the old Wilderness road to Cumberland Ford (Pineville), where they lodged with settler Thomas Gibson. Henderson and Partin had joined the group with something more than sheer adventure or speculation on their minds.

"Aside from hunting and farming, they settled in South America [Frakes, Kentucky] for the purpose of finding Swift's Silver Mine," wrote a descendant of both men, Scott Partin.

Partin, known locally in Bell County, Kentucky, as "Uncle Scott" wrote extensively about his home area, including several articles for the *Middlesboro Daily News* and the *Cincinnati Enquirer*. Most of the stories were written prior to 1920.

"They had in their possession a descriptive map that they received in the English Colony of Kent, Virginia. The map directed them to travel five miles northwest, traveling over many blue mountains and through the rolling limestone region now known as Powell Valley, and through Cumberland Gap and on through a rough and rocky region and into a piney mountain to a high knob between 36th and 37th degrees north latitude," Partin wrote. "They found the furnaces where he [Swift] worked the ore, and they found the marks and trails as described on the map. It is situated in one of the most rough and rocky regions of Bell County,"

Partin noted.

What they found along the waters of the tributary of the Cumberland River was noted by Tennessee Historian Judge John Haywood: "On Clear Creek are two old furnaces, about halfway between the head and the mouth of the creek ____ first discovered by hunters in the time of the first settlement of this country.

"These furnaces exhibited very ancient appearances, about them coals and cinders very unlike iron cinders, as they have no mark of rust which iron cinders are said uniformly to have in a few years," Haywood wrote.

"They got their ore from a cave about three miles from the place where his [Swift's] furnace stood. The walls of the furnaces and horn buttons of European manufacture were found in a rock house, proof that Europeans erected them. In one of these rock shelters we found a furnace and human bones," the judge noted.

Partin wrote that he had, in his possession, Swift's "descriptive maps about the mine and how he came to find it." Partin was born in 1867 and the maps apparently were the same papers carried by his ancestors. Using the map, Partin did some searching himself.

He wrote that he recovered "a tool about six inches long, made sharp on one end and round on the other, with a ring around one end." He also found "various types of crucibles such as used for melting metals, and some human jawbones with teeth." The find was made in 1885 beneath a rock cliff near Chenoa, Kentucky, in the immediate area his forefathers had searched.

Discovery of the smelters, or furnaces, in the isolated part of the Pine Mountain foothills led to the stream and ridge being known locally as "Furnace Ridge" and "Furnace Creek." Certainly the furnaces were found before Partin's people arrived, for an old land grant (in 1790 to Hugh Ross) claims property bounded by "an old furnace near the edge of said creek." Furnace Ridge runs toward Big Clear Creek and, at the junction, is a large rock shelter, or sand cave, where Swift is said to have operated his smelter.

In 1872, another smelter, or furnace, was discovered on Gun Stock Branch off Clear Creek, by John Hubbard. It was located under a rock smelter with a waterfall overhead. Near Chenoa, three cast-iron kettles were found in a small cave on the Fox Family Farm. Railroad crews working near ·Furnace Ridge near Chenoa also reported finding a large iron pot. Traces of silver were found in the remains of the Furnace Ridge smelters, early settlers claimed, along with silver among the ashes.

One local Bell County legend places Swift revisiting the site in 1791 "in the company of others," at a time when Swift was said to be attempting to relocate his lost mines.

"In the date 1860 and 1870, there was a man who came to this country and stayed with my grandfather Henderson, and he was a counterfeiter. He had a silver mine in Pine Mountain where he got his silver ore, and my grandfather had a blacksmith shop that he used to run the metal out," Partin wrote.

"I know it to be true because my grandfather showed me the place where they got their silver ore. He took me to the place in the date 1888, and it had been worked to some extent. I went back to the place about one year later and got some ore and brought it and left it with my grandfather," Partin recorded.

"I never lost trace of the mine, but I stayed away from it for 45 years, and when I went back to where I thought the mine was I could not find the place. The timber had been cut and logged out, and the place had got filled up with the washings from the log roads."

Partin's copy of the Swift journal is unique in that it gives Swift not as John but as William M., and lists some associates not normally found in other versions. One, a female cook named Merry (or Mary) Cartwright, Partin says was still living in the area when his grandfathers arrived there. Also, the journal offers one-half of everything found to the finder and notes that, at the mine, Swift left behind a sledgehammer with a French crown cut into the face, one sheepskin apron, and other tools, including one set of money molds used "to make French Crowns."

"In one place he had thirty thousand dollars (buried four feet down with large stones placed over). At another place he buried four ten-gallon kegs of the same type," Partin wrote.

Also in the Partin copy of the journal, Swift is said to have taken an Indian partner named Marquette, who pinpoints the location of the mine.

Partin wrote that a man named Gibson had a dream about where some of the silver was buried, and hired a man to go with him up the Clear Creek. They dug a hole three or four feet deep, breaking for the night. After dark, the man apparently crept back to the spot and dug something up from the hole. Gibson discovered the empty hole the next day and the helper was never seen again. "Near the spot where this treasure was dug up, I found a cut on a beech tree: Swift and Munday," Partin wrote. He also wrote that Marquette and Munday "fell out" and killed each other and that Merry Cartwright buried them "over the big mountain opposite the furnace." He adds:

"My grandfather told me he found all of Swift's signs and marks on trees and stones, all but a gun-cut on something pointing south, but he never did find the Swift mine. He was always confident it was there."

Just below the Lakely carvings at Henry Bolton Gap, along with an old road that predates settlement of Pine Mountain, is a unique little sand rock arch known as "The Needle's Eye." For eons, the wayside shelter has been a camping place for travelers along the route, and once upon a time the wall and ceiling had carvings and paintings, one of a human hand.

There are similar landmarks in central Appalachia with the same name, and Swift mentions "The Needle's Eye" in one version of the journal. Directly across the old trail is a large overhanging bluff known as "Turtle Rock" or "Turtle Back Rock." Not surprisingly, it looks much like a turtle, and has a top similar to the reptile's shell.

Below this rock an Ohio man spent a summer in recent years digging for a silver cache he believed was buried there, using everything from shovels to bulldozers. All he found was dirt, and even today, evidence of his effort can be seen as a large hole.

The land belongs to Lonnie Fuson, who is often visited by treasure hunters in search of Swift, Lakely's treasure, Cherokee caches, and other treasure. The saddle gap is at Henry Bolton, and the mountain nearby is the subject of various treasure tales. Some believe several different places contain hidden wealth. Fuson says that the large rock outcropping that boasts the Needle's Eye on one end has odd carvings, including turkey tracks.

One Florida treasure hunter believes a Spanish treasure is buried above the formation, along the trail, beneath a rock cut and shaped like a bow tie or a double-bladed axe.

A Kentucky relic-hunter believes that a cave on the north side of Pine Mountain, across from the arch, contains an old Shawnee or Cherokee storehouse of burials and silver. The gap itself contains unexpected rock carvings that seem to lead a searcher from one sign to another.

Near the gap, on the headwaters of Popular Creek, is a limestone cave almost forgotten by modern local people. There, or nearby, Colonel Tye, his son, and a group of men that probably included John Swift, were attacked by Indians as they camped. They had apparently ventured there in aid of Swift in his blinded search to relocate his lost mines. During the surprise nighttime attack, Tye's son was killed.

Just southwest of Henry Bolton Gap are the "three" Log Mountains, where a Kentucky scientist was guided to what was suspected to be an outcrop of silver. The inquiry was part of a geological investigation in 1854 and 1855 by the state of Kentucky. Professor David Dale Owen found the outcrop near an old Indian village said to have been thirty miles square.

Benjamin Herndon, a local mountain man known for his explorations, guided Owen to ore that many believed had been worked by Indians and Swift. Owen reported the ore proved to be a "kidney-shaped mass of dark gray argillaceous iron stone, containing some accidental minerals sparingly disseminated, such as sulphur and lead, which proved to be hydrated silicate of alumina."

The "alumina" was found in shale, within a local outcrop, about 500 or 600 feet up Log Mountain. Within Log Mountain and the surrounding countryside only a few years later in the 1880's, a huge coal boom flourished which has lasted even until today.

Northeast of Bolton Gap, between there and Pineville, Kentucky, is the location of Furnace Ridge, the site of early pioneer finds of silver smelters, ashes with silver content, and human remains buried beneath a rock shelter that had European buttons on the clothing.

Southwest of the gap, still along the "backside" of Pine Mountain, is Clear Fork, which flows eventually through the "Narrows" near Jellico, Tennessee. There, aside from the almost continual hunt for Swift's mine at Primroy Hollow, No Business Hollow, and Bridge Rock Arch, were also found abandoned silver smelters. Still further west, in the headwaters of the Big South Fork River, other smelters were discovered in the region of Chief Doublehead's Silver Mine.

In fact the Pineville, Frakes, Bolton Gap, Primroy, and South Fork tales should all fall under the same category, but because two different states are involved, they have been separated by jurisdiction.

Has part of the treasure at Henry Bolton Gap been found in recent years? There is evidence that in fact a sizable find was made there in 1994.

Rumors of the discovery spread quickly among the Swift buffs in the summer of that year, and the finder (who will not be identified here for various reasons) appeared that September as part of the audience during the "Swift Silver Mine Lost Treasure Weekend" in Jellico. To a few other people who follow the legend he confided his story, showed Polaroid photos of the fifteen silver bars, and displayed some of the bars. One viewer of the find reported that the unidentified man dropped a bar on the pavement and it chimed or rang like precious metal.

The Kentucky finder said he had obtained a copy of the

Lakely papers and contacted Michael Paul Henson about the old tale. Following his instincts, he investigated the gap area and, in a stroke of brilliance, took the manuscript and maps to North Carolina to have a Cherokee "read" them. He was surprised at how easily the Indian interpreted the pages, telling him that several cache sites were located nearby, including a gold and silver cache weighing more than two hundred pounds.

The man returned to the gap and made camp, following the translation of Lakely's old manuscript from the well-known carvings on the bluff beside the road along the Bell-Whitley County line. Within a few yards of the carvings, in a low bluff line, he found a triangle with a dot in the middle, and beneath that, he discovered a rock carved much like an anchor.

Digging below the spot of the "anchor" he removed earth down to about twenty inches and found fifteen silver bars, each shaped like a wedge or an axe, and each weighing about seven ounces. On one of the bars was the imprint of a Spanish king who ruled the nation in the 1700's.

Henson said the triangle carvings were found some fifteen years earlier by Bill Metcalf; he and Henson had walked the low bluff line many times.

The prior year, in 1993, Tommy Veal (a Choctaw Indian specializing in reading signs and carvings) accompanied a group to the area of Bolton Gap and told them a Spanish treasure was located somewhere nearby, according to marks he found.

Other people who have researched the Bolton Gap area, aside from your author, include Roy Price of Jellico and Doug Hammontree of Chenoa. The finder of the silver wedges continues to search the gap area, and has reported that the Cherokees told him that at least twenty-five other caches are hidden there.

Some speculation has the silver found there, and that which is yet undiscovered came from ancient mines nearby, operated by the Indians, the Spanish, and then Swift. Since the initial discovery, the same treasure hunter has found two other caches, and continues to pursue the remaining treasure.

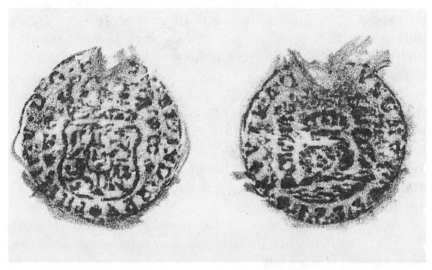

One of the Spanish milled dollars supposedly counterfeited in the Cumberland Mountains by Swift or Mason. This one, unfortunately, was made of lead and not silver.

Uncle Scott Partin

The Flanagan Version

An unusual version of Swift's Journal was published in *Appleton's Magazine* in 1906 by Howard Flanagan. He wrote that he had "reconstructed" it from information from various sources.

It goes as follows (Swift speaking):

> I went to sea, when a boy, and I became a captain of a ship. When I left the sea I settled in Alexandria, Va. I frequently visited villages of North Carolina and traded wares from my wagon, and I frequently went far into the country and traded with the Indians.
>
> One day I met an Indian boy, far away from his people. He was wild-looking, wore tattered garments, and looked very badly kept. He told me that he had come from away across the back mountains, and that he had run away from his people and had avoided the Indian trails, and that he had been many weeks without shelter or sufficient food. He said he was not of Indian blood, that his people were French. They had been killed by Indians and he had been taken captive when he was very young, but still old enough to remember. In the years that he was growing up, the Indians had treated him kindly and adopted him into the tribe, but he had cherished the idea that when he got big enough and had learned the country he would run away and find a home among the white men.
>
> I took him to Alexandria with me and cared for him and nursed him as I would my own. He told me when I met him that if I would be good to him he would take me to a mine known to his people, where vast stores of silver were laid. When Munday was strong again we

departed from Alexandria. Guise and Jefferson, men I know as sturdy hunters and able to stand hardship, went with us, and we had ponies and provisions. We reached the Big Sandy River after much hardship, but without mishap. Munday knew the trails and the habits of the Indians so well that we were able to avoid them. From there we traveled west through a hilly country, following the creek bottoms until we came to a rocky country that looked like the end of the world.

A turbulent river was before us, and following its windings from the heights we came to the mouth of a large creek. Our path fell rapidly to the creek, which has small branches running through deep ravines having great cliffs rising on either side. On the opposite side of the creek from where we were the land rose up to a cliff that stood far back from the creek, and this cliff had a great hole in its side near the top. We called that the "Lighthouse"; we could see clear through it, and see the sky beyond.

Munday did not know where we were, but after following the creek on a southwest course, he recognized the hills on the opposite side, and said that if we were over there, he knew how to reach the Indian Trace, which was some miles below, and having reached the Trace he would know how to go to the mine. He said we had to go through a myrtle thicket and then down a flight of steps that the Indians had cut in the side of the cliff at the top of it; and that across the creek from the foot of the cliff at that point and in the cliffs of the other side was the mine. We crossed the creek by a natural rock bridge, and Munday led us to the place that the Indians used for a camping ground, and for games when on their hunting trips. This was not the time of year for them, and we did not see any of them. We camped there, and a creek flowed by our camp. When we went out with Munday again he could not find the myrtle thicket, and we came again to the rock bridge and from there we went down a rocky branch, and there were vines closing the entrance mouth of the branch. This was near the river and a mile above the mouth of the big creek that we saw first.

We camped in this branch and kept our horses there. We could leave them there grazing while exploring the country, because the cliffs made an enclosure except for the entrance, which was closed by the grapevines. Munday could not find the cliff where the mine was, but one day he called out to us and said: "Here is the myrtle thicket. I know the way now. Through this thicket we reach the steps in the cliff. From there I can point to the mine." It was hard to get through the thicket. We could not take our horses, and we stumbled many times and had to fight and cut our way. We got to the Indian steps which are cut in the side of the cliff. You can stand on top of the rock there and look across the creek, and to your left the creek cuts through the cliff, and the cliffs in front are the shape of a half-moon.

Just above the creek, on the other side, there is a ledge, and higher up another ledge, and up near the top of the cliff a third ledge, and between the second and the third ledges Munday said was the opening to the mine. Now we crossed the creek and we climbed up to between the second and the third ledge, and then we went west a couple of hundred yards and found the mine. There was a big rock that looked like a buffalo sitting down, resting on the slope within a few hundred feet of the opening to the mine. We cut our names on that rock, Swift, Munday, Jefferson and others.

We got ore and we smelted in a rock-house which is in the second ledge. This rockhouse faces the sunrise, and looking out, there is a branch of a creek that comes in from the southwest and just below the mouth of that branch are three monument rocks, one large one and two small ones. They are layers of rock and they taper to a point at the top.

We all returned home with our silver, but we could not carry as much as we wanted the first time, and we came back again and again, better prepared. The time before the last we stayed too long. Munday told us we were staying too long, as we had been in the country almost a year, and the Indians came upon us near the river. We were living in a rockhouse, and we barricaded the front and fought them off all day and escaped.

We had such peril and privation and increasing danger from Indians that we did not go back for some years. Then when we were leaving the country of the mine again, Munday's horse was bitten by a rattlesnake in the leg, and he could not go on. Each one of us had a sack of silver, which was all that a horse could carry besides ourselves and our pack, and Munday insisted that we would have to walk in turn with him and let his sack of silver be carried also. About this we quarreled, and Munday threatened to return to his people and betray us and bring them down upon us; so we killed Munday, and we buried his sack of silver on the rocky branch, beneath a forked white oak; and I marked the tree with a compass and a trowel. For a more particular description I have made diagrams and maps as I remember. It is eight miles from the natural rock bridge to the place where we first camped by the creek, a due south course. One mile northwest from the rock bridge and right below where the branch forks, we smelted ore. Five rods up the creek from where it bends to the south, there is a large fallen rock. A gap in the cliffs ease off there and lets you out of the cliff country.

Now the troubles and hardships of the exposure, particularly of that one long, hard winter, left their marks upon me. My iron frame is unbroken, but my sight is gone. Every rock and hill and creek is clearly before me, but I cannot find the place, and the markings that I have described cannot be found by my party.

I led this last party from the west, seeing as only the blind can see, and we reached the river, but alas! I could not give to other eyes what was stamped behind my own.

The Parsons Version

In the spring of 1982 I held a seminar at Pine Mountain State Park, above Pineville, Kentucky, with fellow researcher Roy Price. During that presentation we sought new information on the amazing Swift legend.

A few weeks later I received a faded copy of yet another Swift journal, this one from Mrs. Maisie Hoskins, of Pineville. Mrs. Hoskins' parents came from Virginia, and the portion of the old journal was found among a stack of Parsons family genealogy papers.

The main variation of the Parsons copy is that of the date given for the operation of the mines, from 1738 to 1739, much earlier than most journals that place the mining from 1750 to 1780, generally.

What follows is a brief sketch of the Parsons copy, which is partly written in first person (as if Swift himself penned it) and partly written in third person.

"He and G. ____Frenchman was captured by Indians and taken through the regions of North Carolina...through the mountains of southwest Virginia.

"He remained with the Indians three years...while he remained with the Indians they took him to a silver mine. He marked the place with an idea of returning.

"After returning to the mine he 'succeeded in coining up lots of rich metal into French Crowns, enough for three horseloads....'"

The Parsons copy repeats other journals as Swift directs searchers to cross mountains, rocky regions, through a large gap filled "with Indians named Mocca," through a bottom "by an old Indian graveyard," and then mentions (for the first time by itself), "Munday's Map."

Swift here directs searchers to a "half-moon shaped rock house...or a little creek filled with cedars...where we smelted our silver ore. Thence back eastward to a ridge that runneth east, west with the ridge to cedar gap...there the mine is on the left as you go eastward.

"At the mouth of the mine a ____tree stands containing the words 'Swift and Munday's Mine and Map.'"

Inside the mine (according to the Parsons journal) is "a canteen, molds, and sheepskin aprons...and a load of coined French Crowns buried on the right as you go in (the) rockhouse.

"The ore is in a gray rock with a sandstone ledge running nearby. The mouth of the mine is as large as a hogshead or barrel and drops down...in the ground about ten feet, then made off level."

The Parsons copy echoes the central Kentucky versions, with Munday joining the crew along with "a woman as a cook." It recalls other journals in referring to a dispute and killing, with the cook and another crew member being buried "just opposite the mine" about four or five miles in a half-moon rockhouse in the large mountains.

The copy also has Munday returning to his home in North Carolina and staying there for several years. "Munday decided to return and mine some more but found the mining region settled up with people...but succeeded in finding the buffalo lick and decided that he could find the mine."

He returned "to get help but was soon taken sick and died."

Swift, being nearly blind, decided he would "return to the rich mine...but found the country settled."

Supposedly Swift offered the directions to the lost mine to various parties, for sale or for a percentage of the treasure if located.

*****

Here, according to the Parsons family copy of the Swift journal, are the directions to the mine, word for word:

"The mine was bound on the west by a creed [creek] and a ____ spring of Indian reeds as run by a gaudred 10 degrees east of 1000 feet from (reeded) spring about 3 miles on the north by a large mountain and on the east by a creek and branch and on the south(east) by Buffalo Lick and south by a river Rockhouse 30 degrees north 1700 poles from _____ Spring. By quadret, 26 degrees N. 1600 poles to Moon Rock House, 36 degrees E. NE., 60 poles.

*****

This copy of the numerous Swift journals offers some unique differences not already mentioned. First, this is the only time that both Swift and Munday return to the mine after being away for years, especially independently or "on their own."

Second, Swift appears here to give specific astrological guidance or tips to the knowledgeable searcher. A quadret (or, spelled correctly, quadrant) is an early device for measuring angles for nautical purposes to decide the altitude of the sun. It was used by sailors and was similar to more current sextants. Given tradition concerning Swift's involvement in shipping interests in the Atlantic, is it not likely that he would be accustomed to such a device?

*****

Scott Partin wrote a newspaper account of Swift's ventures for the *Middlesboro (Kentucky) Daily News*. Two accounts were published in March of 1947, one dealing with the information we have just covered. The other account offers much more information, and is somewhat different than all other stories.

The source of Partin's information for this account is unknown, but here Partin lists many more names and places than formerly available. We begin with his second account of Swift's words, which are similar to those found in the Apperson copy:

Started on 25th of June, 1761, from Alexandria, Virginia, and came to Littles, thence to Pittsburgh, thence to head waters of Wheeling, thence to little Kenawa, thence to Gaundotte, thence to Sandy, from thence to the Long Ridge, thence to the river name not known, thence to Large Rocky Creek, thence to the place were we stayed from the 18th of July to the last of October.

We left the place and went the same road back, and on the 28th discovered savages, but concealed ourselves and got clear of them and on the 30th were re-pursued by savages, got off safe.

Nothing happened until the 9th of November, when savages fired on us and shot a ball in our loading. We returned the fire, they retreated, and we traveled hard and camped on the Kenawa after which nothing happened until we got to the settlements on the 20th of December.

Started back on 15th of April, 1762, and arrived at the place 10th of May without difficulty, except a loss of a gallon of rum. We stayed until 1st of August. Came to Ghost [Host?] camp on 20th, where alarmed by savages, but got off clear and camped on the creek and came through safe and left a valuable prize marking some trees with curious marks. From which place went to Caster [Castle] Woods and from thence to Virginia where we stayed until 1764, then started on 1st May and came by New River from that to Cumberland Valley and crossed the mountain and set our course and went to the place where we arrived on the 20th of June and stayed until 1st of September, when we started and went through Castle Woods and found a man living there by the name of Castleman, where we stayed five days. From thence we went to the settlement and got home on the 1st of October.

Started from home on 1st of October and got to the place on 4th of November where we stayed until the 1st of April, 1768, when we started by Sandy. Meeting with nothing but material on our way home. We started...same year, got safe to the place 1st of July and stayed until the 25th of October, started and went by Sandy and at the forks lost two of our horses stolen [by the savages?]. We left two loads of valuable prizes, a great loss to us but escaped with our lives. Got home on the 1st of September, 176- and was at the place again and came by the place where we left the two horseloads of valuable prizes, and found all the things as we left them in '62 and '63. Made three other trips to place of which I kept no account, except curious marks and particular marks.

1st of September we left between 22 and 30,000 in crowns in a large creek running near a south course. Close by the spot we marked our names, Swift, Jefferson, Munday, and other names on a beach tree. With compass and square, striled [strolled] about 20 or 30 poles from the creek stand a smart rock and between it and the creek you will find a small rock of bluish color with 3 chops in it make by a grit stone by rubbing it on the rock.

By the side of this rock you will find the prize we left, no great distance from the place we left 15,000 of the same kind markings 3 and 4 trees with marks. Not far from these we left the prizes, the prize is near a forked white oak and about four feet under the ground. We laid two large stones across it at the forks of Sandy. Close by the forks is a small rock which has a spring in one end of it.

Between it and a small branch we hid a purse under the ground it was valued at $6,000,000. We likewise left and buried the rock of Rock House. You must go into latitude 30 degrees west north when you will angle triangle find yourself to be in 80 degrees of west latitude when by geometric fraxlon [fraction?] of 90 of 2 degrees of divide as in problem with is explained, it appears by the true altitude and disk of the sun that the fore side place wanted is in the sixth degree, six minutes, and 10 seconds on the west angle of _____ degree of longitude as in plain exicution and division as appears by observation sun 38 degrees _____ minutes north longitude, eighty degree six minutes and 19 seconds.

Description of the country adjacent, the creek where the furnace...on it heads southwest and runs northeast. The creek abounds with plenty of laurel and is so swift that it is almost impossible to get a horse near the place. So extremely rough is the way we never took our horses near than six or seven miles of the place.

There is a thicket of holly a quarter of a mile below the furnace and a small lick about one mile and there is a large buffalo lick two miles from the small lick on another creek, which we called Lick Creek.

...find my name on a birch tree in the year 1867 [1767] and about one mile below you find money, Jefferson and Gist name in the year 1765 and 1767. Between a small lick and the furnace is a removable [remarkable?] rock it hangs over the creek and the creek runs under it, the mountains and hills about with laurel and water crosses so much that a man cannot get along, without difficulty, most of the hills and mountains have but little timber, but are poor and bare.

North of the furnace about three miles is a long ridge seven or eight miles in length which abounds with good timber of different kinds, but south of it there is no timber of notice. Furnace Creek forks about three miles from the Lick and in the forks upon the point of the hill you will find three white oaks from one stump. On each of these trees is cut a small notch with a tomahawk, we sometimes went to a small spring up to the right hand fork and came back that way. Which was the...creek and the river, the first company in search of the object...mine was Steley, Island, Maclintick, and Swift.

You must set your compass on the south side of furnace and steer due south course 200 poles and you will find a tree that grows in this form....

Then set your compass a second time and 20 poles and you will find a large and limb grown out straight to the south. Under this you will find one also. Set your compass on true west side of the furnace under the Rock

House and go due west 50 poles and you will find a tree this shape.

Set your compass a second turn and run due south 20 poles and you will find a large limb growing out of the south side of the tree. Under this we buried 4 - 10 gallon kegs of crowns. You can't miss finding the place if you find the furnace.

This is a true copy of the map Swift used in his travels when he worked the long-lost silver mine.

Castle Rock, in Rockcastle County, Kentucky, was thought by some to be Swift's "remarkable rock." The spot was a meeting place for longhunters. In one journal version, silver mine seekers were looking for a "French Castle" believed to be a rock formation that could be seen for miles.

The Search Continues in Old Virginia

Even today the search for Swift continues. In Tazewell County near Jeffersonville, silver was reportedly found in 1892. Dan Graybeal, a Virginia Mine Safety and Health Administration employee learned of the legend from his grandparents and spent about fifteen years searching and researching.

An issue of "Messenger," the agency's employee newsletter, published several pages on Graybeal and the tale. An enthusiastic treasure hunter then, Graybeal has since given up his hunt and donated all his research to a local library.

"Today there are a number of geologists, engineers and others searching for the lost treasure, and I am totally confident that Swift and his mines did exist," Graybeal is quoted as saying.

The mine inspector lived in Norton, Virginia, and traces the Swift journals back to 1750. He maintained that the original journal contained maps and was taken to Uniontown, Pennsylvania, following Swift's death in 1800. In the 1840's, the journal was obtained by William Forward, of Louisville, Kentucky, who also plays a large role in the search in the Red River Gorge area near Campton.

Graybeal believed that an unidentified judge near Norton, Virginia, came across a partial copy of the original journal. Graybeal's research went much beyond the casual "Swift Buff" and he found that one Jonathan William Swift served under General Washington at the Battle of Fort Duquesne in 1755, as many Swift journals claim. Graybeal believed that he discovered three maps while researching the copies of the different journals.

In the journal that Graybeal spoke of, Swift is given as Johnathan William Swift, of English heritage, born in

Philadelphia on October 3, 1712. Following his colonial military service, Swift is said to have entered the "trading business" and encountered George Munday, who chanced upon a silver mine after following a bear into a cave "west of the Blue Ridge Mountains." Munday's family was killed by Indians and he was taken hostage, learning of many more silver mines before his escape.

"One must forget about today's state boundaries in order to understand Swift's travels," Graybeal noted.

After several years of mining, the crew stored up a huge cache of silver in the "great caverns of the Shawnee" with hopes to return and recover the wealth. Swift sailed to England, is imprisoned, and returned years later blind and ill.

"Swift lists four locations in his journal where he had buried treasure amounting to several thousand dollars, but descriptions of the locations are unreliable because markings indicating directions to the mines were often placed on trees that have long since been felled," Graybeal said.

Swift returns from prison, learns that Munday and some of the other crew members have been killed by Indians, and could not locate the rest of his original crew members. Swift died in 1800, his journal the only remaining clue to his lost mines.

Graybeal told of one report of silver being found in Tazewell County and silver occurring in minute amounts in the rest of the area.

In fact, the extreme western point of Virginia, from Roanoke to Cumberland Gap, is dotted with lost silver mine lore. Probably the earliest mention of Swift's silver mines begins at Martin's Station, near Rose Hill, when early Kentucky historian John Filson requests a land grant for acreage forty or fifty miles north of "Martin's Cabin," where he claimed Swift had operated a silver mine.

In *Shenandoah, the Valley Story*, Alvin Dohme retells the story of "Mad Mary" Greenlee, who had been held captive by the Indians. She appeared in 1734 outside Fort Stanton following an Indian attack. She lay on the ground among the dead enemy and was found to be alive.

Apparently she had fled the colony after having been accused of witchcraft and took up with the Indians. While dressing her wounds the woman babbled of a cave sparkling with diamonds, rubies, silver and other precious gems. Eventually she took a party to the cave but the treasure was not found.

Western Virginia, aside from sharing the Cumberland Gap lore with Tennessee and Kentucky, also has Castlewood, where some versions of the journal have Swift's crew stopping to rest on their way from their mines to the colonies. They visited there with "old man Castle." Jacob Castle, according to *Castle's Wood and Early Russell County, 1769/1799*, by James W. Hagy, was a longhunter who spent long periods of time in the mountains. By some accounts, Castle was an albino and outcast, and a bitter enemy of Adam Harman. Castle had been suspected of aiding the French in 1749.

After leaving the white settlements, Castle lived with the Indians, eventually purchasing the area of Castlewood for a "butcher knife and rusty musket."

Noted longhunters and adventurers known to have visited Castle included John English, Joseph Moore, Nathaniel Gist, John Anderson, William Pittman, William Russell and John Boles. Four of these names, English, Gist, Anderson, and Boles, are names often linked to Swift.

In Virginia versions of the tale, the Clinch and Guest (Gist) Rivers are mentioned, along with streams outside the state, including the Cumberland, Upper Yadkin, Big Sandy, Levisa, and Tug Fork. Creeks and other landmarks include Swift's Camp Creek, Upper and Lower Devil's Creek, Big Stoney, Hoot Owl Branch, Rockhouse and Indian Creek, Bear Den, Bull Run, and John's Creek.

Frontier Virginia versions contended that John's Creek, which runs through New Castle, was named for Swift. Tug Fork, it was also believed, was named because "Swift bored holes in some silver pigs and put a plug through them to tie them together." Swift was thought to have dropped some of these "tugs" in a fork of the Big Sandy while crossing the water during an Indian attack.

The "Draper Papers" carry a brief note that Swift, following his unsuccessful attempt to relocate his mines in Virginia near "Nancy Gap" left his companions and went down the mountains along the river to Limestone, Kentucky, now Maysville, at the junction of Limestone Creek and the Ohio River. The town was established by the Virginia Legislature in 1787, and Daniel Boone and his wife operated a tavern there for three years.

Blackwater, Virginia, just above the Tennessee line, was the home of the Melungeons, who also occupied Newman's Ridge, just a few miles southwest. The Melungeons are a mysterious people long associated with lost silver mines and counterfeiting.

White Rocks, a notable outcrop of white stone on the south face of Cumberland Mountain between Cumberland Gap and Jonesville, has long been the center of silver mine lore.

Big Stone Gap, once a major pass and long known by the Cherokee and other Eastern Indian nations, was the site of a bushwhacking that ended a savage spree by notorious Cherokee war captain Bob Benge. Benge (or Binge, Bench, etc.) was the red-headed son of a French trader and a Cherokee Princess, the daughter of Chief Doublehead. His family has long been rumored to have been involved in silver mining, and Doublehead is believed to have had a secret mine somewhere along the Big South Fork between Jamestown, Tennessee, and Somerset, Kentucky.

Captain Benge, as he was known among the white settlers, had taken his small raiding party into the Tennessee Valley and captured a white woman, hoping to trade her back for money, or sell her to the Shawnee. During their trek from Tennessee, Benge showed her some silver ore and said, "This is what the white man seeks."

On an earlier raid, Benge and female captives Polly Alley and Jane Whitaker stopped somewhere in the Breaks of the Sandy, and paused a day while Benge filled his pockets with silver from an ancient mine there. Local legend has this forgotten mine being the same as that known to the old counterfeiter Sol Mullins, a Melungeon.

When Benge and his captive approached Big Stone Gap that fatal day, the frontier militia had anticipated his route and hid among the rocks and trees in the pass. As the raiding party approached on foot, the white militia opened fire, killing the renegade Cherokee in the first volley and saving the female captive.

Militiaman Vincent Hobbs was recognized as the one who fired the fatal shot, and was awarded a silver-plated rifle by the Virginia governor after Hobbs proved the dead man was Benge by sending along a red-haired scalp.

Benge is also noteworthy for two reasons: He was a cousin to John Watts, a member of Swift's original mining crew by some journal versions; and Benge was the chief of an Indian town known today as Rising Fawn, Georgia, where he and fellow tribe members were said to operate a silver mine somewhere beneath Lookout Mountain.

Near Coeburn, Virginia (once called Gist Station), the remains of a smelter were found in 1935. An old pile of slag lay nearby, and silver ore was separated from the ashes.

The Gist family played not only an important part in the exploration and settlement of the Appalachian states, but also in a few versions of the Swift legend. The name is not only given as Gist, but as Gries, Grist, Gass, Guest, Guess, and Grust. The name frequently appears in Virginia versions of the journal, as a mining crew member, and occasionally in east Tennessee versions. In some Kentucky versions, Swift's journal has his crew stopping or passing through "Ghost Camp" on their way back to Virginia.

Christopher Gist was an experienced backwoodsman, having steered George Washington and others from Williamsburg, Virginia, some 450 miles to Fort LaBoeuf, Pennsylvania, on Lake Erie in 1753. One Kentucky version of the legend says Swift pointed to a rock near the mouth of a mine and told some unknown purchaser of a "waybill" that his name was inscribed there, along with others, including "Gist."

Another legend says Gist located a silver mine while on an exploration in 1750 for the Ohio Company. During his 1750 exploration, Gist reported "Thursday, 21. Set out 545, E15, MS 5M, here I found a place where the stones shined like polished brass, the heat of the sun drew out of them a king of Borax, a saltpetre only something a bit sweeter; some of which I brought in to the Ohio Company, though I believe it was nothing but a sort of sulphur."

One "Grist" is listed in association with Swift in the Scott Partin version of the Swift journal. In Wolfe County, versions of the journal, the associates are given as Munday, Jeffreys, and "Gries."

In *History of Wise County*, Charles A. Johnson speculated on a copy of the journal, reportedly then "150 years old" and badly worn with years and use, and re-tells the legend of having "a Frenchman" captured by the Cherokees in 1738. The captive was taken from North Carolina into the mountains to the west and forced to work an ancient silver mine known only to the Indians.

After escaping, the Frenchman "employs a silversmith named Swift to accompany him." They return to the mine, which Swift declares to be the "richest known," and succeed in coining up lots of ore into French crowns, "enough for two horseloads."

After returning to North Carolina, the men spend three months and travel back to the area of the mine, but are unable to relocate it. The "Frenchman" is identified as "Monda" or Munday. As a result of the experience, the following "journal" passed around western Virginia until the present day:

"Me and my guide coming to the mine, marked our path by rocks, creeks, gaps, and maps on trees. Traveling 35 to 40 miles, crossing a mountain and rocky region, we came through a large gap filled with Indians called Mecca. From there through a bluffy region; thence from there to a cliff on the right, thence up a creek, crossing in the opposite direction to the cliff, thence through a bottom by an old Indian graveyard; thence by said branch to a buffalo or deer lick gap, thence through the gap to a valley running east and west, thence four or five miles to a half-moon shaped rock house in the mountain on a little creek full of cedars and spruce pines where we smelted our silver ore; thence back eastward to a ridge that runneth eastward to a saddle gap in the ridge where the mine is. At the mouth of the mine stands a tree to which is tacked a card bearing the words 'Swift and Munday's Mine Map. Take Notice.'

"In the mine is a pick and canteen we left, also money molds. Our sheepskin aprons was also left in the rock house and loads of coined French Crowns buried on the right side as you go in the rock house. The ore was in a gray rock with a sandstone ridge running nearby."

The mouth of the mine is about as large as a hogshead or barrel, and drops straight down in the ground for about ten feet, then made off level."

The journal is similar to the Partin version, except that Munday hires Swift, not Swift befriending Munday. Also, the "Mecca" Indians may refer to their appearance of Mediterranean extractions, thus may be a reference to Melungeons in the area.

Joe Dougherty, of Russellville, Tennessee, had in his possession an old family manuscript written by his father, Arthur H. Dougherty. Like many families, the Doughertys had their own version of the tale of Swift. Unlike most, with the Shephard family's Kentucky quest an exception, the Dougherty family made an active effort to find the lost mines.

The hunt began about 1812, when Arthur's brother, W.A. Dougherty, obtained a faded document from an old man in Virginia known as Boatwright. One page was a crude map, and the other pages were a detailed journal reportedly written by Swift. The trek of the Dougherty men took them into the mountains of extreme western Virginia with Moccasin Gap, north of Kingsport, as their starting point.

The journal is unusual, yet similar, to other versions in the area, including that of Uncle Scott Partin of Frakes, Kentucky. It begins as follows:

"I, George William Swift, was born at Salisbury, England,

in the year 1689 A.D., a son of William Swift, who was a miner of copper, silver, and lead. Staying with my father until I was eighteen years old, I decided that I would not follow mining any longer and set sail for France, where I gained rank as a sailor for a number of years, until the French decided to colonize America.

"Setting sail for America, in the year 1718, under French Governor Bienville, who succeeded in founding a colony at the mouth of the large river (Mississippi) of several mouths."

The journal goes on to say that Swift decided to go to the English settlement at Portsmouth and try horse trading and became acquainted with regional Indians. The Indians guided him through the "large blue mountains" and into a rolling limestone region to a silver mine.

There they coined up French crowns and returned home to stay three months. When he returned, he brought John Martin Monday, an Englishman, and Mary Cartwright, a cook. A year later Monday murdered Swift's Indian guide, called Marquette, as well as the female cook. In the Partin version, Mary (Merry) Cartwright survived and was living in the area near the mine when Partin's grandfathers arrived there to settle.

Monday and Swift departed the mines and stayed away for several years, with Swift becoming "near blind." Yet the pair decided to make one last trip.

"As my guide and I were coming to the mine, we marked our path by rocks, creeks, gaps and maps on trees. Leaving from Portsmouth in the London Company's grant, and traveling several weeks, we crossed blue mountains, then a limestone region, then a barren-topped mountain and rough and rocky region, coming finally through a large gap filled with spruce and cedar, which in the Indian language (was) Moccasona."

Later the Swift version pinpoints the mine site as twenty miles straight as a crow could fly north from the Moccasona Gap, and on that peg and others in the journal, the Dougherty family began their search. The hunt for the mine is on file with the McClung Museum in Knoxville, and was published, in part, in a series of newspaper articles in the *Morristown Citizen Tribune* in 1985.

James A. Dougherty, in his *Historical Sketches of Southwest Virginia* published in 1966, says that Clinch area versions of the legend offer "differing accounts," but are apparently based on the original source. He reported that Tazewell has been the scene of much prospecting for Swift's ore, but that folklore there says very little about Swift or his associates.

Dougherty wrote that a small vein of silver, locally called "Swift's Silver Mine" was discovered near Jeffersonville, now the town of Tazewell. He also refers to a sizable store of "silver pigs" in some unknown cave near Pound Gap, and notes that near the gap, on the Virginia side of the mountain, was a "natural corridor formed by the lower ridge that could easily be barricaded to form a natural pound for Swift's horses, hence the name "Pound" and "Pound Gap.""

Dougherty also mentions Castle's Camp (Castle Woods) as being in existence early enough to have been visited by Swift. One Virginia legend has Swift and Christopher Gist operating the mine and using Castlewood as an outlet for their growing silver business.

Virginia silver lore also has one of Swift's caches being buried in Stone Mountain or in the backwoods of Dickerson County. Silver-bearing chucks of ore have also been found in a stream near northern Wise County.

The Dougherty family version has Swift's pony falling and breaking a thigh in Moccasona or Indian Gap, where they hid a pony-load of coin on the mountain facing southeastward, by the side of a large rock. The "Swift Journal" was apparently dated April 16, 1775, and signed by Swift.

Taking Moccasona as Moccasin Gap "in the Clinch Mountains" W.A. and Arthur set out, reaching the Clinch River (the "unknown river") beyond which they boarded with a Mr. Greer. Greer told the men that his father had showed him a tree with "Swift and Munday's Mine" carved on it, and agreed to take them to the site. From there the Doughertys crossed a large mountain and came into a narrow valley with spruce and cedars. There along a creek they found a pile of cinders and nearby, the remains of a smelter with five marked sand-stones and a trench leading downhill.

From the cinder pile they recovered a carved stone with a big arrow on one side and figures below the arrow. On the corner of the stone were the dates 1753 and 1755. Above the arrow was the name T. Grover. Nearby was a large rock shelter. The next day they set out again, following the old map and journal, and found some red rocks with small pieces of silver. One rock had twenty-seven pieces, none larger than a wheat grain.

While on their trek, the Doughertys were told an old Indian tradition involving a man named "Munday" who sought to relocate the mine along with a man known only as Jefferson, another known as Grust, and one Thomas Grover. The men ventured into Scott County, Virginia, apparently after Swift abandoned the mines but before his return to England.

Some time later, Arthur Dougherty was traveling through Hancock County and learned that Uncle Lewis Hopkins had a map to the lost silver mines. Hopkins lived on Newman's Ridge, home of the Melungeon people, and had hunted for the mines for several years. Not trusting each other, Hopkins and Dougherty both drew rough directions to the lost mine and had "Captain Jarvis" compare them. There were so many similarities that Hopkins agreed to share his map.

The Hopkins map was in twelve pieces, a result of being folded so long, and the next morning Hopkins agreed to accompany Dougherty for a fee. He agreed to walk across the mountain and meet Dougherty at Hubbard Springs, Virginia. He promised that when Dougherty took him to the smelter he would lay his map down and they could find the mine.

Eventually they arrived at the smelter site, and Hopkins found he only had part of the map on his person. Eventually the two men remembered the missing parts, however, and took off through the mountain to find the mine. They became separated and only met up again at a mountaineer's home, both without any luck in finding the mine.

Dougherty reported that "Captain Jarvis" of Sneedville told him of an encounter by "Colonel Bird" and John Swift at Bean Station. Colonel William Byrd wrote of that adventure that he found "only one case of hunger, and that of a lone miner, with no wife and ten miles from any corn."

A Dickenson County, Virginia, version has the mine located in "the fourth ridge from the Blue Ridge." Swift, Munday, and Jefferson are said to have found the mine but were unable to work it, covering the entrance and planning to return. The men traveled to Castle's Woods, where Munday is said to have been killed over an argument about the mine. Swift then "traveled to the fort" and soon afterwards went blind. He finds help in his search from the ancestors of local men: Morgan Lipps, Covey Holebrook, Eli Hill and "old man Castel himself."

The men followed Swift's instructions to Nancy Gap, on the Sandy Ridge, where he told them to look for a certain tree. When the tree was not found, Swift said he could not show them the mine. This "certain tree" may have been one mentioned in other legends, namely a forked dogwood. Swift was said to have then collapsed and "cried like a baby."

*****

Longhunters William Pitman and Henry Scaggs were contemporaries of Swift, and associated in their frequent trips into Tennessee, Kentucky, and western Virginia with the likes of Ambrose Powell, William Blevins, William Cox and Jasper Walden, among others. On their way to and from colonial Virginia, the hunters stopped at Martin's Station. Pitman and Scaggs, while stopping there in 1776, showed some silver ore they had found. The men had been hunting a short way from their camp and discovered the ore "on a hill that there was no snow upon, while all the surrounding area was covered." They investigated and found the dry spot covered with ore.

Both men were well known and respected, so their story

was taken at face value. They would have continued their silver hunt had it not been for Indian hostilities.

Others associated with silver mine hunts based at Martin's Station were Hugh Ross, William Pitt, and John Reed. The old frontier station even plays a role in a "waybill" published in the Middlesboro *Daily News*, as reported by Joe Brandenbury on January 25, 1984. Directions to one of Swift's mines are given:

Go up Cedar Creek, go through Martin's Station and take up the old Indian Trace up the mountain. Go to the first bench and then take the left and go a west course for a mile and take up the mountain and go through a narrow rack [rock or crack?] about 150 yards before you get to the top of the mountain.

When you get to the top you will find a small oak that has many hacks of a hatchet on it. Then you look a due north course and you will find a marked line. Follow that line till you cross a branch. It is a very clear branch.

When you cross the branch take up a ridge. The line is marked to the top of the same ridge. Then you cross a swag for about 100 yards and then you see the cliff where the mine is.

There is a picture of a bow and arrow cut on a beech tree that stands on the leading ridge that runs from the Flag Pond. The arrow points a direct course to the mine.

The last time I [Swift] was at the mine, we stopped it up with a rock that we cut to fit the hole. There is a tree in the way, about getting in the mine.

You will find our furnace a due east course from a large rock and a northeast course from that we hid two chestnut kegs of money by a large poplar that was about halfway between the mines. The second mine is about opposite the falls of the water about one mile.

You go down a hollow you look to the left you will see a cliff running northeast. You go to it, examine it, and you will find a hole in it about nine feet broad. It is walled up very nice. I guess the mass [moss] has grown over it in this time.

Open it and the sun will shine in it when the it rises in the morning of a summer month.

The silver is pure. One hundred fifty yards below the mine you will find a stooping poplar bending down the hill. On the lower side of it we buried thirty one large bars of silver three feet deep. Then we left and went to old Virginia and have not been back since.

The waybill had been copied or typed from "the original" by Lillian Fugate of Ewing, Virginia. She said that three men from "up north" came to the Rose Hill area in 1916 with the original copy, and searched the area without locating the mines.

An old Indian treasure hunter, Abe Cole, lived in the Cumberland Mountains near Rose Hill, and kept local people stirred up and excited by making continual claims that he had located the silver mine. He would frequent F.L. Graybeal's General Store and speak of the silver mines.

Another local treasure hunter included Herbert Gardner of Ben Hur. He reportedly had a copy of a "waybill" that had belonged to one of the original miners. Gardner and his companions searched for three years.

Ralph Gardner and Russell Mosier also searched for the mines, using dynamite and drills, but found nothing. A Rose Hill resident and historian, Bashie Kincaid, believed that the Swift family lived in Lee County, Virginia, and points to a marriage between Polly Swift and James Overton recorded there in 1755.

Mrs. Kincaid reported that she believed the silver mine was located "above the Hagan." She says an arrow like the one mentioned in the Fugate waybill was located in the 1970's in the mountain above Rose Hill.

Her brother, Frank Rowlette, is a retired federal cryptanalyst, specializing in breaking codes. He says the Swift "code" was sent to the War Department but the secrets could not be decoded. He believes two Swift cryptographs existed, but are now lost. Rowlette was, at last report, trying to locate copies of the cryptograms in hopes the American Cryptogram Association could solve them.

Martin's Station was built in 1769 by Captain Joseph Martin and a party of twenty men. When Boone passed down the old Indian trace he was surprised to find a station located there, and reported that the men were "building cabins and planting corn."

The same year, the station was abandoned and destroyed by Indians. Martin returned in 1775 and rebuilt the isolated station, some twenty miles east of Cumberland Gap. He became "Colonel" Martin, a noted pioneer and commissioner of the Cherokee Nation.

In 1786, Martin and others attempted to establish a new state, and wrote that Charles Robertson had been authorized to mine "$30,000 specie." Three different silver coins were proposed with a coat of arms on one side and the outline of the mountains on the other. They were to mint one dollar, fifty cents, and quarter pieces. Apparently these "State of Franklin" coins were never produced.

Colonel Martin eventually married Betsy Ward, daughter of the Cherokee's "Beloved Woman" Nancy Ward and a trader known only as Bryant.

Other places in western Virginia connected with the Swift lost silver mine legend include his mention in various journals of passing across New River, Ingles Ferry, a "big gap" above Castlewood, and a "door in the Cumberlands." Journal versions also refer to gaps being used at the head of the Sandy River.

Pound and the Great Cave

Two places in western Virginia have played a larger role in the Swift legends than any other place, except possibly for Martin's Station. Pound Gap and the Breaks of the Sandy have, for more than 240 years, been searched for silver mines, treasure caves, and caches left by Swift and the Indians before him. The Breaks of the Sandy, shared by Virginia and Kentucky, more fittingly belong in the Kentucky lore, but Pound and the continuing legend there are mostly Virginia tales.

As mentioned earlier, Pound may have been named for the "impound" of horses on the south side of the gap by Swift's mining crew. Even most historians believe that the name comes from the sound that horse hooves made (and still make) on the rock in the area: an echo or hollow sound, which echoes back as the horses pass. The hollow sound also supports the perpetual rumors that the gap contains a large cave beneath it, supposedly the Great Cave of the Shawnee.

As related in the chapter about the Great Cave, Chief Charles Blue Jacket mentioned Pound Gap as being sacred to his Shawnee nation. Blue Jacket claimed to be a descendant of one of Swift's Indian helpers. One Swift journal points to the Pound area by saying, "Thence to one of the forks of the Great Sandy Creek, near its headwaters. We had two workings; the other went southwest along a great ridge."

The Great Cave of the Shawnee, according to Blue Jacket, extended from one side of the mountain to the other, being many miles in length, and could also be entered at different mouths. According to tribal history, the Shawnee hid their women and children there during a great battle with their enemy, the Cherokee.

One of Swift's principal mines is supposedly near the cave,

according to Kentucky historian Collins; and in many versions of the journals, Swift and his men stored their final year's coinage and silver bars there, never to return to get them.

"They...covered the entrances to the cavern when they departed the country," Collins wrote. Chief Cornstalk and Blue Jacket's father were said to have gone into the cave more than once and worked the nearby mines with Swift. "Some parts of the journal of John Swift contain terms that are unmistakable to this region," Collins concluded.

Among prospectors in the Sandy Ridge area were Hick Baker, Elijah Rasnick, and Noah K. Counts. In a version of the journal mentioned by Jasper Sutherland in *The Babe of Virginia*, a mine was found by Swift, Jefferson, and Munday. They worked the silver and covered up the mine entrance, heading to Castle Woods. On their way, Munday was killed in a fight over sharing the silver, and the other men were captured and robbed by Indians. Swift escaped, found his way back to the settlements, goes blind, and cannot relocate the mine.

Hick Baker reportedly found a large amount of silver in a "water hole" to the "south of Cumberland Mountain" but could not relocate the site. Sutherland said the Swift tale was first told to early white settlers by the Cherokee.

A man named "Hammons" found some ore "on McClure" and took it to Dump's Creek Forge, where it was run out and found to be silver. He later dug a hundred-foot hole near "where Nathan Phillips now lives [before 1936] below the mouth of Roaring Fork." Members of the Wampler family helped him build a long ladder for use in the mine, which was near a "corncob rock" pile.

Also looking in the area of Roaring Fork were Kelly and John Erwin and Dr. Lige Rasnick. Rasnick reported that he found a beech tree on Coon Branch with "H. Swift 1813" carved into the bark. Rasnick also claimed that James Simmons, near Johnson City, Tennessee, had a "deerskin map" made by Swift. Simmons and his brother apparently taught school in Oklahoma, and an old Indian Chief gave them the map. On it, Swift says the mines "were on the fourth ridge of the Blue Ridge," which was believed to be Sandy Ridge.

"The land...being thin and nearly level, with big timber on the north side of the mountain and little scrubby timber on the south side. One hundred miles as the eagle flies from Guyandotte River was placed a stone monument with six notches in the northeast corner," the map, or journal, reads.

Dr. Rasnick also found other clues and an old furnace beneath a rock shelter. He was directed by Simmons to a tree with a wild turkey cut into it, which he found. Yet Rasnick never found the letters "M, N, and G" which were mentioned on the deerskin map.

"They drew up several maps and sold them to rich people at a thousand dollars apiece," the doctor said. Some of these journals or maps fell into the hands of Morgan Lipps and his son David.

*****

The Spurlock version of the journal has Swift and his men returning to "Munday's house" in 1763 by way of the New River. Two years later, on their way to "the lower mines" they again travel to the New River and cross at "Ingles Ferry." This is historically possible, because Ingles Ferry had been authorized in 1762, and was located in old Montgomery County, Virginia, on the Great Valley Road. It was operated by William Ingles (sometimes given as English instead of Ingles) and the ferry became a noted resting place for travelers into the Kentucky wilderness along the later Wilderness Road.

One continuing mystery mentioned in the Spurlock version, and in a few other copies of the Swift journal, is the identity of the "Scottish Company." There are several possible answers.

For one, Scottish immigrants were often employed by Colonel governments to collect taxes, enforce financial laws, collect duties, etc. This may have added to or created the "skinflint" or "tightfisted" jokes and stereotypes in America about the Scotch. William Connelley was quoted in the

Greenup (Kentucky) *Independent* in 1873 about an incident:

"When Swift was driven from the silver mines in Kentucky by the approach of hostile Indians, he returned to his home in North Carolina. The money which he had with him created suspicion among his neighbors and he was arrested as a counterfeiter.

"Upon trial of the case against Swift it was proven the coins in his possession were pure silver, and the charges were dismissed.

"At an early day silver money which was circulated in the settlements of what is now West Virginia [and Kentucky] is said to have been made by Swift. It was free of alloy, and of such description as to indicate that it never passed through an established mint."

The most likely identity of the "Scottish Company" comes from a version of the journal held by Judge Apperson, and reads, "We bought five more ships from the Scotch Company."

This would explain Swift's complaint abut money the company attempted to collect, causing many "Swift Buffs" to believe that much of the silver from Appalachia went to expand Swift's sailing fleet. Some researchers contend that the passage of text points to Swift acquiring his "silver" from pirating the high seas and preying on Spanish ships, taking the booty inland to melt and recoin, then taking it back into the colonies with claims of a very wealthy silver mine.

More Valuable Than Silver

The discovery of silver in large amounts in the new territories would have meant vast wealth for someone, aside from Swift, but the discovery of silver's sister ore, lead, helped to protect the new settlements. Pioneers might make jewelry and tableware from silver, but from lead they could make bullets.

Western Virginia history says that Colonel John Chiswell discovered lead and zinc deposits while hiding in a cave from warring Cherokee. A short while later, about 1756, Chiswell and his son-in-law, Colonel William Byrd (or Bird) opened a lead mine and established the town of Leadmine, later called Austinville.

Fort Chiswell was founded "a short distance east," and became the county seat of old Montgomery County. It became both a frontier trading post and a refuge for pioneer families.

"Colonel Chiswell had been engaged in mining operations near Fredricksburg, Virginia, for some time previous to this time, and was an intimate friend of Colonel Byrd," wrote Lewis Preston Summers in *History of Southwest Virginia.*

The mines were apparently sold in 1783 to Thomas Madison. The location of the mines was then given as being on the "east side of New River."

"Colonel Chiswell, sometime prior to 1775, killed a man in Cumberland County, Virginia, and while awaiting trial he committed suicide," Summers wrote. The Chiswell mines were near the present site of Wytheville, Virginia, although John Adair's early map places the mines in old North Carolina.

Old lead mines became less important, and settlers in Tennessee and Kentucky became acquainted with their new region and discovered lead deposits there. Lead mines were established within six miles of Lexington, on North Elk Horn Creek, in Kentucky, and in a bend of the Clinch River in Anderson County, Tennessee (known today as Lead Mine Bend). Lead was also reportedly found in Laurel County, Kentucky, near Hazel Patch along the banks of Cane Creek in south Whitley County, Kentucky. The Swingle lead mines operated in Tennessee in old Jefferson County.

Ramsey's *Annals of Tennessee* reports that lead mines were located in 1787 by Jacob Kimberlin in old Claiborne County.

"It was found south of the French Broad, not far from Gap Creek, on a farm owned by Jeremiah Johnson, Esq.," Ramsey noted.

Notable here is something many people do not know: Most silver in public circulation comes as a by-product during the release, or smelting, of copper, zinc, gold, and lead.

George Dougherty, in 1788, was granted over 11,000 acres along the Clinch River and Walden's Ridge in Anderson County, Tennessee. Dougherty was believed to have found a secret lead mine, which may in fact be the one at Lead Mine Bend, which is said to have been worked since early white settlement. The lead mines operated there until 1942 and, over those years, for at least three periods of time.

An elderly man who prospects the "Bend" said that the mines produced lead, zinc, and silver. The mine opening, or one of them, was reported to be "as big as a barn."

"There's lots of silver still up there," the old man claimed in 1984.

Ouasiota Pass, near Station Camp Creek in Kentucky, was said to be the site of an old lead mine as well. Indians were said to use the lead there to color their body. Bumpass Cove, in Washington and Unicoi Counties, was the site of a lead mine which opened in 1780 and was known as the "Colyer Mine." By 1812 most of the ore being sought there was zinc and iron. By 1970, the site had become a regional trash fill.

Lead was also produced, along with silver, zinc, and other

minerals, at the Ducktown Copper Basin beginning in 1847. Silver recovered during the copper processing in 1948 reportedly brought $35,923. By 1963, the silver output was estimated at $138,000.

*****

While the research into Swift and other lost silver mine lore covers Kentucky, Tennessee, West Virginia, Virginia, North Carolina, and to a lesser extent Alabama, Georgia, and Ohio, it should be noted that historians have routinely included Pennsylvania in the legend. This may have been included by earlier researchers because of the double connection of Swift with Pittsburgh, and his early routes along the old Braddock Road to Alexandria, Virginia.

In several versions of the tale, Swift makes Fort Pitt a stopping-off place, where he picks up additional crew members and buys supplies. From there he proceeds down through present-day West Virginia, crossing the Quindotte and Kannawa Rivers and entering the modern state of Kentucky across the Big Sandy River, often at the Forks of the Sandy.

Yet Swift and his original mining crew had an earlier connection with Fort Pitt. He and several of the men had served the British under Colonel George Washington's Colonial Army against the French and Indians at the French fort there. Monday, or Munday, was a captive of the American militia forces and eventually was befriended by Swift, who took him back to Alexandria where he soon learned of the existence of the ancient silver mines.

While most of the search for silver has occurred south and southwest of Pennsylvania, a few silver legends persist in that state, including an Indian mine said to be located near Deep Run close to the Maryland state line. Also, early Spanish were said to be in the area of Spanish Hill, and to have left fortifications there.

The Secret Silver Mines
of Captain Bob Benge

What do Big Stone Gap, Virginia, and Rising Fawn, Georgia, have in common? What is the link between the Sciota villages of Ohio and the shadowy rock shelters of Rock Castle County, Kentucky? What is the best-kept secret silver mine legend in Central Appalachia? The answer to all these questions is "Benge." Captain Bob Benge.

No, not a Revolutionary War patriot or a Civil War hero, nor even a western cavalry officer, but the final hope of the fading Cherokee, and the last great warrior along the old frontiers of an expanding United States.

From the ancient Overhill villages along the Tennessee and Georgia border to the mound-centered Shawnee towns along the Ohio River, to the Kentucky Barrens on the old trails, to Nashville and the ill-manned forts in the Cumberlands of old Virginia, Benge led a small hit-and-run force of mixed-blood warriors and renegade whites for several years. His trail of brilliant tactics and revolting slaughter scared the stuffing out of pioneer families in four states. All the while, Bob Benge may have had an unknown silver mine that could have made him a wealthy man had he not chosen war.

Benge was probably born in Running Water or Lookout Mountain town below Chattanooga, the son of an English or French trader and a Cherokee maiden who was sister to the noted War Chief Dragging Canoe. He was also a nephew to Chief Doublehead and a cousin to another mixed blood chief, John Watts. The shrinking Cherokee nation was undergoing a cultural change at the time of Benge's birth, full-blooded warriors being replaced by mixed-breed sons who held much honor and trust in the tribe. By the time Benge reached maturity he had seen numerous treaties already broken, both his uncles carrying on campaigns against the growing white population in their historic homeland, and had learned some valuable and horrible lessons.

Benge, who was red-headed and spoke perfect English, was equally at ease in Indian villages or white settlements. Early in his years as a warrior, he is credited with talking settlers out of their stations, or forts, and into surrendering to some attacking force. Sadly, many of these prisoners were then killed on the orders of Doublehead, who is known to have bashed out the brains of white babies on convenient trees because they cried.

Doublehead earned his nickname, apparently, from whites who learned of his psychotic behavior. At one moment, the War Chief could be civil and compassionate, and at the next, aided by rum or other liquor, could change his character and butcher people.

One legend has Doublehead operating an ongoing silver mine somewhere near his land on the Big South Fork, between Jamestown, Tennessee, and Burnsides, Kentucky. There, at what is today known as Hines Cave, many warring parties met to plan their attacks. Bob Benge was probably among those war councils, even as a young man, and was certainly used by Doublehead for his speaking abilities.

Following the death of Chief Dragging Canoe, who is said to have danced himself to death celebrating a victory, several attempts to launch large attacks against white forts were abandoned because word spread too fast among the settlers and they were always prepared. The duty of keeping the struggle against expansion of white settlements fell to the subchiefs, then called "Captains" because of English and French influences in the tribe.

Captain Bob Benge had grown to adulthood, taken a wife and fathered children. He was Chief of a beautiful little town in what is now extreme northwest Georgia, wedged between Alabama and Tennessee. Known today as Rising Fawn (also the name of a daughter Benge had and named after the first thing he saw on the day of her birth) the community is split now by Interstate 59. Just north is the county seat of Trenton, and all around Rising Fawn are the bluffs, gorges, and wonders of Lookout Mountain.

While some modern researchers link Rising Fawn with a chief of the same name who ruled a village north of Atlanta, and attempt to place old Cherokee gold mines within the mountains there, Rising Fawn's little-known silver and lead mine is said to be somewhere in the hills near the present town, according to a community history by Kathleen W. Thomas.

Ironically, as Bob Benge became the last noted warrior against the white settlers, a descendant (probably his son) led one of the first groups of Cherokees to exile in Oklahoma along the Trail of Tears.

During his youth, Benge had accompanied his uncle, Doublehead, on occasional raiding parties, and one time, in the barren country between Lexington, Kentucky, and Nashville, Tennessee, the Indians captured two white hunters whom they knew to be spies. Among their belongings was found a large amount of liquor, and Doublehead's party drank heavily. After awhile, Doublehead stripped flesh from the hides of the two white victims and ate it, passing it around to Benge and the other warriors. The flesh-eating was not a normal Cherokee custom, but Doublehead believed, in his drunkenness, that the Indians might obtain the strength of the fallen enemy by eating the flesh.

Early in the 1780's, Benge (who was mistakenly called "The Bench" by many white settlers) and John Watts began their guerrilla-type raids on white settlers and travelers in a spree that lasted more than a dozen years. Benge developed a unique strategy that confused the enemy and even left questions as to his identity and, at the same time, protected his village from revenge.

Leaving the security of the old Overhill towns which were cradled by the Smokies and Lookout Mountain, Benge and his warriors headquartered in the wilds of the Kentucky and Tennessee Mountains, apparently within the holdings of Doublehead in the Miro district that extended from above Knoxville, Tennessee, to Somerset, Kentucky. From there they swept down on the travelers along the old Wilderness Road and Scagg's Trace, or took old Indian trails along the mountains and surprised lone cabins and stations in east Tennessee and western Virginia.

Many times the white settlers were killed in battles or butchered afterwards; often the white women and children were captured and taken to the Shawnee towns of Ohio to be sold as slaves or traded back for captured Indian prisoners. Benge forged a strange alliance with the Shawnee, the historic enemy of the Cherokee, and a few members of that nation served within the ranks of his little force. He also took in white renegades and fellow Cherokee. The history of both North Carolina and Tennessee is dotted with raids credited to Benge, so much so that pioneer mothers often told their children to "Watch out or Captain Benge will get you."

Benge's lessons under Chief Doublehead and his own weakness for liquor may well have originated the now-common phrase "Going on a drunken binge."

The raids are too numerous to list in their entirety, but briefly, here are some notable accounts:

On June 20, 1875, Benge and his band killed the members of the Scott family at the headwaters of Wallen Creek, Virginia, taking Mrs. Scott prisoner to the Sciota villages where she eventually escaped.

A year earlier Benge is credited with the killing of white boys in Powell Valley, Tennessee, the kidnapping of a small girl, and the killing of three travelers along the "Kentucky Road." His type of warfare and his retreat to the Ohio towns caused many settlers to mistakenly believe Benge was a Shawnee, and the mistake often appears in regional histories.

In August of 1791, Benge, again called "Captain Bench," hits the Elisha Ferris home near "Mockison Gap," killing Ferris and taking Mrs. Ferris, Mrs. Livingston, and a child captive. All but Nancy Ferris were killed the first day. During one of the raids, Benge became more friendly toward one of his white women captives, and engaged her in conversation, showing all the women some chunks of silver and saying, "This is what the white man seeks."

During another adventure, while taking two women captives through the mountains above Castle Woods, Benge and his party stopped somewhere in the Breaks of the Sandy and "filled their pockets" with silver ore from an ancient mine there. Polly Alley and Jane Whitaker reported on the incident upon returning to the Virginia settlements. The ore was said to be from the same site that a well-known counterfeiter, the Melungeon "Sol" Mullins, obtained his ore.

So Benge had a knowledge of several secret silver mines along the frontier: his own mine near Rising Fawn, Doublehead's Mine on the Big South Fork, and the old mine in the rugged Breaks area. Because of evidence of looting of cabins and stations during his raids, he apparently had a good knowledge of the value of coins and jewelry, much of which was probably carried into the Shawnee towns for exchange.

Some Swift researchers might note the Breaks captive as being a member of the Alley family, later to foster Robert Alley and a continual search for the old lost silver mines from Cumberland Gap to Johnson County, Kentucky.

Numerous other raids took place under Benge and, in 1792, he joined his small band with John Watts and others and attacked Buchanan's Fort near Knoxville, Tennessee, under the command of Chief Doublehead. The Indians were driven back after fifteen of their numbers were killed. The Cherokees again began resorting to smaller raiding parties and hit-and-run operations.

Following a quick raid on Carter's Valley stations in northeast Tennessee, Benge and his crew, followed closely by white militia, retreated to a favorite camping grounds atop Pine Mountain above the current town of Jellico, Tennessee. There, in the middle of the night, the white militia caught up with them and attacked them as they slept. Benge and others managed to get away in the darkness, but a trusted warrior known as Big Aaron (or "Big Apron") was killed, and much of the plunder from the white station recovered.

Benge's captives, aside from white women and children,

included as many black slaves as he could accumulate, which he sold to other Indians and whites. He once told a white captive that he would venture into Tennessee and steal all of Isaac Shelby's slaves as punishment to the patriot for his actions against the Indians.

His deeds and bravery, as well as his cold-blooded murders, so captivated some early historians that they described the raids in detail, and even wrote paragraphs about the character of Benge himself, including a detailed account of a day's running battle, on foot, with a noted white enemy, Ensign Moses Crockrell. Crockrell and two militia men were approaching Rye Cove in Powell Valley when Benge ordered his band to shoot and kill Crockrell's two companions and save Crockrell for Benge. Benge and the white militiaman then began a chase through the mountains that pitted both men, one on one, against each other and ended with Benge's tomahawk being embedded in a cabin right behind Crockrell's fleeing head.

Crockrell survived to tell the story, but the same week Benge and his band probably murdered fourteen persons inside Kentucky along the Wilderness Road.

In April of 1793, Benge's raiding party killed six members of the Harper Ratcliff family in Hawkins County and, one year later, murdered members of the Livingston family near Mendota, Virginia. It is probably true that Benge was also responsible for the murder of some notable regional patriots, including Isaac Bledsoe, who was killed on the Laurel River in Kentucky.

"He was remarkable for his strength, activity, endurance, and great speed as a runner," one early historian noted.

Benge's final campaign began in April of 1794, when he attacked the Livingston family, and after much murdering, captured Mrs. Elizabeth Livingston. The lady wrote a detailed account of the attack and the incidents that followed; it was dated only nine days after the event, before she had forgotten the details.

She noted that as the band passed over Powell's Mountain and approached "near the foot of the Stone Mountain," a group of thirteen militia including Lieutenant Vincent Hobbs bushwhacked them, killing Benge in the first blast of rifle fire. Virginia historian Lewis Preston Summers, in *History of Southwest Virginia*, gives the battle site as near Dorchester in Wise County, while others give the site of Benge's death as Big Stone Gap.

Hobbs, afterwards noted for his deeds, headed the militia group tracking Benge, and arrived at Big Stone Gap to find the Indians and their captive had already passed. He went on, finding two of Benge's advance party making a fire, and killed both of them, discovering that in fact Benge had not yet entered the gap area.

The Virginia militia then hid among the rocks at the gap, and surprised the Indian as they entered the pass, firing without notice, and killing Benge and others. Mrs. Livingston was wounded by an Indian's tomahawk during the fight, but recovered.

Lieutenant Hobbs then inspected the dead Indians, scalping Benge, and sending the scalp to the governor of Virginia, who noted that indeed the scalp was that of Benge because "the hair is red" and rewarded Hobbs with a silver-plated rifle. One of the creeks in Wise County, Virginia, still carries Benge's name.

The way Benge's death came was ironic, for had he not spared a captive he could have moved more quickly, and would have passed through the gaps ahead of the enemy militia. It is also ironic that this Cherokee half-breed warrior, with his secret knowledge of silver and silver mines along the frontier, would be killed by a man who was to receive a very expensive silver-plated gun as a reward.

Goin' to Carolina

"Early explorers in North Carolina were fascinated by the Indian's tobacco pipes tipped with silver, and by copper and gold ornaments," wrote Hugh Talmage and Albert Ray Newsome in their *History of a Southern State, North Carolina*.

Just as Virginia supplied a growing colonial population for its daughter Kentucky, North Carolina's claim eventually stretched to the Mississippi River, and she became the mother of the state of Tennessee. North Carolina's Yadkin Valley, her most westward frontier before 1770, also supplied some exceptional people who became patriots of the new frontier, including Daniel Boone.

According to many Swift journals, some of Swift's men also hailed from the Yadkin. Swift claims that Munday had a home there as well, and many of the trips back from the mines involved "wintering" in North Carolina rather than at Swift's Alexandria, Virginia, home. One legend tells of Swift's arrest for counterfeiting while in North Carolina. He was set free because the amount of silver in his coins was greater than the silver content of British, French, or Spanish coins in general circulation.

The mountains of western North Carolina, which we call the Blue Ridge and the Smokies today, formed both a natural and a political barrier. Reports of rich mines of gold, silver and friendly Indians filtered through the rugged gaps and tickled the spirit of Yadkin Valley settlers.

Even after westward settlement began, much of the legend of the Swift mines was housed in the Piedmont section of the state. Silver hunter James McLeMoore is said to have obtained his copy of the "original" journal on the Upper Yadkin. Not surprisingly, most of the "silver mine" lore in the mountains of North Carolina is deeply woven with Cherokee and Spanish lore.

Despite claims of Kentucky, Tennessee, or Virginia mines made by Swift, some researchers believe that the ore actually came from deposits within current North Carolina. The first commercial silver mine operated in the United States was near Lexington, North Carolina, and was incorporated in 1839. Lexington is south of Winston Salem and in the immediate vicinity of the old Yadkin Valley. It is also only a short distance from Salisbury, rumored home of John Swift in two different versions of the tale.

North Carolina, surprisingly, was the leading center of gold mining in the nation until 1860. Gold was discovered in Cabarrus County in 1799, and in stream beds and on the ground in Warren and Moore Counties. By 1830, there were some fifty-six active gold mines operating in the state.

The 1799 gold find, made by Conrad Reed, involved a huge nugget weighing seventeen pounds, and this find kicked off the first gold rush in the nation. The Georgia Gold Rush, which led to the removal of the Cherokee, followed, and in 1849 the better-known California Gold Rush began.

Silver mines operated in Davidson County, possibly earlier than 1818, at Silver Hill. Mines also operated near Thomasville: the Eureka Mine; the Fair Grove Gold and Copper Mine on the Nathan Kendall property; the Silver Valley Mine northeast of Silver Hill; the Welborn or Smith Mine west of Silver Hill; and the Cid Mine and Emmons Mine, fifteen miles south of Lexington.

About two miles south of Thomasville were the Loftin, Lalor, and Black mines. Other active gold and silver mines within the region included the Dodge Hill, Billy Allred, Morgan, Biggs, Plyer and Liberty Mines, Nooe, Ida, Secrest, Hepler, Ward, Peters, Hunt, Cross, and Brown mines. The Washington and Conrad Mine was probably the most active and productive. The mine reached a depth at an angle in the earth of about 400 feet. Much information about the old Conrad Mine and other sites is available at the Washington County Library on South Main Street in Lexington.

The Conrad Mine operated for fifty years under four different owners, including John M. Lisle, Mrs. Fredrick Cammann, John F. McKee, and James E. Clayton. McKee is said to have found a very good copper vein in the depths of the mine. All that remains of the Conrad Mine following its 1880 closing is a very deep hole and a huge pile of waste rock. One modern-day owner believed that much silver is left unmined.

By 1825, North Carolina boasted of gold and silver mines in 13 counties and, in 1830, the Bechtler family began a private mint near Rutherfordton. Their coins, very rare today, are valuable collector pieces.

Ancient silver and copper mines once operated in Madison County, and ore was certainly taken by ancient Indians from the Copper Basin in extreme western North Carolina.

The Cherokees were rumored to have a silver mine somewhere near Silver Creek or in the bluffs overlooking Wesser Creek. An old Indian named Bigfoot shared the story with the Grant family. When the early whites learned of the mine they came to investigate, but the Indians had moved the silver to a hollowed-out bluff, concealing it there. After Bigfoot's death, a deerskin map he carried was used by W.I. Grant to locate the cache, but he failed to remove it from its resting place for fear of an Indian curse. The Bigfoot tale became a part of a series of silver legends to grow and prosper in the rugged region of North Carolina known as the Nantahala Gorge.

John Wikle wrote of his family's lore in an Asheville newspaper in 1965. He noted that much attention has been given to Wesser Creek and Silvermine Creek in Swain County for more than 200 years.

Three Spaniards were said to have lived "at the mouth of Silver Creek" more than 100 years ago. James Swancey was a native of "the gorge," and said that a young man of Spanish blood visited there with a map showing where the Spanish hid three bushels of money. The Latin visitor apparently failed to find the treasure, and disappeared without notice. Nantahala Gorge is said to be honeycombed with caves and "manmade caves" which are supposed to interlock or connect and "some contain traces of valuable ore."

Cliff Wikle, a boy living near Silver Mine Creek, chanced upon the old Spanish silver mine while looking for a lost cow. He tried to relocate it later, but could not. Legend has a group of local Cherokee burying a "black pot of silver" sometime prior to the removal of the tribe. The treasure spot is marked by "a crow's foot on a tree" and has never been found.

One avid searcher along Wiggins Creek was Jasper Truett, who died about 1895, leaving behind wonderful stories of silver, silver mines, and even silver bullets. Truett is mentioned often in connection with Nantahala Gorge, and was said to have molded his own bullets from lead found there in some secret place. He claimed the ore was so pure he could cut it off with his knife. Truett sold other white settlers lead shot for their rifles, but there was so much silver in the ore that it gummed up the barrels of their guns.

The mountain across from the Truett Cemetery on Wesser Creek is supposed to contain the secret mine, on a high ridge. Other men reportedly associated with Truett in the silver and lead mine were from the communities of Needmore and Wiggins Creek, and included Jonathan Morgan and Jeff Wikle.

The lost silver mines of the Nantahala Gorge have been passed down through generations of whites and Cherokees in the region and often published in local newspaper and magazines. One good account appears in *Buried Treasure of the Appalachians* by W.C. Jameson. Horse Mountain, in Rowan County, North Carolina, was the site of a silver find in the 1760's by a Pennsylvania prospector known as Thomas Clapum, according to Michael Paul Henson's *America's Lost Treasure*.

Clapum, aided by a black slave, found silver nuggets and then the "mother lode" in a cove on the west side of the mountain. The men smelted up two horseloads of silver and concealed the mine, burying a large pot full of acorn-sized silver "wads" and marking the spot on rocks and trees, somewhere along Richland Creek.

Clampum died before returning to reopen the mine or

recover the pot. A relative visited the area about 1850, but was unable to find the treasure. The story was kept alive by members of the Elliott family, with whom Clampum reportedly stayed after closing his mine. The tale was retold in the *Evergreen Magazine* of Ashboro, North Carolina, in 1851.

Whiteside Mountain is said to have old Spanish carvings hinting of a silver mine. The carvings are located high up on the impressive landmark.

Treasure tales also abound in the western North Carolina sites of Black Mountain, Grandfather Mountain, Table Rock, Flat Rock, and Luftee Creek. Another tale from the Nantahala area has a very rich silver mine being operated there by the Cherokee, under the supervision of an old brave named Sontechee. He lived along Factory Creek and was chosen to guard a natural cave because it had a rich silver vein near the back of the cavern.

Eventually the Indians were removed from the area, and whites searched for the silver mine. A landslide may have sealed up the mouth of the cavern, but whites found an old smelter, cinders, and a pile of burned ore.

James McLeMoore came to Kentucky from North Carolina in 1878 with the express purpose of locating Swift's silver mine, and caches left by Swift and his men. Having spent time in the gold fields of the Carolinas, he had a knowledge of ores and geology. McLeMoore was a Baptist minister, and had obtained journals and maps of the Yadkin Valley where he believed Swift and some of his men lived.

McLeMoore believed Swift returned to the Upper Yadkin and died there. One of his journals, noted William Connelley, contained some sixteen pages of information, and was much longer than other versions he had seen. The North Carolina man conducted his search in the area of Johnson and Magoffin Counties, joined by a number of local people.

Another Tarheel native mentioned earlier, Lakely, traveled to the Frakes area of southeastern Kentucky in the 1930's, there to meet a tragic fate: dropping dead suddenly after finding the rock carvings he said pointed to a portion of Swift's treasure.

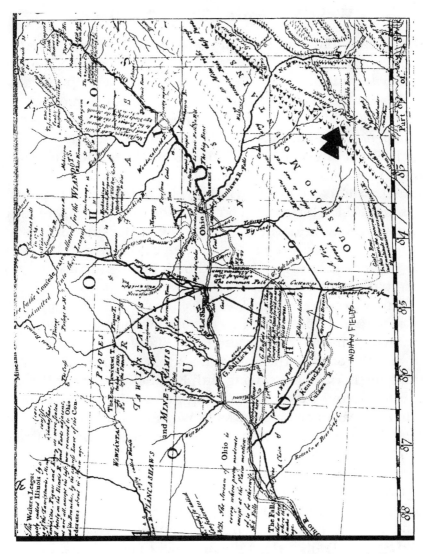

This old map of the Indian towns in North Carolina and Tennessee indicates a "Remarkable Rock," the same term used by Swift in many versions of the Journal.

West Virginia, Take Me Home

"At early day, silver money was circulated in the settlements of what is now West Virginia, said to have been made by Swift...it was free of alloy and of such a description as to indicate it never passed through an established mint."

This is a quote from a newspaper article in the *Greenup Independent*, a Kentucky publication dated February 1873.

The lost silver mines of John Swift have roots in every state in mid-Appalachia, including West Virginia. In the various versions of his journal, Swift notes several places through which he traveled on his way to and from Fort Pitt to the Kentucky wilderness, some only in passing, others as campsites, and a few places as sites where he and his crew concealed silver ore, coins, and bars during Indian attacks and pack train troubles.

Other treasure sites in West Virginia predate Swift's 1760's mining trips, going back to regional Indian lore and even involving Spanish caches about the state.

Swift's journey through the state, then part of the Virginia territorial claims along with Kentucky, mention the Big Kanawah and Guyandotte River, the Big Sandy River, and what appear to be landmarks in Wayne County. Other areas suspected to be involved in the silver mine lore include Braxton, Clay, and Nicholas counties.

One lost silver mine was supposed to be somewhere between Workmans and Meadow creeks, fifteen miles from Beckley, on the "old Jarell farm" in Randolph. A treasure cave is reported to be near the Buchanannon River on the Old Seneca Trail, a short distance south of Pickens, in Randolph County. Some accounts have Swift's crew passing on an old road through Charleston to the Forks of the Sandy River. Swift, in his blinded effort to relocate the mines, is said to have searched Twelve Pole Creek in the company of seven men, one of them Colonel John Tye, a constant companion in Swift's final days.

President Thomas Jefferson is said to have surveyed a portion of Wayne, Lincoln, and Mingo counties along the "coordinates given by John Swift in his journals." The survey area also included land between the Tug Fork and the Sandy River, just inside Kentucky, in the 1775 survey conducted by Peter Jefferson and Joshua Fry. The Jefferson (or Jeffers) name has long been associated with Swift, as crew members and later associates.

The Thomas Jefferson claim that resulted from the survey later became the holdings of Kentucky Colonel Richard Apperson, who also held what he believed to be a copy of the original Swift Journal, which came to him by way of William Spurlock and Robert Alley. Alley searched much of eastern Kentucky and probably lower West Virginia for years in search of the lost mines.

Doddridge County was the site of a little "silver rush" when local residents found pieces of silver in the creek beds just prior to the Civil War. An old silver mine was believed to be located above Dry Fork on Big Issac Mountain. The site has since collapsed, but a smelter and counterfeiting operations were thought to be inside.

Along the Gauley River in Fayette County, a silver mine was said to exist in colonial days, operated by a Richmond, Virginia, man who coined silver from silver ore.

Swift reports crossing the Kanawha River at least three times, and during one crossing wrote that he buried some $52,000 in English crowns nearby. Another Swift cache site is said to be located on a creek that empties into the Big Kanawha near Point Pleasant.

Tea Creek, in Pocahontas County, was searched in the 1920's by George P. Moore and others, following a survey map made by Sam Young. Young had given Moore a lump of ore, suspected of being silver, which he found during a land survey. The treasure hunters used a "transit" but failed to locate the silver vein. A few years later, gold was discovered along the creek and at the head of Stoney Creek by a railroad construction crew.

Probably the most interesting of the silver treasure tales of West Virginia involves Indian Camp Rock. Lucullus Virgil McWhorter, in *The Border Settlers of Northwest Virginia, 1768 to 1795*, details the story. Indian Camp Rock is located some fourteen miles above old Fort Buchanon. The rockhouse is an amphitheater-like structure at the end of the valley, making it an ideal campsite for ancient Indian and early whites as well. The entrance is fifty feet wide by twelve feet high, is formed of limestone, and faces due east. It is large enough to house an entire family, but shallow enough for the first rays of the sun to light up its entire depth.

Ash Camp Cave is located nearby and both caves have been known to contain Indian relics and remains. In Ash Camp, at least fifteen skeletons were uncovered in a mass grave, all apparently dying about the same time.

"About Indian Camp there hovers an interesting tradition of a lost mine and buried treasures of fabulous riches. This origin antedates the Revolution, with some apparent foundation in truth, although this region is not alone in its claim to be the scene of original operations, but covers Kentucky and Tennessee as well," McWhorter wrote.

"The mine was worked by a party of Spanish and English adventurers, who were nearly exterminated by their Indian allies. It appears that there were Spaniards by the name of Petro, or Pedro, on the Upper Monongahela as early as 1777, whose descendants are still living in Randolph County.

"Near Indian Camp, in 1883, I was shown a set of ruins of the 'ancient mine' and a small polished stone relic, resembling a disc, and a fragment of dossy lead, claimed to have been taken from the debris or waste of the mine. With these relics were found pieces of basketry and a buckskin moccasin. I have examined an interesting figure carved on a large sandstone boulder in a nearby grotto, known as the 'Chimney Rocks.'" he said. He added that the carving appeared to be that of a "rude compass."

Stone Coal Creek is another site of a lost mine legend,

The rugged, cliffy mountains of North Carolina's Nantahala Gorge are said to be the site of a secret Spanish and Indian silver mine.

and several carvings were found there by a hunter known as Calvin Smith. On a large flat stone near the head of a creek was read the following: WAS FOUGHT FOR THE RICH MINDS. SWARTUS CNANCU 1555. RITEN BY SNATH. DONE WHILE THE BATEL...

Some three-fourths of a mile northwest of the site was another stone, looking like a tombstone, with the following (the S. is supposed to represent silver): 1555 LBS OF GOLD AND S. SEPERAT ED FROM THE OAR. SNATH 1777.

Both carvings were visited and noted by Dr. L.S.S. Farnsworth on July 15, 1867, in the company of Valentine Lorenz, both of Buchannon. The local dentist kept the last stone in his office for several years.

Three-fourths a mile farther northwest of the last stone was a small cave or rock shelter. Inside was another stone that had apparently fallen from the ceiling. It was also engraved, with a compass pointing south southeast, and portions of the words GOLD and SNATH and the date 1777.

Dr. Farnsworth believed the compass directed searchers to a point on the Buchannon River just below the crossing at the village of Sago. Following the directions, other searchers claimed to find similar carvings near the Sago ford. The find echoed an earlier story that about 1740 three Frenchmen came to the area of the Little Kanawha, near Cave Rock Post Office in Upshur County. They searched for silver ore and spent much time in a rock shelter nearby. One of the Frenchmen died or was killed under the shelters, and the other two crossed the mountains, never to return. Years later a "caucasian" skull was found in one of the local shelters.

The Indian Camp tale began when an Indian appeared in Jamestown, Virginia, prior to the revolution. He wore silver arm bands and other silver ornaments, and offered to take local inhabitants across the mountains to find the silver. He led them to the area around Buchannon River. The Indians and whites got along well at first, working the silver mine until one of the whites struck one of the hosts. The other Indians attacked the white miners at the cave.

The survivors, fearing their impending death, tried to hide

all visible signs of mining by blasting out the face of the over-hanging cliff and closing the mine. While this was being done the man named SNATH made his carvings. The battle ended and a few whites survived, making their way back across the mountains after setting up markers to help them relocate the mine. Only one or two lived to reach the colonies.

In 1883, in a cave on Grass Run not far from Indian Camp Cave, some ancient tools were recovered and found to be made of metal. They were very rusty. A map in the possession of Joseph M. Wilson (who got it from his grandfather) shows the old Indian trace through the region, several rivers, and supposedly the location of the old silver mine.

In another account, Swift's crew is attacked while camping on the Buckhannon River. The men take shelter in a cave and stash their load of silver there, hoping to return for it later. There have also been rumors of a silver mine known to Swift in the Buckhannon Valley. Old mining tools were once found there, as well as two mine shafts.

WA2 FOUGHT FOR
THE RICH MINDS
2WARTU2 CNANCW
1555
RITEN BY 2NATH
DONE WHILE THE BATEL

Message on the Stone Coal Creek rock number one.

The message on Stone Coal Creek rock number two.

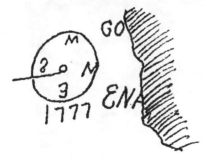

The message on the Stone Coal Creek Cave wall.

The "master" sign to the Lakely mystery at Henry Holton Gap near Frakes, Kentucky. The odd figure and several carved letters atop the small bluff apparently caused a North Carolina treasure hunter to "drop dead."

One of many carvings found in Pine Mountain along the Kentucky, Tennessee, and Virginia line. Most "Swift" researchers believe the 125-mile-long ridge to be the mountain called "Laurel" in several versions of the infamous journal.

From the Cumberlands to the Smokies
The Legend in East Tennessee

When you ask treasure hunters about Swift's mines and eastern Tennessee, most would usually answer "Bean Station," the little crossroads village where John Swift romanced the Widow Renfro during his final search, and more importantly, left her the "original" copy of his notorious journal.

Certainly Bean Station plays heavily in the entire tale, but is only a small part of the east Tennessee lore. Much of that state's link with Swift comes by way of Kentucky, not only in proximity, but in fact. Until the states settled their dispute over boundaries after 1830, much of upper Tennessee was part of Kentucky, or so Kentucky thought. The upper portions of counties such as Grainger, Claiborne, Campbell, Scott and Pickett were settled by pioneers, through Virginia and Kentucky land grants.

While Bean Station is the subject of another chapter, the rest of east Tennessee, including the Melungeon tales, plays an important part in the continuing search for lost silver mines.

Interest in silver goes back long before the first colonists or longhunters entered the region about 1760. Being located on the old Warrior's Path and then along the "southern" bend of the Wilderness Trail blazed by Boone, much of the Swift connection has to do with Swift and others passing through the area. Yet the French, Spanish, and Cherokee contribute to the legend long before our better-known adventurers.

While some historians dispute it, the Spanish penetrated into east Tennessee as far as the Chattanooga area. When a shallow grave was excavated just inside the now-commercial cave at Raccoon Mountain, the skeleton and uniform of a

Spanish soldier were discovered. Spanish armor, helmets, and artifacts have been found in the Cumberland Mountains, and even as far north as West Virginia.

There is reliable evidence that the Spanish had some commerce and contact with the Melungeons, as explained elsewhere, and may have constructed forts in northern Georgia at Fort Mountain, on a bluff-top near Jellico, Tennessee, and at Ancient Fort near Murfreesboro, Tennessee (although the latter fort is apparently of Indian origin).

Some early North Carolina histories claim that the village DeSoto visited was located in the extreme western part of that state.

The French certainly operated openly in Tennessee, and thus the French Broad River was named. An old French store operated between the Clinch and Holston Rivers, and others were located here and there throughout the state. When the English arrived in the region they learned of the French activities, and heard rumors of Spanish silver miners. English and colonial traders marvelled at the silver jewelry and tools used by the Cherokee, and were told of other mines.

As early as 1630, the Virginia colonial governor was told of "silver mines within four days of the mouth of the James River." Governor William Berkley wrote to a friend in 1669 that he was taking a ten-day journey inland to find Spanish silver mines located at "37 minutes and 38 minutes" latitude.

Governor Berkley wrote in 1868 that "I did this last spring resolve to do his Majesty a memorable service, which was in the company of 200 gents who had engaged to go along with me to find out the East India Sea. We had hopes in our journey we should find some mines of silver; for certain it is that the Spanish in the same degree of latitude has found many."

James Moore's journal, published in *Early Travels in the Tennessee Country* by Samuel Cole Williams, wrote about his venture:

"I made a journey in 1690 over the Apalatheas Mountains and took up seven sorts of ore of mineral stones, all differing either in weight, color, smell, or some other qualities.

"By my friend Colonel Maurice Matthews, I had these tried

in England. He sent word that two were very good and one indifferent. On the same journey I was informed that the Spanish have been at work within twenty miles of me. The natives described to me their bellows and furnaces, and said they killed the Spanish for fear they would make slaves of them to work the mines, as they had other Indians," wrote Moore.

Nicholas Cresswell, an English-born journalist, claimed to have visited a silver mine site within three days of Leesburg, Virginia, according to *Legends of Loudoun* by Harrison Williams. John Smith and one Captain Newport reportedly explored westward beyond the falls of the James River, where silver mines were reported.

As early as 1654, Governor Francis Yeardly of North Carolina visited "South Virginia and Carolina" (the Tennessee territory) and boasted of land "experimentally rich in precious minerals."

One hundred and fifty years later, Abraham Steiner visited the Overhill Cherokees in east Tennessee and wrote: "a young Indian was here today who had very cleverly inlaid his tomahawk with silver, having graved in a small flower design the initial letters of his name. Their rings and plates for nose and ears are covered with drawings of wild animals and the like.

"Mr. Dick Fields had a rifle with silver mountings and the finest trimmings on the stock. The work done by an artist in the State of Tennessee, the gun having been sold for eighty dollars," he wrote.

Steiner also saw another Indian, Ole Crowee of Chota, with a silver metal on his breast, apparently a reward or gift from the English or French. Andre Michaux, French botanist in the region in 1793, made mineral and metal inquiries.

Tennessee pioneer hero James Adair noted that "within twenty miles of the late Fort Loudoun (near Vonore, Tennessee), there is a great plenty of whetstones for razors, of red, white, and black colours. The silver mines are so rich that by digging ten yards deep, some desperate vagrants found at sundry times so much rich ore to enable them to counterfeit dollars to a great amount, a horseload of which was detected when passed for the purchase of negros in Augusta."

Historian Dr. J.G.M. Ramsey wrote that "a tradition still continues of the existence of the silver mines mentioned by Adair," and added that the legend was "derived from hunters and traders who had seen the locality and assisted in smelting the metal."

Not far from Fort Loudoun, a man known only as Leffew was known to have operated a secret silver mine shortly after the Civil War. The location was said to be northwest of Pennine, between Milo and Spring City. The tale has Leffew and his black helper murdered by unknown parties. Local people sought the mine near Stinking Fork, inside Rhea County near "Dead Negro Hollow."

Adair's *History of the American Indian* was published in London in 1775. In it he notes, "On the tops of these mountains I have observed tufts of grass deeply tinctured by mineral exhalations of the earth...from which we may rationally conjecture that a quantity of subterranean treasures is contained therein; the Spanish generally found out their southern mines by such superficial indications."

Ramsey mentioned "the late Mr. Delogier" of Sevier County having testified to the existence and riches of mines of silver, one of which he worked at, in the "very section of the Cherokee country described by Adair. Ramsey's *Annals of Tennessee* was first published in 1853.

As early as 1730, Sir Alexander Cumings, who adopted himself into the Cherokee tribe, visited iron and copper sites and prospected for other metals, sending some to England to be tested.

Much of the suspected mineral wealth of east Tennessee has been realized, and some are now over-mined. A journey to Ducktown on the copper basin east of Cleveland might shock many who would see the amount of earth turned there. One of the by-products of decades of copper mining there, surprisingly, was silver and gold.

The same might be said of Bumpass Cove, four miles from Erwin, where ore deposits have been known since before the Revolutionary War. Streams from the cove flow into the Nolichucky River, and the natural cove area was once a large Indian settlement. Lead mined there was said to have been fired against the British at the Battle of Kings Mountain.

The first Bumpass Cove lead mine was operated by William Colyer, and was known as the "Colyer Mine." This mine was opened about 1780. By 1812, the main ore from Bumpass Cove became iron and then zinc, but by the 1970's the cove had become a regional landfill.

The Nolichucky River region, which includes the Unaka Mountains, has been the scene of various silver mine searches, including a search by a Greene County man named Fred Cansler.

Cansler hired college students to research the Swift legend, and offers the idea that the journals may deliberately mislead searchers into Kentucky. He found many of the same landmarks in Tennessee. In 1992 he displayed a silver coin he found, and maintains a large file cabinet containing the research.

Buddy Johnson's *Silver in the Unaka* tells of his family's search for the mine, based on the Swift legend. The story is fictionalized for easier reading, but in it Johnson relates the search, gives landmarks, and writes that in 1794 a fifteen-year-old boy stumbled into an old mining shaft near Red Fork, Clear Fork, and Poplar Creek.

Johnson writes that his grandfather's uncle got a map from the body of a Civil War victim killed at Limestone Cove. One of the men killed was a J. Blackburn, possibly a descendant of the Blackburn in Swift's mining crew. Johnson places the old mine, supposedly filled with silver bars, near the junction of the Clear Fork with the Nolichucky River, and places charcoal pits on a ridge of the Unaka. Johnson also tells of initials being found of "J.S." and "G.M. Munroe."

Bulls Gap, the site of a pioneer iron furnace, was also the site of a private lead mine operated by the little town's second settler, James Parker. He lived in the gap and found the mine near his home but, being a hermit, kept the location private.

Another noted east Tennessee lead mine, which also produced silver as a by-product, was located on Leadmine Bend in the northernmost portion of Union County. Speculation has the forefather of the Daugherty (or Dougherty) family first finding ore there. George Dougherty was granted over 11,000 acres of land along the Clinch River and Walden's Ridge in 1788.

Continual mining of zinc and other metals deep in the earth near Jefferson City echoes early rumors of lead in the White Pine Community. Other sites said to have had early lead mines sought by pioneers include Blount, Loudon, Cocke, and Anderson Counties.

Early settlers of Powell Valley, between Lafollette and Tazewell, sought silver and lead along the waters of Davis Creek, across Cumberland Mountain. Obviously the Kincaid family of the valley may have found such either there or in the Lead Mine Bend area.

Many versions of the Swift journal, including the Partin version, have Swift and his men crossing "a large, bald mountain" on their way to the mines. Roan Mountain, on the North Carolina border above Elizabethton, features "Bald Knob," which may have been cleared annually by regional Cherokee so they could hunt game there. The mountain stands between the old Yadkin Valley area of North Carolina, and Cumberland Gap.

East Tennessee has many more claims to the Swift legend, including being the home of the Melungeons, the location of Moccasin Gap above Kingsport, the site of Cumberland Gap, and the doorway to the settlement of the west. The region may also claim to be the home of many well-organized and impromptu searches for the silver mines, including those of Bland Ballard's search of the Clear Fork near Jellico, and a shared claim with Kentucky to lost silver mines along the Big South Fork River.

Spring City, Tennessee, is the site of an old Cherokee silver mine tale that involved several white families, murder, and mystery. W.C. Jameson, in his *Buried Treasures of the Appalachians*, tells of a small group of Indians returning to the region of Piney Creek some time after the removal and apparently recovering a wagonload of silver. Despite attempts by early settlers to locate the mine, they could not until a local farmer named Leffew found it.

Leffew searched the Cumberland Mountains above Spring City and eventually showed up at his home, showing his wife a lump of silver he had recovered from the old mine. Unfortunately he took the find to town and boasted about it over drinks, telling people in the bar that the mine was located not far from a landmark known as "Big Rock."

Leffew apparently hired a black man to help in the mine, and dispatched him to buy supplies, including dynamite. The two men went off toward the mine and were never again seen alive. When the black man's body was found, he had been shot in the head, and the area soon became known as "Dead Negro Hollow."

What was presumed to be Leffew's body was found near Vinegar Hill hanging from a tree, choked to death in his leather suspenders. During the time both were missing, a rough-looking bunch of men was seen wandering around the Leffew farm.

Years later, another local farmer named Thurman was searching for stray livestock in the Piney Creek gorge when he found a narrow slit in a bluff. A pole of nearby rock indicated that the place had been mined. Thurman abandoned the mine and continued to search for his cattle; later he tried, unsuccessfully, to relocate it.

Thurman's search was followed by a local man named Warrick, who was familiar with Piney Creek gorge and spent much time there looking for the Leffew mine. One evening he appeared at his home and showed his sister silver he had found at the old mine.

Warrick hid part of his workings beneath a large boulder at Warrick Fork, showing his sister the site. For some time he mined ore and hid it below the boulder. One day he went off to the mine and was never seen again. His sister and others looked for him without success, and then went for the cache below the rock, which was also missing.

A Sevier County man named Delozier told Tennessee historian Ramsey that he knew of silver mines somewhere in Cherokee Country, and attested to the richness of them because he had worked there.

"The face of a man" looking toward one of Swift's mines is mentioned in several journals. Raven Rock, also known as Indian Face Rock, is located in "The Narrows" south of Jellico, Tennessee, and the huge bluff stands guard on the Primroy Hollow, where searches for lost silver mines have been conducted since 1770. The mountain floor below the unusual bluff is pitted with glory holes and old mine shafts. (Photo by Mike Steely)

Bland Ballard's Search

In *The Land of the Lake*, a history of Campbell County, Tennessee, by Dr. G.L. Ridenour, the author says: "The first company of men in this section to promote a systematic search for Swift's Silver Mine was composed of Bland W. Ballard, James Bradshaw, William Renfroe, Chester B. Benson, John Blackburn, and Isaac Renfro of Kentucky, and Elisha Walden, John Walden, and James Renfroe of Tennessee."

Ridenour was referring to a wild gorge section of the Clear Fork River about five miles south of the current Kentucky state line today called "The Narrows." The area, cut out by rushing white water, features unusual bluffs of sandstone and limestone that stand some 1600 feet above the valley. It is a slice of scenery more typical of the mesa area "out west" than from the old mountains along the Kentucky and Tennessee border. When Ballard and the Kentucky capitalist came to the region to attempt to find the lost silver mines, the cliffy gorge was inside Kentucky. The area was "lost" to Tennessee in 1859 after the Cox/Pebbles survey.

Between the first settlement of the Jellico area, about 1780, until present, people have sought the legendary silver mines along the Clear Fork, on No Business Creek, on Stinking Creek along the headwaters, and between High Cliff and Frakes on Pine Mountain. Most of the search has been by local family members, but a few massive, well-financed groups have also prospected. The Ballard search was one of those, and occurred in the early settlement years. Another serious prospecting effort for silver, gold, and other ores took place in the 1880's, immediately prior to the railroad construction through the Narrows.

The articles of partnership drawn up by the Ballard group state that they "have this day flattering prospect of obtaining and finding a silver mine said formerly to be occupied and worked by a Mr. John Swift, together with the hopes of finding a number of dollars and crowns said to be hid by Swift."

This group was led to the Narrows, and more particularly to Primroy Hollow there, because of several reasons: The area is similar to that mentioned in various versions of Swift's "journal"; supposedly Swift wintered there with Aaron Whitecotton, an early settler of Hich Cliff prior to 1800 while blindly attempting to relocate his mines; much of the land was claimed by a Tennessean (James Renfro) who had a copy of Swift's journal and searched for the mines; and Ohio pioneer and patriot John Bryan sought silver earlier nearby along a creek known today as Silver Mine Branch.

In looking back at the Ballard search, there are some other obvious reasons for the search of the Clear Fork Narrows. Among the men in Ballard's association were the Renfroes of Kentucky and Tennessee, who may well have had a connection with "Mrs. Renfro" of Bean Station, to whom Swift gave the original copy of the now-famous journal. Bean Station, the last white outpost on the expanding frontier, is only about fifty miles southeast of the Narrows.

The Waldens, who still have descendants in the region, had early explored the area of Pine and Cumberland Mountain. By some versions of the journal, the Waldens (as Walten and Waldrum) were associated with Swift.

The closest connection to the Ballard search is probably John Blackburn, for the name Blackburn, Blackbourne, and Blackberry have long been associated with Swift, both as an original silver-mining crew member and in Swift's fruitless attempt to relocate his mines. The name is usually given as J.C. or Samual Blackburn. Swift says Blackburn was a trader among the Cherokee "of the Carolinas" before joining his expeditions back and forth from Virginia to the various hidden silver mines. One Samual Blackburn resided in North Cumberland County, Virginia, at the same time as John and Thomas Swift lived there in the mid-1700's.

By some legends, Blackburn was the sole survivor of Swift's original company, the others killed by Indians in their attempt to relocate the mines while Swift suffered in prison in England for his public support of freedom for the colonies.

Most of Elisha Walden's interest centered around the Cumberland Gap area, and Walden's Ridge is named for him. The fact that he was in the region with other longhunters about 1761 may have associated him in time with Swift, who operated his silver mines from 1761 until 1769. Walden's hunts included "Laurel Mountain," today known as Pine Mountain. His interest in minerals is evident by his naming "Copper Ridge" for the ore he found there.

Bland Ballard, such an important Kentucky settler and political figure that a county was named for him, was born in 1761 in Spotsylvania County, Virginia. In 1779 his family moved to Kentucky, and Ballard joined the militia. Bland's family was attacked by Delaware Indians, and many, including his father, two brothers, and his stepmother, were killed. He bragged about killing more than thirty Indians in revenge.

Ballard represented Shelby County for three terms in the Kentucky General Assembly, served as trustee of Shelby Academy, and helped survey the route from Shelbyville to the Falls of the Ohio. He was six feet tall and a gifted public speaker. He and his wife, Elizabeth Williamson, had seven children.

The grounds about the bottom of Raven Rock (Indian Head Rock) are pitted with old "glory holes" made by silver-mine hunters. Beneath the Bee (or Honey) Hole, just around the bluff, is a long, low mine dug by some unknown treasure hunter.

Ballard's search in the old Kentucky state placed him in good company. Despite his failure to locate the lost silver mine, he joined, among other noted searchers, John Filson, James Harrod, John Breckenridge, and even Thomas Jefferson.

The Clear Fork silver mine legends should rightfully fall under those of "Southeastern Kentucky," for the area was claimed by Virginia and then Kentucky until the early 1800's. Early land grants, including those of James Renfro for the

High Cliff region which included Primroy Hollow, were issued by Kentucky.

Early maps of both states show the "old" state line, questionably surveyed by Dr. Thomas Walker, as being estimated between the Pine and Cumberland Mountains. Today the line is much more north, cutting through the town of Jellico and then climbing Pine Mountain to the east and Jellico Mountain to the west.

Near the head of Stinking Creek, which joins the waters of Lick Creek near the Habersham community, is an all-but-forgotten mountain branch strongly connected with the old treasure legends.

Silver Mine Branch begins near the top of Pine Mountain, where Interstate 75 now runs, and snakes its way down the south side of the ancient uplift to enter Stinking Creek only a mile or so from what is now the Stinking Creek exit of the modern four-lane highway. The branch comes by its name through history, because an old pioneer stayed there briefly long before the area was settled.

John Bryan (or Bryant or Brian) was a noted settler of Ohio and well-known explorer and longhunter. He was a companion of Daniel Boone, James Harrod, and others who eventually settled and farmed near Yellow Springs, Ohio, near the Shawnee town of old Chilhowee (now Old Town). For some unknown reason, Bryan came to the wilds of the mountains, and is said to have had a silver mine somewhere in the bluffs along Silver Mine Branch. Apparently he stayed there no more than a few years, but was in the region about 1770 or 1780, at the same time Swift reportedly returned and searched for his lost mines.

An associate of Bryan, one Samuel Mason, operated a station or fort on Lick Creek, between present-day Jellico and LaFollette, along the old Indian trail from Big Creek Gap to the Clear Fork Gorge. Mason, later to be known as the bloody Mississippi bandit and cutthroat companion of the beastly Harpe Brothers at Cave in Rock on the Ohio River, became involved in counterfeiting Spanish coins and trafficking with river men along the Tennessee River. Eventually he was "ran out" of the mountains by pioneer lawmen headed by John Sevier.

Much of the land which includes Silver Mine Branch was owned by a man who lived near Norris Dam and who claims that a vein of silver exists in the bluffs along the stream.

Bland Ballard, Kentucky patriot and politician, is said to have organized one of the first corporations to find Swift's lost silver mines. Ballard, along with survivors of the Renfro family, searched the Clear Fork River Gorge area south of Jellico, Tennessee, near the Kentucky state line, apparently after 1820.

At the Ancient Pass

Any modern visitor to Cumberland Gap is first struck by the view from atop the Pinnacle Rock, and then by the ghosts of more than 100,000 settlers who passed through the ancient gateway on their way to Kentucky, Ohio, western Tennessee, and beyond. Today, as work on a massive traffic tunnel continues, there are plans to restore the gap to its condition during those pioneering days.

While it is known that Swift ventured through Cumberland Gap while searching to relocate his lost mines and headquartering with Mrs. Renfro at Bean Station, it is less obvious that he used the gap during actual mining trips. In the various journals he is quoted as indicating trips back and forth to the upper, middle, and lower mines via "The Large Gap" and "The Big Gap." References to places in western Virginia, especially Castlewood and the Big Sandy River when mentioning the "large" gap, indicate the Breaks of the Sandy. Possibly the "big gap" mentioned during trips from the Yadkin Valley via the New River and Holston River involved Cumberland Gap.

Several journals mention Swift's hiding bars and coins on the south side of the gap and, it is at Cumberland Gap that many searchers have begun their quest. Both William Spurlock and Robert Alley, who eventually traced the legend to eastern Kentucky, searched the Cumberland Gap area.

The historic pass is ripe with treasure lore, involving not only Swift but tales of Spanish, Indian, and Civil War sites as well. Tales of silver mines elsewhere detailed should rightfully fall within the section on Cumberland Gap, including those of White Rocks and Martin Station, Virginia; Pineville and Frakes, Kentucky; and Pine Mountain and Jellico, Tennessee. However, because of their length and importance, those tales are dealt with separately.

If Swift moved through Cumberland Gap during his years of mining, he made little note of the odd things there. Even Dr. Thomas Walker, who ventured through the gap in 1750 and later, noted the cave on the south side, its powerful stream issuing forth, and the many carvings of crosses and animals he discovered in the gap.

Yet if Swift chose a gap to cross the Cumberland Mountains from the Holston River area, he must have used the old pass. No other convenient gap exists for many miles to the northeast until Pound or Big Stone Gap. To the southwest only Big Creek Gap, at Lafollette, Tennessee, offered early travelers a way into Kentucky.

Some modern-day Tennessee "Swift Buffs" believe the entire question is moot anyway, claiming that Swift's mines were in the Nolichucky or Unicoi Mountains, or spurs of the Smokies. The idea is that Swift deliberately misled searchers by guiding them into Kentucky. Odd as this theory is, it has several adherents.

Other Swift researchers point to a large Indian village in the region of Town Creek, just southwest of Cumberland Gap, as being the Indian town mentioned by Swift. Others believe he crossed Newman's Ridge or Moccasin Gap near Kingsport, and noticed the Melungeons, calling them Mecca Indians.

At least one settler in the Cumberland Gap region seemed to have prospered from a secret silver mine in the Cumberlands. When local Union loyalists murdered John Kincaid II shortly after the close of the Civil War, they may have achieved their revenge on the rich slave owner of Powell Valley, but they may also have silenced the one man who could have made the area rich.

When Kincaid settled in the fertile valley at the base of Cumberland Mountain between Jacksboro, Tennessee, and Cumberland Gap, he is said to have found and operated a hidden silver mine. He grew so wealthy that he built a brick mansion in 1842 along Davis Creek. According to legend, Kincaid found the silver mine across the mountain along the headwaters of the Clear Fork or Clear Creek. Immediately north of his home, across Cumberland Mountain, are the three "Log Mountains" of silver lore fame in Bell County, Kentucky, and Claiborne County, Tennessee.

Dr. G.L. Ridenour, in his book *The Land of the Lake*, tells of Kincaid, and notes that early settlers of Powell Valley sought lost silver mines along Davis Creek north of the mountain. This "Davis" creek is not the same one where Kincaid lived.

More modern silver mine hunters have searched the area of Alum Cave, or Sand Cave, up and down No Business Creek, and in the headwaters of the Clear Fork River along Tackett Creek. More accurate speculation of Kincaid's find, from which he was said to have minted coins more valuable than the U.S. specie, might have the ore coming from the Lead Mine Bend area of the Powell River. Much of the old mines are now covered by the waters of Norris Lake.

The large deposit of lead may have been discovered by a longhunter known as Daugherty. One George Dougherty, in 1788, was granted more than 11,000 acres along the Clinch River and Walden's Ridge. Evidence of the operations are still visible, and the lead mines, which also produced other ores, were worked at least three different times, as late as 1942.

Davis Creek, where Kincaid made his home, is a few miles north of the Lead Mine Bend area.

Swift's Final Search

For purposes of accuracy, I should say at the onset that I have taken some poetic license in reconstructing the events, times and people involved in Swift's final search of central Appalachia, as depicted here.

By most journal accounts, John Swift was imprisoned in the Tower of London in England in 1774 because he was heard voicing his opinion that the colonies should be independent of Britain. Since he had served in the American/British Army under George Washington during Braddock's Campaign, where it is said that he chanced to meet the French captive Munday, Swift no doubt had strong feelings for the American colonies.

From 1774 until about 1789 he was held there, finally gaining his release and making his way back to his beloved homeland. One account says Swift was recognized at Fort Pitt as he was on his way back into the wilderness to relocate his fabulous mines.

Since he had left his journal with Colonel John (?) Tye, he returned to Uniontown, Pennsylvania, picked up his maps and journals, and was accompanied by Tye and others to Bean Station, Tennessee, below Cumberland Gap. There he headquartered, staying with the widowed Margaret Renfro. He had apparently known the Renfro family in the Yadkin Valley of North Carolina during the 1760's. When he reached Bean Station he learned that Munday and some other mining crew members had attempted to return to the wilderness and retrieve the silver, only to be murdered by the Indians.

During the long attempt to relocate the mines, and the caches hidden here and there along the mining crew's pathways to and from the colonies, Swift was handicapped by near-total blindness, age, and the drastic change of the country during the years of his absence. He had abandoned the mines in 1769 and now, only fifteen years later, found new roads blazed, new forts and outposts where there were none before, and settlers everywhere from Wolf Hills in Abingdon, Virginia, to Harrodsburg, Kentucky, and beyond.

As best as can be recounted, Swift's search began near Cumberland Gap in the mountains of Bell County, Kentucky, and Caliborne and Campbell counties, Tennessee. Most of the search took place on Pine Mountain near natural landmarks similar to those listed in his journal, and centered on the Henry Bolton Gap region and the Narrows of the Clear Fork, plus a possible search of the Furnace Ridge region of Chenoa in the Narrows of the Clear Fork.

Aaron Whitecotton, the first settler of the High Cliff region of Jellico, is said to have hosted Swift and his companions for one winter. Swift is also believed to have associated with the outlaw Samuel Mason at his station in the wilds of Lick Creek, north of LaFollete, Tennessee. During the time of his return, much of the search area around the Narrows and especially High Cliff and the Primroy Hollow area, was held by the first legal landowner there, one James Renfro. This man is believed by some to be the son of Bean Station's Mrs. Renfro, and to have had a copy of Swift's journal. A few years after Swift left the area, James Renfro and his slave boy were killed by lightning while searching for the lost mine. Some tales have them killed in the mountains above Flat Lick, Kentucky, while others have the incident in Pine Mountain on Clear Creek or the Clear Fork.

Following the search of Pine Mountain along the current Kentucky/Tennessee line, Swift apparently returned to Bean Station. There he warned Mrs. Renfro that he did not trust some of the "Frenchmen" in his party, and left a copy of his journal with her.

Sometime prior to this, while camping with Colonel Tye near Popular Creek in the Pine Mountain foothills north of Henry Bolton Gap, the search party was attacked in the middle of the night by Indians. Tye's son and another man were killed, but the attackers were eventually driven away. Listed in the party with Tye were John Burlinson, Sherrard and Thomas Mays, and the son (John Tye, Jr.). The incident is recorded in Tennessee history, and says that an "old man" was injured, never identifying him as Swift.

The Mays brothers were apparently associated in the building of Limestone, on the Ohio River, later known as "Maysville." Following his unsuccessful search of the Big Sandy area, Swift is said to have departed down the river, landing in Limestone, there to resume his search in central Kentucky. Swift had traveled to the two known "doors" in the Cumberland in extreme western Virginia, namely Pound and the Breaks of the Sandy River. Just to the east, in the foothills of the Blue Ridge, Swift had written that he stayed with "old man Castleman" at Castlewoods on various trips back and forth to his mine.

In the frontiers of Virginia, Swift's last search was said to have been assisted by "the ancestors of local men" named Morgan Lipps, Covey Holebrook, Eli Hill, and even "old man Castle" himself.

The search of the area there ended at Nancy Gap, on the Sandy Ridge, where Swift directed the men to look for a certain tree, a forked Dogwood. Swift was said to have collapsed upon learning that the tree could not be found, and to have cried "like a baby."

Within the area of search along the Virginia/Kentucky border are two places supposedly named for Swift: John's Creek (and John's Creek Mountain between New River and New Castle); and Tug Fork, in Kentucky, said to be named for the "Tugs" of silver fashioned by Swift's mining crew.

"Swift bores holes in some silver pigs and puts a plug through them to tie them together," one researcher wrote. Pound Gap plays heavily in the legend, said to be the location of the "Great Shawnee Cave" by Shawnee legends. The name comes from the "pounding" sound horse hooves make when crossing the "hollow" mountain. Several versions of the legend have Swift murdering his miners and storing up all the final year's successes (1769) in the Great Cave.

The Breaks of the Sandy is also heavily associated with the

Swift legend, especially a huge formation there known as "The Towers."

Searchers after Swift's death have, until the present day, combed the mountains around Wise and Coeburn, some silver-bearing ore reportedly being found there, and a heap of old cinders containing silver ore also located.

After Swift abandoned the Virginia search, he was reported to have traveled down the Big Sandy to the Ohio, and then on to present-day Maysville. There he may have gone overland to the Red River Gorge, assisted there by Colonel Tye, John Anderson, a man named Townsend, and others. Certainly more "Swift" evidence, carvings, landmarks, and other clues have been found in the Wolfe County natural wonder area than at any other site in Appalachia. While places here and there bear some appearance to his noted landmarks, the gorge area has dozens, including some carvings said to be made by Swift.

Following 1800 and Swift's supposed death in Lexington, many people undertook the search in the gorge area, including the descendants of Anderson. Copies of the journal, given either to Colonel Tye, Anderson, Townsend, or others, were circulated widely, and encouraged many attempts to search the gorge. The search continued until recently, when the state gained ownership and opened a park there.

Other versions of the legend say that Swift died in Bean Station in 1800 or 1812, still others have him traveling to North Carolina to seek out the treatment of Dr. Hicks, a Cherokee physician, and later dying in the Yadkin Valley.

Whether the Swift Silver Mines of Appalachia ever existed is much a matter of debate, but the following is certain: A man calling himself John Swift certainly traveled about the middle mountains prior to 1800, and was assisted by many local settlers in different areas, in search of the fabled mines. Who he really was is in question, and some speculate that the "last days" Swift was really John Filson, the historian and initial claimer of "Swift's Mines" in a Virginia land request.

Filson disappeared off the face of the earth in the years prior to Kentucky statehood, as did other Swift searchers, including Kentucky patriot James Harrod. Much of the information we have today about Swift and the various lost mines and buried caches comes from those last dozen or so years that "Swift" and early settlers searched the mountains for clues.

Tommy Veal inspects a bow and arrow carved into a rock in the Cumberland Mountains. A Choctaw Indian and the past national "Long Distance" treasure hunting champion, he is often sought for his ability to find and read old signs and symbols. (Photo by Mike Steely)

Who Was John Swift?

Amid all the debate as to whether or not the lost silver mines of John Swift ever existed within the confines of the wild Appalachian Mountains are deeper questions that, if answered in the correct manner, may point to the answer of the first. For the next few pages I will pursue those questions, starting with the first one: Who was John Swift?

Without considering the possibility that Kentucky's first historian (and the biographer of Daniel Boone) John Filson may have, indeed, penned the Swift journal, I will draw on my twenty or so years of research to find the elusive Swift and reveal him. Filson, it is recorded, made an early land claim for acreage in Kentucky, land which he claimed contained the Swift mine. Some believe that after Filson disappeared, literally, into the Kentucky territory and from the pages of history, the journal was found among his belongings and then sold as an authentic guide to the lost mines.

A few other people believe Filson disappeared only to take on the identity of Swift and seek funds and backers to search for mines he once claimed to have worked. Certainly, with that type of claim in writing, almost any silver discovered in the region could be claimed by an imposter.

And yet among all this speculation, it turns out that a man named John (or Jonathan) Swift did, in fact, exist and prosper in the very colonial community he claims in most versions of the journal, Alexandria, Virginia. The dates and events that encircle that Swift seem to be in exactly the right time frame for anyone to claim him as the authentic character in this old and confusing tale.

Judge John Haywood, whose early history of the settlement of Tennessee and Kentucky was as accurate as he could make it, and who was closer to the time of the legend than anything else written, describes Swift as follows:

"That there was actually such a man as John Swift, that he is not a mythical character. That he was known to be in the western wilderness. That he was reputed to have worked silver mines...that he was of good character and entitled to credit. That he kept a journal of his transactions. That neither the genuineness of his journal nor the probability of its truth and accuracy were ever questioned by those having the best opportunity to judge of it in these respects...."

Although some versions of the journal claim Swift was born in England and came to America to seek his fortune, most probably John Swift (according to records) was born about 1727 in Philadelphia. In 1752 he married a lady whose Christian name was Desire. Shortly before their marriage in 1750, he is listed as being a Loyal Collector of Customs. Shortly after the union, Swift moved to Alexandria, Virginia.

Some legends have Swift serving with General Washington in the French and Indian Wars, alongside the likes of Daniel Boone. There he met future members of his mining crew, befriended a French captive named Munday who later showed him the old mines, and afterwards became a trapper or trader in the Ohio and Kentucky valleys.

James A. Dougherty, in searching for the historic Swift, wrote that a "man by the name of Jonathan Swift, J.W. Swift, Jonathan W. Swift, or J. Swift did live in Alexandria...and was considered a prominent citizen. In 1786 he signed a petition to the Virginia General Assembly regarding aid for the Alexandria Academy...he signed a petition regarding wheat inspection...soon after the death of Washington he became a charter member of the Washington Society and was their first treasurer."

Certainly the "Alexandria Swift" existed. But some journals, or versions of the original, claim Kent Colony, Virginia, as his home base and, indeed, a Swift family lived there as well. One Jonathan Swift was granted 22 acres in Christian County, on the New River, in 1807. The 1790 census lists various Swifts, including John, in the North Carolina count, yet the man was only thirty-four years old and may have been a son or distant relative. In 1667, one Jonathan Swift was living in New Kent Colony, one hundred years before the time of the legend.

Interestingly, the John Swift of Alexandria was granted two tracts of land in Kentucky, in 1795 and 1809, on the Green River. In 1801 the same Swift, along with William Mattock Rogers of Boston, was allotted acres on the Green River, in old Hardin County, Kentucky. Additional land grants were issued to Swift in 1803, and can currently be found on file in Kentucky's capital.

One copy of the numerous Swift journals seems to, again, point to the Alexandria man as the right character. It reads: "I was born on October 3, 1712, in Philadelphia, Pennsylvania, my ancestors first came to America in 1637. I married Desiree Ann Swift, April 21, 1748. When I left the sea in 1752 I settled in Alexandria, Virginia."

In Alexandria Swift not only got to know George Washington, under whom he had served in the colonies, but also came to know Thomas Jefferson. Records indicate that Jefferson surveyed a large pat of what is now the Kentucky and West Virginia border in search of silver mines. Also, one of Swift's crew members was (by most versions) a man named Jefferson or Jeffers.

So, all other claims aside, it appears that the Philadelphia-born Alexandria shipping merchant named John Swift may have been the same Swift of legend and lore in the Kentucky mountains.

The Reams Version

William J. Reams, of Wyandotte County, Kansas, was a native of Laurel County, Kentucky, and had a large interest in the Swift legend. He shared his information with William E. Connelley, and his account was published in *History of Kentucky*.

Reams tells a somewhat familiar tale but with some large differences, including having Swift assemble his former men, including Munday and McClintock, in 1790 and return to the old mines.

"The party arrived at the mines and examined the treasure hidden at the different points in the vicinity of their various furnaces. Nothing had been disturbed. The last place of concealment to be examined was the great cave. When Swift saw the immense sums lying on the floor of this ancient retreat of the Shawnee, the evil spirit of his nature was aroused, and he resolved to possess the whole of the great riches," the Reams tale says.

Swift then kills all the sleeping men in his greed, and is punished for his act by being blinded. He goes to Bean Station and tells Mrs. Renfro of the murders and she refuses to wed him. Then, according to Reams, Swift departs for North Carolina to seek out the Cherokee Doctor Hicks in hopes of curing his blindness, leaving the original journal to Mrs. Renfro's hands.

Reams said he believed Swift and his men were pirates who got their silver from ships on the Spanish seas and carted it into the mountains, there to melt it down and recoin it. He did believe, however, that much of the treasure was left at various places, including the Great Cave, where it remains to this day.

Reams did an extensive search about Swift himself, and came up with the following, which argues powerfully that Swift was not a fictional character:

- That he was known to have been in the western wilderness.
- That he was reputed to have worked silver mines there, and to have concealed much treasure in those wilds.
- That he was of good character and entitled to credit.
- That he kept a journal of his transactions.
- That the knowledge of the existence of his journal was common to part of the country of considerable extent.
- That neither the genuineness of his journal nor the probability of its truth and accuracy was ever questioned by those having the best opportunity to judge of it in these respects.
- And that he left his journal in the possession of Mrs. Renfro when he went away, never to be heard of again.

Who Knew Swift?

Over the years Swift claimed to have been in the wilderness mining silver, and in various versions of his "journal," many individuals are named. These names vary from journal to journal, and some also appear in local histories of the exploration and settlement of central Appalachia. Other names are associated with John Swift during his last search for the lost mines. Many of these were early settlers of western Virginia, eastern Tennessee, and central and southeastern Kentucky. Some names can be found and documented; some cannot. Here, in alphabetical order, are part of those mentioned:

ANDERSON. According to a southwest Virginia, Clinch River version of the journal, the Anderson name was associated with Swift. This "constant companion" assisted a blind and aged Swift not only in the search there, but in the Red River area of Kentucky as well, in the company of one Colonel Tye. Anderson's widow later moved to the Red River Gorge area to continue the hunt.

BALLARD. According to a Campbell County tale, Ballard was an associate of John Blackbourne (a partner with Swift) in the attempt to locate silver in the Narrows region of the Clear Fork gorge. Bland W. Ballard and his companions formed the Swift Silver Mining Company sometime around 1880, along with members of the Renfro families of Kentucky and Tennessee. Ballard also played an important part in Kentucky history.

BARTOL. Alexander Bartol is also given as BARTOW, and was a member of Swift's "Pack Train" into the mountains.

He and Jeremiah Bates settled in southwestern Virginia, and their names were popular there. Bartol is listed in the Spurlock version of Swift's journal, along with James Mott, Bates, Fletcher, and others.

BATES. Mentioned above, Jeremiah Bates is given in the Spurlock version of the journal.

BEATY. Andrew Beaty is linked with silver mining along the Kinney Creek section of upper Kentucky. He was associated with Joseph Sprinkle (or Springle) and a company of counterfeiters at Saltpeter Cave in Carter County.

BLACKBURN. Also given as Blackbourne, Blackberry, and Blackberne, he was an "original crew" member. His Christian name is given as J.C., John, Samuel, and even Hans. Blackburn is believed to have been a partner who came from England to assist Swift. By one account (from Henry W. Tomkins of Detroit), Blackburn was the sole survivor of the Swift Crew. The Red River Gorge area has him buried there.

Hans Blackburn is given in the Big South Fork version as the murderer of Tuckahoe at Doublehead's Silver Mine, in the company of Munday. Legend says Princess Cornblossom killed him in revenge for the murder of her brother. A probable descendant of Blackburn, one John Blackburn, was a member of Ballard's Silver Mine Company on the Clear Fork River just inside Tennessee in the 1800's, along with the Renfro family.

BLUE JACKET. This Chief of the Shawnee has long been associated with Swift in many Kentucky and Ohio legends. Actually, Blue Jacket was a German youth captured and raised by the Sciota Shawnee. He adopted their ways and eventually became a war chief. After the Indian Removal, Chief Blue Jacket returned to Kentucky as a guide for a group of Kentucky capitalists, headed by Ohio Major James Galloway, to lead them to the lost silver mines. He did so for several days, but then refused to take them any farther. He promised to send his son to lead them, but did not. Years later a descendant, Peter Cornstalk, returned to Rules Mill in Kentucky, and searched for the lost mines.

BRYAN. Probably John and also given as Bryant, was associated with Swift during the unfruitful final search for the mines. John Bryan was an early member of the Henderson Survey of the Cumberland, and led a party of longhunters into Kentucky as early as 1775. Bryan had been captured by the Indians and held for years prior to his activities. The 1775 hunt extended from Sulphur Fork of the Middle Tennessee to Red River in Kentucky.

Bryan is also given as Brian, Bryan, etc., and was believed to have known Samual Mason, the Ohio River outlaw, and is thought to have worked with river pirates in Tennessee. John Bryan lived for some time on Silver Mine Branch in Campbell County, Tennessee.

CAMPBELL. Isaac Campbell, by many versions, was a six-year member of the original mining crew under Swift. He is mentioned more than six times in various journal versions. One journal says Campbell was killed by Indians in November of 1767 on the way to the silver mines. A man by the same name played an important role in the settlement of Kentucky and Tennessee. Campbell may have come to know Swift while both were members of Colonel Washington's colonial army under General Braddock.

CARTWRIGHT. Mary (or Merry) Cartwright was supposedly Swift's cook. This German woman was never permitted to see the mines, and according to one version, was killed by Swift himself. She is mentioned twice in the southeastern Kentucky journal versions, and may have been the widow of Robert Cartwright. Scott Partin of Bell County claims that Merry Cartwright was still living in the area when his forefathers came there searching for the lost mines.

CARTY. One northeastern version of the journal has him

as a member of the Jonathan Swift crew. Could also be spelled McCarty.

CASTLEMAN. Probably Jacob, possibly Castle. He was a famous frontier hunter who worked from his camp in southwest Virginia, the place known today as Castlewood. Swift, in different journals, refers to spending time with "Old Castleman" annually on his way to and from the mines. By one Kentucky River account, Castle (or "old man Castle") accompanied Swift on his aged search to relocate the treasures down Swift's Creek in Central Kentucky prior to 1800.

CORNSTALK. Chief of the Shawnee, he claimed to have been part of Swift's original expedition, presumably as a guide. His descendants searched for the mines along Paint Creek and Mud Lick Creek in Kentucky.

DE BOIS. This is the name of a French family long associated with Swift. Some of them may have been early crew members listed simply as Frenchmen.

FINLEY. Probably John Finley. He is listed in a single journal version as a mining crew member. Finley, who plays heavily in early Kentucky history as Daniel Boone's guide into the wilderness is also given as Findley, Finney, or Flynn.

FLETCHER. Moses Fletcher is often mentioned as one of Swift's mining crew members. Fletcher is said to have fought with Flint over their shares, and recovered from his wounds at Munday's Yadkin Valley, North Carolina, home. Most accounts list Fletcher as one of Swift's unfortunate murder victims in the Great Shawnee Cave.

FLINT. Abram or Abraham Flint is given in a few journals as one of the winter crew members left behind one year to work the mines. He is said to have been killed during a fight with Fletcher over shares of silver. The name is also given as Abraham Flynn.

FRENCHMAN. G. Frenchman is a general French associate in two accounts, probably corrupted from George Munday, Frenchman. Frenchman is listed in the Partin version as a mining crew member.

GREYSER. He is listed in one Virginia version as a latter-day associate of Swift in the unsuccessful search to relocate the mines.

GROVER. By one account, a member of the original crew.

GUEST. Or Guess, Gist, etc. Probably refers to Christopher Guest, the noted explorer of Swift's time. Guest, Gries, Grise, Guise, and Guess are all given as members in various journals in the border area of Virginia and Kentucky.

HALL. He is mentioned in southwestern Virginia legends in accounts of the late search by John Swift. It is said that Hall purchased or somehow obtained a copy of Swift's journal.

HAZLETT. Usually given as Henry Hazlett, it can also be spelled "Hazlip," "Heaslup," or "Haxlett." Was a crew member for several years during the original mining. He was wounded by Indians on the way to Fort Pitt, and died at Munday's North Carolina home on December 24, 1767. Hazlett is often mentioned with Montgomery and Staley, and may have served with Swift under Colonel Washington.

HOLEBROOK. This was a latter-day associate of Swift's in southwestern Virginia. He reportedly bought a copy of the journal and accompanied the aged Swift on the final search.

IRELAND. James Ireland (also given as England) was an acquaintance of Swift during the Braddock Campaign, and is mentioned as a mining crew member in a Tennessee version of the journal. Also given in southwest Virginia lore as

"Island."

JEFFERSON. Shadrack Jefferson is mentioned in some versions as an original crew member. Also, a "Jeffries" was a Peruvian miner hired in Cuba and taken into Appalachia to oversee the silver mining. In most versions it is spelled "Jefferson," and is sometimes believed to be Thomas Jefferson's father. Also listed as Jeffers.

LIPPS. He is mentioned in legends in southwestern Virginia as a last search companion of Swift. Was a forefather of Morgan Lipps.

MARQUETTE. He is mentioned in one southeastern Kentucky journal as Swift's trusted Indian guide. Another version, from central Kentucky, gives Marquette as one of the French members of the crew.

MONTGOMERY. Seth or Alexander Montgomery was, by most versions, a major associate of Swift's during the original excursions. Montgomery is listed as a financial backer from Maryland or Virginia, or as an expert on silversmithing trained in the Tower of London.

MOTT. John Mott is mentioned with Lipps, and is usually given as James or John Mott. A financial supporter of Swift's in the last search along the Virginia and Kentucky line. Also found as "Motts."

MUNDAY. Or Monday. Usually George, George Martin, Alexander or Jonathan Munday. He was the most-mentioned member of the Swift crew. By most versions, Munday was a young Frenchman who was captured by the Shawnee and forced to help mine silver from their ancient mines. Serving with the French against General Washington's colonial force, Munday was captured and befriended by Swift. After nursing Munday to health in his Alexandria, Virginia, home, Munday told Swift of the mines and agreed to lead him to them.

He is mentioned as a crew member during the years of 1760 until 1769. While Swift was imprisoned in England for his patriotic American speech, Munday reportedly headed an expedition to the mines and was killed by Indians.

He is also given as John Martin Monday, Jonathan Mondeaux, Monie, Money, and in one account, Alfred Munday. Such an important part did Munday play that some versions give the find not as Swift's mines but as Munday's.

Some journals by Swift list Munday as eventually settling on the Yadkin River of North Carolina.

McCLINTOCK. Joshua McClintock is given as a latter-day associate in the Swift search to relocate the mines in the 1770's. Also given as MacIntosh.

RENAUD. Andre or Andrew Renaud was supposedly a French crew member on the original mining trips back and forth from Alexandria to Appalachia. Given as Renaud in the accounts of early mining, his name could nevertheless be a version of Renfro.

RENFRO. Probably Margaret or Mrs. Joseph or James. The female love at Bean Station, Tennessee, with whom Swift left his famous original copy of the journal. (This may also be the Spurlock, Tye, Apperson, Alley, and Connelly version of the same journal, with variations.) Renfro may also be found as Renfroe, Rentrow, Rentfrew, Rentfroe, or Renaud.

Other Renfro family members of interest: James Renfro of Bell County, Kentucky, who was associated with Bland Ballard in a search on the Clear Fork in Campbell County, Tennessee.

ST. MARTIN. Pierre St. Martin (sometimes just Martin) is listed in three journals as a member of the French accompanying Swift in the original crew. This could be a variation of the name John Martin Munday.

STALEY. Also Slatey, Steley, etc., first name probably Harmon. He was an original crew member, and is listed in many journal versions. Staley was reportedly wounded by Indians on the way to the mines, and probably served with Swift under General Washington.

STEWART. Probably James, a survivor of the Fort Loudoun massacre by Cherokee, who resettled in Bell County, Kentucky. Said to have known Swift during the fruitless attempt to relocate the mines.

TIMMONS. Becky Timmons is believed by some researchers to be the granddaughter of McIntyre or McClintock, one of Swift's original crew members who searched the Red River Gorge area of Kentucky.

TOWNSEND. Chanced across Swift while the old man was searching the Red River Gorge area in Kentucky. He befriended him and took him to Lexington, Kentucky, for medical treatment. Swift gave him a copy of his journal and then, around 1800, is said to have died. This copy apparently passed to Becky Timmons, who continued the search in the area.

TYE. Colonel John Tye, a latter-day associate of Swift's who may have watched over his journal while Swift was in the English prison. Tye accompanied Swift back into the new territories afterwards, and along several sites in an attempt to relocate the mines.

WAITE. By one southwest Virginia legend a latter-day associate in the fruitless search.

WATTS. John Watts is mentioned as a 1761 member who (along with sixteen others) followed Swift into the wilds of Kentucky. Watts might have been the father of Cherokee Chief John Watts, a half-breed nephew of Chief Doublehead.

WHITECOTTON. Issac or Aaron Whitecotton of the High

Cliff area of Campbell County, Tennessee, with whom Swift wintered during his unsuccessful attempt to relocate his lost mines. Whitecotton is linked to John Bryan, Sam Mason, and James Renfro.

WILTON. William Wilton, also given as Wilholt, was a mining crew member in one Virginia version. May also be Walden, the name of an early family of explorers of Kentucky and Tennessee.

WRIGHT. He is listed as a mining crew member in one journal.

WYANDOTT WOMAN. Unnamed, by one version, with whom Swift fathered several children, apparently while he was a trader on the Ohio, before finding the silver mines.

One of the few authentic clues as to what became of Swift's crew, corresponding to some legends, comes from a footnote in *Trans Allegheny Pioneers* by John P. Hale, published in 1886:
"This party of Indians next went to a house occupied by Thomas Drennon and a Mr. Smith, and captured Mrs. Drennon, Mrs. Smith, and a child. Thence, coming down toward their home, they wounded Captain Samuel McClug and killed an old man named Monday."
This account was dated in 1780, and details an attack along the Kanawha River in present West Virginia. A separate account refers to the same band of Indians who killed Monday's wife as well.

Who Was Mrs. Renfro?

The better question might be: Where was Bean Station? Swift does not specify Tennessee, although most people point to the current Bean Station, north of Morristown. Actually, that community is old enough to have hosted him in the 1780's, but barely. With the creation of Cherokee Lake and the backup of the local creek, the Tennessee Valley Authority moved the town about two miles east of its original location.

An earlier Bean Station was located north of Johnson City, on the banks of the Watauga River. The Bean family, prominent in east Tennessee history, relocated to the current Bean Station north of Morristown.

Interestingly enough, Pineville, Kentucky, and Cumberland Falls, Kentucky, both lay claim to the Bean Station name. And Mrs. Renfro, commonly believed to be the widow of Joseph Renfro, is also claimed by Pineville to be the widow of James Renfro, Sr.

H.H. Fuson, in a history of Bell County, Kentucky, wrote that James Renfro came to operate a ferry at Cumberland Ford in 1821. Title passed from him and his wife, Darcus, to their son James, Jr., in 1832. Renfro, Sr., had been a member of the Claiborne County, Tennessee, county government in 1801, and was on the Donelson voyage down the Tennessee River to Nashville in 1779.

There must have been a connection between James Renfro, Sr., and Swift. Some, like your author, believe the man was either the love-child of Swift and Mrs. Renfro, or Mrs. Renfro's son who was at Swift's knee during those latter days in 1780.

When James Renfro wasn't making money operating the ferry and toll gate at the ford (now Pineville) he was hunting for the lost Silver Mine using a map or journal he had which probably came from Swift.

The Bean Station, Tennessee, Mrs. Renfro became a widow when her husband, Joseph, was killed by Indians during the tragic Donelson River Voyage from Long Island in Kingsport to Nashville. The voyage included not only Joseph, but Moses and James Renfro as well. Joseph was killed near Battle Creek on the Red River near its junction with the Tennessee River when he and the other Renfros took charge of the women and children on the voyage.

The Renfro family apparently came from North Carolina about 1770. William Connelley researched Mrs. Renfro and wrote that she was romanced by Swift, who wanted her hand in marriage. Following her husband's death, the state of North Carolina granted her a "large tract of land as a compensation for his loss and for claims he had then pending against the state for settlement." The grant was made in 1784. Connelley wrote that:

"Renfro was a man of standing and consequence and...he left his widow with a large estate. She is reputed to have been a woman of beauty and rare accomplishments, and to have lived on a large plantation near Bean's Station."

Judge Haywood wrote that Swift visited Bean Station during his frustrating search to find his mines, and left there in 1790 after hunting the region with several Frenchmen who were not the same French who had accompanied him during his mine operation. Other tales have Swift's visit to Bean Station about 1784, and his companions include some of those, including Munday, who had served in his original crew.

Fearing that the new companions might overpower him and take his maps and journal, Swift gave the journal to Mrs. Renfro for safekeeping.

Another version has Swift and his former companions actually locating some of the cache they had previously hidden, and storing it in the Great Shawnee Cave. There, as his companions slept, Swift murdered them one by one in order to claim the entire treasure for himself. When he returned to Bean Station he confided his deed to Mrs. Renfro, who abruptly refused to marry him. Then he departed for Virginia, or by some versions for Yadkin Valley, North Carolina, or even Kent Colony, Virginia.

Haywood has Swift returning the following year, 1791, again visiting with Mrs. Renfro, and continuing to search for his lost mines. On this final search, which apparently ended about 1800 with his death, his associates include Colonel John Tye, a man named Anderson who assisted him in his blindness, and others. Haywood has Swift making his search with dark bandages bound closely to his face and eyes.

"In this condition," the author says, "he was mounted upon his horse, which was led by an attendant, while other attendants or persons employed by him endeavored vainly to trace the course to the silver mines."

As noted in the Kentucky legends, Swift may have died in Lexington, Kentucky, attended by a man known as Townsend, or may have returned to Virginia or North Carolina after treatment by an Indian physician called Hicks (or "Kicks") for his illness. In any case, he died; a few versions even have him dying at Bean Station. Swift reportedly left Mrs. Renfro a large sum of money before departing. The "Kicks" mentioned above was supposedly educated in Paris, France, and was a leading surgeon in North Carolina at the time.

Charles R. Hicks was a Moravian Christian convert of mixed blood. By 1827 he was chosen as principal Chief of the Cherokee Nation, with John Ross as his assistant. Hicks is said to have taught the Cherokee hero Sequoyah to write in English, and was a friend to the half-breed son of Nathaniel Gist. Some versions of the Swift Journal have a crew member named "Gist," and mention stopping at Gist Station, in Virginia.

Hicks was born in Tomatley, on the Hiwasee River in Tennessee, in 1867. His father was a white trader, his mother a

Cherokee. Although crippled in childhood, he overcame his handicap and became a leader of his people. He was said to have taken part in the Battle of Kings Mountain, fighting for the Americans, providing medical attention to fallen patriots.

Roy Price (center) shares photos and maps with other "Swift Buffs." Price has been the spokesman for his community's annual "Swift Silver Mine Lost Treasure Week-end."

Even Today They Search

Forget, for a moment, Granny Anderson, Cud Hanks, John Filson, James Harrod, Scott Partin, William Spurlock, Blue Jacket, Cornstalk, or the hundreds of other searchers for the lost silver mines. Today, aided by aerial photos, topo maps, computers, and metal detectors, a new breed of treasure hunter seeks the treasures supposedly left here and there by Swift and his men.

Possibly two sites have actually yielded silver bars and coins, and both fit neatly into descriptions of landmarks in some journals.

The current crop of "Swift Buffs" often share clues and maps with each other. A few do not share anything and are extremely secretive about their efforts. A handful publish stories about the legend or their own searches, most often when the search has been unsuccessful.

Speculation about the legend continues to grow and sometimes takes on twisted notions and unexpected locations.

One treasure writer, Don Viles, wrote in *Treasure Cache* in 1995 that Swift's Silver Mines were actually situated in Colorado, between Colorado Springs and the Garden of the Gods. I've visited the Garden a couple of times while on vacation and found it beautiful and unusual, but believe there's no way Swift could have traveled to Colorado and back to the colonies within the time frame most journals give.

The Viles article was the last piece of mail I received from Michael Paul Henson, along with a note and a chuckle from his wife, Nancy. We often shared information about the legend and other Appalachian tales and I had recently sent them a few pages from a book on Chattanooga that dealt with a Celtic or Viking settlement there.

Another searcher believes that he has found the Great

Cave of the Shawnee and located a nearby grave and glory hole. The problem is that the suspect cave is within the boundaries of the Daniel Boone National Forest.

One writer believes that the Knights of the Golden Circle were reactivated following the Civil War by former rebels and continue to pursue Swift and other treasures. This "secret society" is rumored to also leave many false clues to tease and confuse others.

James Powers of Eagan, Tennessee, has searched the mountains along the Tennessee and Kentucky line. He and his wife have found old coins, scrip, old guns, odd metal objects, and many marks and signs. Powers is eager and willing to share his knowledge of Swift and other treasure lore.

Bill Landry, host of *Appalachian Tales* and *The Heartland Series* on television, hails from southern Tennessee and wasn't familiar with the Swift legend until Roy Price and I invited his production team. Two shows resulted, and the response was so great that he did a third program. He continues to get mail on the subject and has said he'd like to do a full length movie on the lost mines.

Several slide and video presentations have featured the legend, including one produced by Ed Henson, Director of Kentucky's Recreational State Parks, and one by John Tierney, a ranger at Carter Caves State Park in Olive Hill, Kentucky.

Both Henson and Tierney have appeared as speakers at the annual Swift's Silver Mine Lost Treasure Weekend held in September in Jellico, Tennessee, each year. Several other well-known authors, magazine writers, treasure hunters, and researchers have appeared as well, including Bryan Crawford, columnist for the *Louisville Courier Journal*; Dr. Howard Grimm, treasure and legal advocate; magazine and treasure writer Dorian Cook; author and treasure hunter W.C. Jameson; Michael Paul and Nancy Henson; long range treasure champion and sign reader Tommy Veal; and many others. The annual event draws hundreds and continues to grow. Those involved in the event, which takes much work and gets little praise, includes myself and Roy and Melinda

Price, Joanne Watts, Eva Dolcini, Brenda Brown, Gail Sharp, Fay Begluitti, Trula Housley, James Sharp, Phillip Watts, Betty Vermillion, and others. Local merchants, city officials including Mayor Forester Baird, and community leaders such as Granville Moses, Allen McClary, Allen Douglas, Gary Harp, Jerry Llewellyn, Charles Cox, and many, many others have contributed.

By far the most popular event during the three days of speakers, outings, and visiting is a large metal detector competition hunt. The success of the event is directly due to the work and promotion of Tom and Marie Copeland of Knoxville and Bill and Sharron Leon, formerly of Oak Ridge.

The Swift weekend draws people from across the U.S. and is unique in that nationally known treasure hunters and writers mingle with anyone who attends; and lots of information, clues, and tips are shared freely.

Since the idea of "Swift" weekend arose, Michael Paul Henson was a rock-solid supporter, lending not only organizational ideas and suggesting speakers, but also by promoting the weekend himself, and always appearing to see the growing number of "TRer's" and speaking to very interested crowds.

Henson's interest in Appalachian and national treasure goes back to his boyhood home in Quicksand, Kentucky. In the 1950's he put all the old stories he had heard together, bought a Detectron detector, and began hunting treasure. Today his files are full of interesting information, so much so that he wrote several magazine articles each month, answered questions from people from Maine to Alaska, and has several books in print.

Among his many books, which range from ghost stories to a treasure hunter's logbook, are two that many Swift buffs consider to be bibles of Swift lore: *John Swift's Lost Silver Mines* (Journal, Map, Research) was first published in 1975, and contains the Uniontown, Pennsylvania, version of the journal.

Henson's *Lost Mines and Buried Treasures in Kentucky* contains the Alley journal, considered by most researchers to be the most complete and most similar to any "original" journal yet published.

While I have presented small pieces of previously published versions of both journals, only Henson has the right to publish full and complete versions. He also lists historic and personal observations about similar finds, legends, etc., and has certainly earned the title "Dean of Treasure Hunters."

Henson heard almost daily from other treasure hunters, being sought out for his information, or simply being informed about the progress of this or that search. The natural reactions of jealousy and suspicion seemed to stop at Henson's door, and he opened his mind and his library to all serious history and treasure researchers.

"I first heard of John Swift when I was about ten years old, from my grandmother," Henson said in 1994. "The version she told in those days, and she was from down south of Pineville, Kentucky, was that Swift came back in, looking for his mines, and had a fourteen-year-old boy to lead him around."

"My own personal belief is that the lower mines, if they exist, are in Bell County," he added, basing his reasoning on language used in the Alley version of the journal. This version was given to Henson by Alva Rice of Oil Springs, Kentucky. In the Journal, Swift talks about going to the headwaters of the Great Sandy Creek.

"To get to the lower mines, we traveled in a southwesterly direction, north of a great ridge, for a considerable distance," Henson quotes from the journal.

"We crossed a river, the name of which was unknown to us, thence to a long rocky branch, and thence to the mine," Henson continues, explaining the landmarks mentioned as Pine Mountain, the Cumberland River, and Clear Creek.

Henson says he visited the rock shelter on Furnace Ridge, southeast of Pineville, where buttons and pieces of ore were found. He says the mine would have to be above Clear Creek near Frakes, or somewhere on Log Mountain, given the general directions.

The upper mines may be in Wolfe County, or around

Paintsville, or near Ashland, Kentucky, according to Henson, who also points to evidence of a silver mine in McCreary County, Kentucky, evidence which is associated with Chief Doublehead.

"Personally I have sixteen different versions of the journal of Jonathan Swift," Henson said. "The earliest one I have is from a newspaper clipping from 1882, and the Collins part goes back to about 1800. Which one of them is the truth, and how much truth is in any of them, nobody can say.

"Although they are all basically the same, they have different authors, different times, and different versions of the same story. There can only be one basic fact in anything, and how it is distorted is up to the individual writer," he explains.

"Any time you are likely to get as many versions from as many different sources, the more likely you are to solve the mystery," he said.

Michael Paul and his wife, Nancy, teamed their efforts and were both open to any question, clue, new journal or map version, and to sharing what they had accumulated over the years. Henson said the most surprising find came when a friend of his, an attorney for the L&N Railroad, was in Virginia visiting a maritime museum, and chanced across an old copy of *Lloyd's Registry*.

"Jonathan Swift and Seth Montgomery were both insured by Lloyd's Registry from 1761 to 1767 as merchants and sea captains sailing out of Alexandria, Virginia, which proves beyond doubt, as far as I'm concerned, that Swift did exist and was an actual person, as was Seth Montgomery," Henson says.

Along with all the treasure and ghost stories, Henson also wrote two columns. One of these is published in *Kentucky Farmer*, and the other in *Kentucky Living*. His unexpected death in 1995 leaves a huge empty hole among treasure hunters.

A Parker's Lake lady who attended one of the Swift weekends claims to know the location of one lost mine and says she has a family deed to the site. Near the community is a little rural route known as Lead Mine Road.

Jerry Dunn, a Kentucky treasure hunter, has spent much time in Bell, Whitley, and Elliott counties. By 1995 Dunn was hot on the trail of Swift's "upper mine" and had found several carvings.

A Powell Valley, Tennessee, man was hot on the trail of Swift in the 1980's. The fellow ran a country store and was presented some old silver slag from a smelter a friend found somewhere in Cumberland Mountain. The grocer and several other men returned to the old furnace and reportedly uncovered bars of wedge-shaped ore, each weighing about four ounces each.

Fred Cansler, a builder and farmer in Greene County, Tennessee, has many files of Swift research. He believes that one of the mines is located in the mountains of the Nolichucky area and has a very old German coin of the Swift period.

A Louisville, Kentucky, businessman is collecting every scrap of information he can get on Swift, focusing on directions to the mine and anything dealing with a "Saddle Gap" or a horse saddle in a tree in a gap.

Michael Paul Henson was a touchstone for many Swift searchers and researchers. I asked him to provide a list of current people involved in the hunt for the lost mines. He gave me the following a few months before his death in 1995:

William "Bill" Metcalf, retired salesman, LaGrange,
   Kentucky
James Scott, state highway employee, Martin, Kentucky
Roy Stidham, General Motors retiree, Dayton, Ohio
Michael Durch, real estate agent, Akron, Ohio
Morris Woods, retired school teacher, Clarksville, Indiana
James Smith, antique dealer, New Albany, Indiana
Floyd Ferguson, government employee, Oak Ridge,
   Tennessee
William Adkins, pharmacy owner, Knoxville, Tennessee
John Treadway, coal miner, Wise, Virginia
Clyde White, airline pilot, Roanoke, Virginia
Emiual Likens, retired coal miner, Frenchburg, Kentucky

A Red Bird, Kentucky, man attended a brief lecture that Roy Price and I gave at Pine Mountain State Park in Pineville a few years ago. After our talk we took questions and the fellow stood up in the back of the audience and asked if I had any references to Red Bird in my Swift research.

I found two or three paragraphs and read them aloud, pointing out other references to the area and that part of the Kentucky river system.

"Damn," he said.

I asked him if he knew where the mines were and he replied, "Yes."

Then I asked if he would share his information with the audience, and he shouted, "Hell, no!"

Another time, when we had finished speaking before a very large crowd at Cumberland College in Williamsburg, Kentucky, we began taking questions and comments. One fellow came forward and displayed huge aerial photos and core samples he had taken from Central Kentucky. Apparently he was looking for investors, believing he had found some of the silver Swift claimed to have mined.

The Swift legend takes turns and twists and gets into some strange points of views.

One of the most unusual books based on the legend is a nicely done piece of research by Ralph Volker.

In his *Mysteries of the Mountains, a Story of Lost Treasure*, Volker takes the common Swift Journal and tracks down landmarks and carvings to the Lower Devil's Creek in Wolfe County below the Red River Gorge. Volker also notes the "Masonic" ties in the carved clues and finds a "Bell" on an old Swift map, locating it on a topo map of Central Kentucky.

Volker's red-covered book, a welcomed addition to any history or treasure collection, is available from R&R Enterprises, P.O. Box 205, Benton, Kentucky 42025.

Another part of any library on Appalachian treasure should be Betty Jo Shepherd Chandler's *The Mysteries of Swift Creek*.

I spoke with the Chandlers in preparing this book and understand she had reprinted the book and would like to spend more time actually exploring for the mine. Wouldn't we all?

Mrs. Chandler believes that Swift had been a house to house peddler in Virginia and North Carolina before being caught up in the silver mine lore. Her research involves the Red River Gorge area, starting at the Rock Bridge arch across Swift Camp Creek.

The Shepherd family search touched on family tradition, spiritualism, possession, legal and bureaucratic paperwork, and teamwork.

She writes that Becky Timmons may have been Swift's granddaughter and places Blue Jacket as a member of the mining crew.

The late Tom Troxwell of Scott County, Tennessee, wrote of lost silver mines, Cherokee Chief Doublehead, and other historical tales and myths. Unfortunately, two of his books are now out of print and very hard to find. I found a copy of *The Legend of the Mine* at the public library in Whitley City and *The County Scott* in the city library in Jellico, Tennessee.

W.C. Jameson, an Arkansas professor and treasure hunter, has collected various treasure tales and stories of lost silver mines. He has published several fine books, including *Buried Treasure in the Appalachians* and *Buried Treasures of the South*. Both contain such tales and are published by August House Publishers, Inc., P.O. Box 3223, Little Rock, Arkansas 72203.

Buddy Johnson's *Silver in the Unaka* tells a family story in fictional form of the search for silver mines in extreme eastern Tennessee and ties in with Swift and Indian legends. The book is available from The Overmountain Press, 325 W. Walnut Street, Johnson City, Tennessee 37604.

Southern Treasures is a quick view of several lost treasure sites in "old Dixie" by Nina and William Anderson and available from The Globe Pequot Press, Old Chester Road, Chester, Connecticut 06412.

There are many, many other examples of modern treasure writers and hunters who are expanding and exploring the legend of Swift's Lost Silver Mines. Many more of the books, magazines, manuscripts, and sources are found in the final pages of this book.

Probably the most contemporary information resource is *Kentucky Explorer*, a monthly magazine published by Charles Hayes of Jackson, Kentucky. Charles periodically publishes all types of treasure tales, some on the silver mines and others on outlaw or pioneer treasure. Many regional writers, including myself, often contribute to the *Explorer* and you'll find it on most newsstands in that state or can subscribe by writing *Kentucky Explorer*, P.O. Box 227, Highway 15N, Jackson, Kentucky 41339.

Land of the Lake by Dr. G.L. Ridenour is printed by The Campbell County (Tennessee) Historical Society and contains many lines about the Swift legend and lost silver mines in the Cumberland and Pine Mountain range.

The Wilderness Road by Robert Kincaid has mentions of the legend and the Renfro Family and was reprinted by Lincoln Memorial University, Harrogate, Tennessee, in 1992 as part of Bell County's participation in Kentucky's 200th Birthday.

Many other pieces of information about Swift and the lost mines have never before seen print:

A Kentucky man has shown me, and a few others, a mostly silver axe head, or wedge, he found near an old smelter. He has other relics and the axe head weighs many pounds.

An Ohio man has several "fingers" of silver he found a few years ago while searching for the mines. He believes they were "poured off" onto rough sand or clay moulds simply made by pressing or running a finger along the natural mould.

Several Spanish coins from the Swift era were found on the land of an elderly North Carolina woman. Her sons found them by chance, causing a small silver rush in the western mountains.

An Ohio businessman spent a summer and a small fortune to bring in heavy equipment in his search.

Lonnie Fuson, who lives near Frakes, Kentucky, and owns

the land which takes in Turtle Back Rock and The Needle's Eye natural arch, says the man dug here and there, especially beneath the Turtle-looking rock, but turned up nothing. Fuson is often asked for information or permission to search his beautiful mountainside, which is situated immediately below Henry Bolton Gap and the "Lakely" treasure carvings.

He can point out many carvings in the rocks, including turkey tracks.

A middle-aged Shawnee man came to Jellico, Tennessee, annually for several years in the 1970's and 1980's, using a World War II surplus metal detector to search the areas of No Business and Primroy Hollows for silver and the silver mines.

Since the idea of having a weekend devoted to the legend began, I and other members of the event committee have been approached for radio and television interviews, magazine and newspaper stories, and often receive mail and telephone (and now fax) inquiries from around the nation. The legend continues to grow and certainly all the facts and information cannot be contained in this book.

Simply because of the size limitations, some facts and related tales have been briefly mentioned or left out entirely. Certainly new facts will and do continue to come to light and several books could be published, in the future, on the subject.

If, at times, I have been too skeptical and, at other times too believing, it is because I seem to ebb and flow with the fact and myth of the lost mines.

The difficulty I have with the tale is that each time I pull away from believing parts of it I am presented with new facts or relics. It is hard to hold an old silver bar or coin in your hand and not believe a bit.

I know a man who dynamited his way into a small side room of a cave. He claimed he could look through the small opening he made and see stacks of silver bars. Unfortunately, he says the state official caught on to his being somewhere he wasn't allowed and forced him to leave, unaware of his find or where he discovered it. He left the area, but only after concealing his works and thinking of returning there some day, or night, to complete his effort.

All of these events have taken place within the last twenty-five years. There are hundreds, if not thousands, of people who firmly believe the Swift legend. For many the tale is just that, a tale that goes back in the region, and in their family, for many generations.

Technical developments may in the future answer the questions surrounding Jonathan Swift and his lost mines. Thus the legend will become fact and the myth reality. Thus the romance of the tale itself will fade.

Or maybe not.

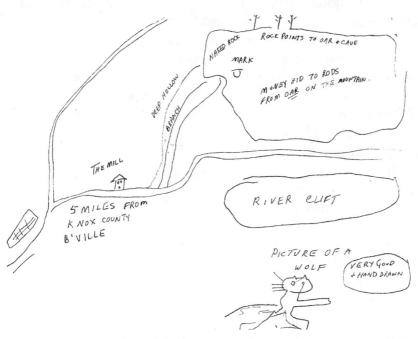

This map, and similar ones, have drawn silver mine treasure hunters to the Jellico, Tennessee, area since early settlement. It is supposed to indicate the area of "The Narrows" and Primroy Hollow.

Author's Final Note

It is May 14, 1995. As of today there is little evidence that Swift's Lost Silver Mines ever existed. There are also thousands of people who believe otherwise.

Aside from Filson's land claim and Judge Haywood's note that the aged Swift was in the region trying to find his mines, there is little to bring historic proof that the man or his mines are anything but legend.

Yet evidence may be there nevertheless. The search and the research continues.

About a month ago, while working to finish this book and prepare for printing, I stopped by a Lexington, Kentucky, public library. Swift, some believe, died in or near that Bluegrass city sometime around 1800. Certainly, if so, something should be on record.

I chanced across an old official record called *Lexington, 1779* and skimmed through it. A short, single note proved to me, if no other, that someone known as Swift had been in the area. It simply read: "Jon. Swift, it was said, the Indians blindfolded him and would not let him see anywhere when he approached the cave."

The passage was handwritten by an early settler who apparently was visiting Logan's Fort (now Stanford, Kentucky) during a "court day." Whether Swift himself was there or whether the information came from others at the event isn't known.

Other new information about Swift came recently in a local history which claimed that Swift stopped by the Stewart family house near the junction of Stinking Creek and Cumberland River (at Flat Lick, Kentucky) while on his hunt for the lost mines in 1779.

Michael Paul Henson wrote that Swift was recognized at

Fort Pitt in 1789, still searching for his mine, some nine years after he was supposed to have died in Lexington or Bean Station.

The Legend of Swift's Lost Silver Mines, the mystery around the man himself and those men he employed and associated with, and the hundreds of Appalachian families who are interwoven in the search all combine to create a continuing historic drama. With such history and myth it really doesn't matter if the treasure exists or not.

Jerry Dunn, a Kentucky treasure hunter, is seen inspecting an old map carved atop a natural arch. Dunn (with binoculars) has spent considerable time in recent years searching for silver caches in the Frakes, Kentucky, area. (Photo by Mike Steely)

John Swift Calls The Dance

So come with me to the treasure trove
To the hanging rock in the high knob cove,
Mount up your burros and we shall ride
Till we reach that watercourse on the divide.
Climb the hill to the top, but go slow
Till you stand at the rock, called old "Buffalo"
See the hole in the cliff and the sky beyond
Far to the west is the big dry pond.
The mouth of the cave is walled with stone
A door you'll find, if you lie down prone.
A remarkable rock, like a chestnut burr,
Is above the mine, on the mountain spur.
A towering rock, like an old haystack
Stands over the hill from the turkey track.
The way is plain, tough rough and hard
But don't turn back, old friend, old pard.
So come on lads and keep in line,
We'll soon be at the old Swift mine.
We'll all be rich, but don't speak loud,
We'll be hijacked by the revenue crowd.

—WJE
Ashland Daily, April 1964

The Ballad of Swift's Silver

In the hills of Kentucky, deep under the ground,
And close to the tall hemlock tree,
Lies Swift's hoard of silver waiting to be found
And I wish that lucky finder I could be.
Swift came with the Indians in dark days of old
Who showed him that rich silver ore.
He dug a fortune then covered up the hole
For he thought he'd never need it any more.

Chorus:
Swift's Silver Mine, Swift's Silver Mine
Wouldn't I like to find ole Swift's Silver Mine.
Swift's Silver Mine, Swift's Silver Mine
Wouldn't I like to find John Swift's Silver Mine.

He left old Kentucky a proud wealthy man
As did his companions, they say.
The wealth they had gathered was spent with lavish hands
They knew where plenty more was hid away.
That rich, gleaming silver it played upon his mind
Till John Swift so greedy had grown
He killed his companions so they could never find
The treasure that he thought was all his own.

Chorus

He came back to the mountains old, feeble and blind
After twenty years had passed away.
But the wealth he had hidden he never found at all
Though he searched for it till his dying day.
And all up the river the old people still,
When the wind is moaning through the pines

Say it's old John Swift a wailing through the hills
A'looking for his lost silver mine.

Chorus

   (Written by Jim Lair, as performed by Jim Gaskin, Renfro
Valley Barn Dance, Kentucky. Used with permission of the
heirs of Jim Lair.)

Linda Veal, Fred Daugherty, and treasure author W.C. Jameson chat with each other
about Appalachian treasure lore. (Photo by Mike Steely)

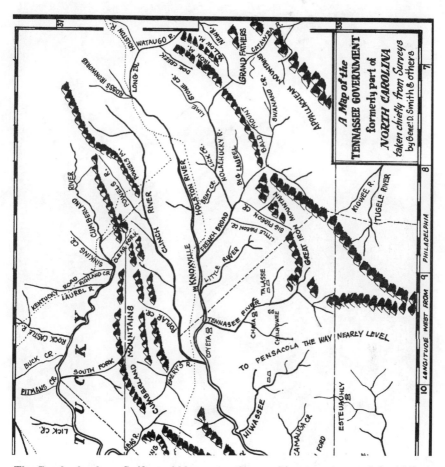

The Cumberlands, as Swift would have seen them on his return to search for his lost mines, with sites of the legend drawn in: 1. Primroy Hollow, 2. Bridge Rock, 3. Silvermine Branch, 4. Lakely signs, 5. Log Mountains, 6. Furnace Ridge, 7. Straight Creek, 8. Renfro's search, 9. Doublehead Mine, 10. Melungeons, 11. Bean Station, Tennessee, 12. Martin's Station.

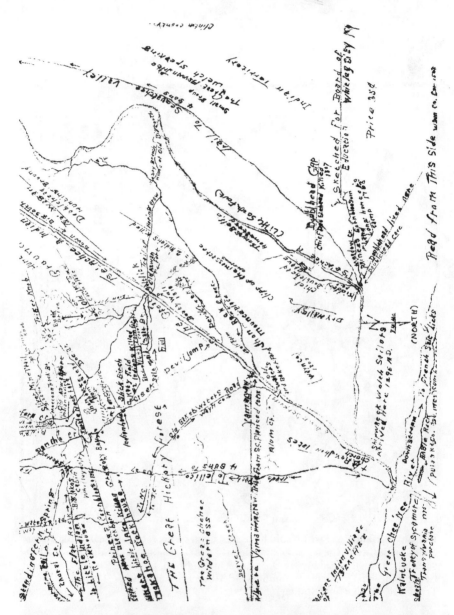

The silver mine trail is sketched here on a freehand map by the late Tom Troxell. The map also shows the vicinity of Doublehead's silver mine. Troxell was a descendant of the noted Cherokee chief, who held much land in the area of the Big South Fork of the Cumberland River.

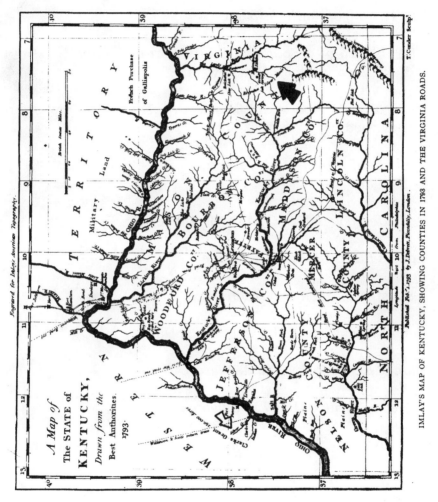

The famous Imlay's map, including the words "Reputed Silver Mines" at the headwaters of the Big Sandy and Kentucky rivers.

Recommended Reading

The History of North Carolina

The History of a Southern State, North Carolina by Hugh Talmage and Albert Ray Newsome

Natural and Aboriginal History of Tennessee by John Haywood

History of Clay County, Kentucky by Mr. and Mrs. Kelly Morgan

A Guide Book to U.S. Coins by R.S. Yoeman

Life As It Is by J.W.M. Breaseale

Goodspeed's History of Tennessee

Jenny Wiley Country by C. Mitchell Hall

Lure of Kentucky by Maude Ward Lafferty

Collected Writings by W.R. Jillson

The History of Southwest Virginia by Lewis Preston Summers

The Kentucky by Thomas D. Clark

Myths of the Cherokee by James Mooney

Antiquities of the Southern Indians by William James

Famous First Facts by Joseph Nathan Kane

Reports of the Washington Silver Mine by Richard Cowling

Historic Sketches of Southwest Virginia by James A Dougherty

Draper Papers by John D. Shane

The History of Wise County by Charles A. Johnson

Old Kentucky Entries and Deeds by W.R. Jillson

Kentucky Historic Society Library and Archives

Filson Library, Louisville, Kentucky

Bradley County Historic Library, Cleveland, Tennessee

Writings of James A. Dougherty

Writings of Michael Paul Henson

Office of the Secretary of State, Frankfort, Kentucky

Writings of Scott Partin, Frakes, Kentucky

Kentucky, a Pictorial History, by J. Winston Coleman, Jr.

Files of the Pineville, Kentucky, *Sun-Courier*

The Asheville Daily Independent

The Middlesboro Daily News

The Louisville Courier-Journal, articles by Joe Creason

"The History of Jellico," manuscript by James Hayden Siler

The Cincinnati Inquirer, 1916

Newsletter of Mine Safety and Health Administration, 1982, Mary Wells.

Bristol Herald article on Dan Graybeal, Norton, Virginia

Lost Silver Mines and Buried Treasures of Kentucky, by M.P. Henson

John Swift's Lost Silver Mines, by M.P. Hensen

A Guide to Treasure in Virginia and West Virginia, by M.P. Henson

The Register, 1980, Harry M. Caudill

History of Bell County, by F.H. Fuson

History of Knox County, Kentucky, by K.S. (Sol) Warren

Land of the Lake, by G.L. Ridenour

History of Kentucky, by William E. Connelley

The Annals of Tennessee, by J.G.M. Ramsey

Early Travels in Tennessee Country, by Samuel Cole Williams

Legends of Loudon, by Harrison Williams

Historic Sketches of Kentucky, by Lewis Collins

The writings of William J. Reams

The Big Sandy, by W.R. Jillson

Kentucky Land Grants, by W.R. Jillson

The Greenup Independent, February, 1873

History of Scott County, Virginia, by R.M. Addington

Writings of Henry W. Tomkins

The Devils of Backbone by Jonathan Daniels

Shenandoah, The Valley Story, by Alvin Dohme

The History of Kentucky, by Thomas Clark

The Red River Gorge, by Robert H. Ruchhoft

The writings of J. Emerson Miller

The Melungeons, The Resurrection of a Proud People, by N. Brent Kennedy

The Melungeons, Yesterday and Today, by Jean Patterson Bible

Tribes That Slumber, by M.N. Thomas and Madeline Kneberg

The writings of Mrs. John Trotwood

Pioneer Families of Eastern and Southeastern Kentucky, by William C. Kozee

The Border Settlers of Northwest Virginia, by Lucullus Virgil McWhorter

The Big Sandy, by Carol Crowe Carraco

The Captive, by Caroline Gordon

The Big Sandy Valley, by W.R. Jillson

The writings of Jim Jayde

The Brooks Manuscripts, Bureau of American Ethnology

Lost Tribes of Tennessee's Mountains, by James Aswell

The Thomas Walker Journals

The Journal Enquirer, April 16, 1964

"The Legend of Swift Silver Mine," by Winfred Partin, *Rural Kentuckian*, April, 1986

The Babe of Virginia, by Jasper Sutherland

An Encyclopedia of East Tennessee, by Allen D. Swan

Article, *The Wolfe County News*, by Mrs. Roy Cecil

Kentucky, Land of Contrast, by Thomas D. Clark

The Mysteries of Swift Creek, by Betty Shepherd Chandler

Kentucky, the Land of the Arches, by R.H. Ruchcroft

The Wilderness Road, by Robert L. Kincaid

Civil and Political History of Tennessee, by John Haywood

The County Scott, by Tom Troxell

Legion of the Lost Mine, by Tom Troxell

Legends of Loudoun, by Harrison Williams

History of the American Indian, by John Adair

The Shawnee, by Jerry E. Clark

The Legend of Swift's Silver Mine, by James Dougherty

Article, *The Louisville Courier Journal*, by Joe Creason, March 13, 1969

The Licking Valley Courier, 1968, by Willis Everman

The Melungeons, by Bonnie Ball

Buried Treasures of Appalachia, by W. C. Jameson

Silver in the Unaka, by Buddy Johnson

Munday leads Swift to the lost silver mine. This depiction is by commercial caricature artist Dennis Porter of Dayton, Ohio.

INDEX